The Truth In Crisis
The Controversy in the Southern Baptist Convention

JAMES CARL HEFLEY, PH.D.

Criterion Publications
Dallas, Texas

Other Books by James C. Hefley

Dawn Over Amazonia *Word*
Peril By Choice *Zondervan*
By Life Or By Death *Zondervan*
Intrigue in Santo Domingo *Word*
Christ in Bangladesh *Harper & Row*
The Church That Produced A President *Wyden/Simon and Schuster*
Where In The World Are The Jews Today? *Victor*
My Anchor Held *Revell*
One Nation Under God *Victor*
Washington: Christians In The Corridors' of Power *Tyndale*
Textbooks on Trial *Victor and Mott Media*
Cloning: Miracle or Menace *Tyndale*
How Sweet The Sound *Tyndale*
Masterpiece In Progress *Tyndale*
Way Back In The Hills *Tyndale*

Copyright Criterion Publications 1986
First Edition printed April, 1986
All Rights Reserved
Printed in the United States of America
Dewey Decimal Number: 286.132
Library of Congress Number: BX6462.3.H43
Library of Congress Catalog Card Number: 86-70962
ISBN Number: 0-937969-00-1

Dedicated to my Seminary Professors at
New Orleans Seminary Who Taught
me to Love the **Word.**

FORWARD

Church historians 100 years from now will likely still be studying the dramatic conflict that emerged in the Southern Baptist Convention in 1979 and remains fully-charged today, in 1986. The dynamics at work in this current situation have far-reaching implications for Southern Baptists as well as Evangelical Christians throughout the United States and the rest of the world.

Being the largest non-Catholic denomination in the U.S. today, the Southern Baptist Convention casts a broad and lengthy shadow over Protestant life in the nation. The shift to the right which has already taken place in the 14.6 million member SBC signaled the future for possibly other major church groups.

This has been no easy conflict to cover, for me as a journalist on a secular newspaper, or for a Christian freelance writer such as Jim Hefley. I have sources, acquaintances and friends on both sides of the battle. And I know that Jim Hefley does too. It is disturbing to see friends fighting with one another and sometimes using tactics that would embarrass the Savior whom they claim to worship.

Yet the story needs to be told—even in its incomplete form. God is not finished with Southern Baptists, and the final chapter to this eight-year conflict has not been written. We do not know how or even when this story will end.

Even so, in this book, Jim Hefley offers insights and details that bring the conflict into focus and offers clues about the eventual outcome. Historians in coming years will want to use this book as a manual for their master's theses and doctoral dissertations on the SBC conflict.

I have worked alongside Jim Hefley during all of the years of the raging crisis in the SBC. He was a friend and colleague before the upheaval began. And I have admired greatly his skills in ferreting out the essential details in reporting the turmoil. He has doggedly pursued angles to the story when other reporters have given up and gone home for rest and recovery from the tumultuous annual conventions.

My journalism professors at Baylor University in the late 1960s taught me that different parties in a dispute deserve and have a right to be heard. They taught me that one clear sign of fair and balanced reporting was either criticism or praise from both sides at the same time. Like myself, Jim Hefley has received praise and criticism from both sides in the conflict. In his quest for truth, there have been times that I have wondered where he personally stands on the issues involved. And it is good that I have had to wonder! Being the type of people that we are, we professional journalists like to play "devil's advocate" as a means of resurrecting the truth from a tormented situation. This means challenging our friends as well as our enemies and enduring their misunderstanding of our roles.

Some will see in this book an apologetic for the fundamentalists (or conservatives, as Hefley calls them in this book). That would be a hollow reading, for Jim Hefley lays out facts that can be embarrassing to both sides. Yes, he does tell the fundamentalists' side, for they too have a right to be heard just as the moderates have that right. To see this book as only a defense of the conservatives is to miss the challenging, probing questions Jim Hefley asks of them.

I do not agree with every word in this book. There are some parts that I would have written differently. Indeed, I would be disappointed if Jim Hefley agreed with every word in the hundreds of columns and articles I have written about the SBC conflict. Yet I glean from his words a thoughtful, insightful, deliberate attempt to lay out for the reader facts as he sees them.

Those who do not want to believe that the other side has a right to present its case with precision and clarity will likely spurn this book. To do that is to err.

Jim Hefley presents the facts in a readable and informative way. I have enormous confidence in the actions of well-informed people, and this book will go a long way to educate its readers.

Louis Moore
Houston Chronicle
Houston, Texas
March 31, 1986

CONTENTS

1 THE EDUCATION OF AN INNOCENT

Saturday morning, in my little Ozark village of Mt. Judea, Arkansas, Uncle Dan, Uncle Bill, and Riley, the brawny woodsman, were at it again on the post office porch. They were arguing over Bible doctrines as they did most every Saturday with a sizable audience listening in.

Uncle Bill Hefley, the town squire, believed baptism was essential to salvation. Uncle Dan Hefley, the grizzled Pentecostal farmer-preacher, didn't. Riley Sexton, who had arms like Paul Bunyan and didn't hold to any organized religion, took first one side, then the other.

Uncle Bill held up his thick King James Bible. "Hyar it is, Boys, in Acts, chapter two and verse thirty-eight, 'Repent and be baptized . . . fer the remission of sins.' Hit's as plain as the nose on y'er face, Boys. Why cain't ye 'cept it?"

"Aw, pshaw, Bill, " Riley chortled. "Hit's symbolic, that's all. Cold creek water don't warsh away nobody's sins. If a man has to be baptized, what air ye goin' to do with the thief on the cross. The Lord tolt 'em, 'Today, ye will be with me in the kingdom.'"

They shifted to foot washing in the church, then to praying for healing, then to Uncle Dan's practice of shouting and dancing in brush arbor meetings. "There's nuthin' in the Bible that tells us to dance and jump around in church like a frog," Uncle Bill declared.

"Ah, Bill," the mountain preacher snorted, "if ye got the Holy Ghost, ye wouldn't talk like that."

On and on they argued while the warm sun rose in the clear sky. Almost every Saturday I heard them and other elders debating doctrine. Occasionally, my Aunt Lucy dropped by to offer Jehovah's Witness literature. They all meant well, but they helped turn me against Christianity.

Then two lady "independent" missionaries, Florence and Helen, came to hold "young people" meetings on Monday evenings. I attended at first only for fun and mischief. Week after week, I tried to make them angry and couldn't. Finally, I began listening to their lessons on the life of Christ. Slowly, I accepted the possibility that Christianity and the Bible might be truth and that Christ might indeed be the Son of God and Savior of sinners.

Florence and Helen left for the foreign mission field. I stayed busy in college at Arkansas Tech and came home on week-ends to operate a small gambling business. Jesus and religion began fading in my mind. Then I was home one Sunday when a Baptist missionary, Ottis Denney came to Mt. Judea and persuaded my parents to let him hold an evening service in our living room. At Mother's insistence, I slipped in to hear him. That night, I took the decisive step and received Christ into my life. I was born again.

The next morning, I started reading the New Testament and loved it. Two weeks later, I sensed God was calling me to the ministry. But I was still trying to decide which church to join.

Uncle Bill tried to show me that his Church of Christ was the right one. Uncle Dan urged me to seek the baptism of the Holy Spirit and become a Pentecostal. My dear Aunt Lucy kept giving me *Watchtowers* and other Jehovah's Witness literature. Ottis Denney dropped by every couple of weeks. He wouldn't argue with my relatives. He simply prayed with me and encouraged me to keep reading the New Testament. "God will lead you in the right way," he predicted.

That summer, Denney arranged for me to attend the week-long Arkansas Baptist Youth Assembly in the far northwest corner of the state. I loved every minute of it, Bible studies with young people my own age, heart-lifting singing and stirring sermons in the "tabernacle" and "study courses" with specialists from the Baptist Sunday School Board. I hung on to every word, listening with deep reverential respect. I never doubted that the Bible, all the Bible, was entirely true and the divinely inspired Word of God.

I became a Baptist and transferred to Ouachita Baptist College in 1947 where all went well until my senior year. During a one-month period the dean of men and the coach committed suicide (the latter shooting himself in the First Baptist Church), the academic dean resigned, and the administration building was struck by lightning and burned to the ground. I heard rumors of "problems" and that there was to be an investigation by a committee of Arkansas Baptist pastors. Apparently nothing was ever done, and to this day I do not know what was going on.

My faith in religious institutions a little tarnished, I took an interim pastorate in a small, troubled northern Arkansas town while waiting for my 20th birthday, when I would be eligible to enroll in New Orleans Baptist Theological Seminary. A new dam had been built downstream on the White River and, with the water behind it steadily rising, the town and church faced a deadline to relocate.

When I arrived, the town had already split between two locations and the church was soon scheduled to vote on where it would go. With leaders from both factions active in the church, it was an ugly situation. The night of the business meeting, I pleaded with both sides to compromise and vote to build the new church halfway between the new towns, where the school board had already wisely agreed to build the new high school. One side had already told me they would accept the center site. The other side declined any compromise and the night of the business meeting I learned why. They had taken the church roll and persuaded enough non-resident members (some had not been in the church in years!) to return and vote for their site. This group won and the faction willing to compromise pulled out and started their own church. For the first time I saw raw politics brutalize a church fellowship.

Deciding to take a stand was a gut-wrenching experience. I finally went with the group which I felt had been wronged, led them in a quick three-month building program, and went off to seminary a little wiser of Baptist nature than before.

I've often relived the experience, rolling the "what-ifs" through my mind, pondering what else might have been done to keep the old church together. Today—35 years later—there are two Southern Baptist churches and two towns three miles apart in the area. The two churches have five or more times the membership of the old congregation. I've preached for both and talked with long-time members about old times. Hard feelings appear to be gone and members of both churches visit back and forth.

From seminary church history courses, I learned more about Baptists than I ever cared to know. Scholars disagree on the origin of Baptists. Some fervently maintain that a succession of Baptist churches can be traced back to the church of the apostles at Jerusalem. Others, with whom I personally agree, hold that successionism cannot be proved. We know only for certain that the first so-called Baptists split away from the English state church in the early 17th century, fled to Holland to avoid persecution, and there split over rebaptism, with one group returning to England to establish, in 1611, the first Baptist church on English soil. Sad to say, Baptists, like other denominations, have been splitting ever since.

Seminary also indoctrinated me into the Southern Baptist way of cooperation and missions. I was convinced then, as I am now that our representative democracy expressed through agencies under the direction of trustees elected at the annual convention is the best way to do cooperative missions until a better plan is found.

At seminary I saw my first real "heresy" hunters, a pack of zealous young preachers, who were tape recording lectures of professors they suspected of straying from Bible truth. I didn't pay them much mind. For one thing, their leader was a "Landmark" Baptist, who was accepting free tuition while seemingly trying to undermine the denomination that was helping him. For another, I felt there were more important things to do than trying to "trap" a professor and ruin his career. For still another, their chief target, Frank Stagg, was one of the best liked teachers on campus.

I had Dr. Stagg for senior Greek and textual criticism. He was gentlemanly to a fault and never sought to make a student look foolish. I had no problems with his assertions, backed by evidence, that a few verses in the King James translation were not in the oldest and best New Testament manuscripts. Nor did I question his dynamic theory of inspiration, perhaps because he didn't go into much detail except to say that he believed God inspired the thoughts of the Biblical writers, allowing them to set down their own words. I assumed he believed that the text was inerrant in the originals. He never said otherwise. Dr. Stagg encouraged me to take additional graduate studies under him in New Testament theology. In the seminars, we argued a lot, particularly about theories of the atonement. After awhile I became more interested in writing for publication and dropped out, although I had almost an "A" average in the graduate studies.

After seminary, and while serving as a pastor in New Orleans, I wrote curriculum for the Baptist Sunday School Board. Editors informed me that certain personalities should not be mentioned to avoid "trouble." The "no-no" list included such disputants as John R. Rice and J. Frank Norris on the fundamentalist right and Harry Emerson Fosdick on the liberal left--all Baptists. Doctrines on which many Southern Baptists disagreed, such as millenialism, were also to be handled cautiously, if at all. Theories of the atonement and how the Bible is inspired were to be handled with extreme care. Tension points in Baptist history were to be touched gingerly, with ambiguity preferable to dogmatism. Once I suggested an article on Baptist succession to youth editor Josephine Pile. Josephine—one of my favorite people—almost froze in horror. "Heavens, no," she said. "We tried that once and almost got our hair ripped out by some preachers."

Every three or four years, I attended the Southern Baptist Convention, if it was within driving distance and if there was a friend or relative who could provide free lodging. My church couldn't afford a convention allowance.

Once there, I attended the inspirational sessions—Foreign Missions Night was always a favorite—and skipped the cut-and-dried business sessions to "fellowship" with old college and seminary buddies. We were quite willing to let the "big preachers" manage denominational affairs. And why shouldn't we? Everything we read in our denominational newspapers and periodicals lauded their skills and greatness. Those were the good old days of trust and deference.

While in the pastorate, I became more involved in writing. In 1961, the David C. Cook Publishing Company of Elgin, Illinois invited me to join their staff as a youth editor. I discussed the possibility with friends at the Baptist Sunday School Board. A Board executive vigorously objected. "You'll be leaving the denomination," he said. I insisted that would not happen. Upon moving to northern Illinois, I immediately contacted Bill Powell, the SBC "missionary" for the metro-Chicago area (he would later become a major participant in denominational controversy), and offered to help as a supply or interim pastor when needed. Bill had known me in seminary. "Okay with me," he said, "but you'll have to convince the denominational servants in the state office that you are a loyal Southern Baptist."

I did—pledging not to promote non-Southern Baptist literature in churches, even though the publication I edited, *Sunday Pix*, was not a Sunday School quarterly—and soon was receiving invitations to preach in Southern Baptist churches. It was another learning experience of how denominational commitments are maintained.

My intentions all along were to become a full-time, free-lance Christian writer. In 1964, with backing from my wife Marti, I made the leap. My forte was "inspirational" writing. For the next two decades, I traveled much of the globe, with Marti joining me after our children were older, researching missionary biographies and other subjects of keen interest to evangelical Christians. Gradually, almost imperceptibly, I moved from "public relations" writing for Christian organizations to more objective journalism. In the process, I discovered that "objective" writing wasn't desired by many church agencies, Southern Baptist and otherwise. As one ministry executive put it, "We shouldn't hang out our dirty linen before the world." Translated, that meant the "Christian" writer should tell only the successes and hold back on problems of the organization.

Inevitably, I transgressed in a biography. On balance, I felt the book was positive, presenting accomplishments which canceled out difficulties in the group. "Nobody's perfect," I told the in-house editor. He smiled and passed the manuscript to his superiors. They asked that the "offensive" material be removed. I offered to move the "conflict" to the appendix. They grudgingly agreed, then, when the book was published, refused to promote the book.

In another book, a missionary biography, I told of the split-up of two world famous women missionaries over twenty years earlier. The public relations director saw red when he got the manuscript. "In the name of God," he screamed over the phone, "what are you doing to us? We can't have the account of their quarrel in there!"

"The Bible tells us that Paul and Barnabas couldn't get along," I countered.

"That was two thousand years ago. These people are still living."

I tried to tone down the conflict, along with other "problems" he objected to in the book. This wasn't acceptable. When I stood my ground against more laundering, he took the matter to his board and then to the publisher who had contracted for the book. A few days later I got a long letter from the president of the publishing house, praising my work, but asking as "a personal favor" to be released from the contract. We made a financial settlement and I presented the manuscript to another publisher who "couldn't see what the fuss was all about" and published the book.

By this time, I had developed a friendship with Ed Plowman, then news editor for *Christianity Today.* "Face it," Ed said, "most Christian organizations and denominations want public relations, not objective journalism."

"Do you get flack for telling both sides in a controversy?" I asked.

"All the time. One preacher, who claimed to be smuggling Bibles Communist countries , went to the magazine's trustees and tried to get me fired when I was writing a story about some financial hanky-panky in his organization. The *Christianity Today* trustees hung with me.

"You can get cynical after awhile in this business," Ed said. "Some good Christian folks honestly believe that on principle we should never write anything negative about anyone. I disagree, but I respect their position. Then there are those whose primary motive is to keep their constituency loyal and those checks coming in. I say the public needs to be protected, or at least made aware of what's going on in the organizations they support. How else are they going to know?"

"Are denominations any different than independent Christian organizations?"

Ed grinned, "What do you think?"

"I think the Lord must have a lot of patience and love for us all."

In 1975, Ed asked me to cover the Southern Baptist Convention in Miami for *Christianity Today*."Pay close attention to the parliamentary sessions," he said. "Do a good job, and we'll give you the Southern Baptists again."

Southern Baptist deacon Jerry Clower, the self-styled "mouth from the south," was there to give an inspirational sermon. I enjoyed interviewing him afterwards. Then I went and sat in on a business session where a messenger named M.O. Owens was asking the convention to clarify the meaning of a clause in the Baptist Faith and Message: "It [the Bible] is . . . truth, without any mixture of error for its matter . . ."

I knew that denominational employees were supposed to believe in the Baptist Faith and Message:, but I had never read the "Confession", as denominational writers called it.

"Does 'without any mixture of error' mean the Bible is without any error, or that truth contained in the Bible is without error?" Owens persisted. The chairman of the Order of Business Committee accepted the question in the form of a motion and said it would be considered at the Thursday morning business session.

Later, Bill Powell, whom I had not seen since Chicago, stopped me in the press room. Bill was now editor of *The Southern Baptist Journal* which I had heard was a muck-raking tabloid. "Did you get M.O. Owens' motion?" he asked. "You watch, they'll never let it be voted on. That's how the liberals keep covering up the heresy in the seminaries."

I turned aside and made a wry face. For one thing, I was puzzled at Bill. He had not appeared to be a heresy hunter in the seminary or later in Chicago.

Still I watched. It was nearly 12 o'clock when the time came for business. The first four items on the agenda were non-controversial and disposed of quickly. The Chairman of the Committee on Order of Business then rose and moved that Owens' motion and another item be postponed until the afternoon business session at four p.m. Owens tried to get the floor, but was prevented when someone moved the previous question (the Chairman's request for postponement), which called for a vote. The business was postponed.

I thought it strange that Owens wasn't present at the afternoon session to present his motion. Bill Powell was on me like a bloodhound when I walked back into the press room. "Do you know why M.O. Owens wasn't there to present his motion? He had a death in his family and had to go home right after noon for the funeral. He told that to the Chairman of the Committee on Order of Business, but he postponed action anyway 'cause he knew M.O. would be gone then. But we'll be back next year," Bill assured, "and the next, until we get the Convention on record about Bible truth. Then the liberals in the seminaries can't hide their unbelief. You wait, just wait and see. We're not going to give up."

I walked away shaking my head at the change that had come over Bill Powell. Actually I thought the whole business was funny so long as it didn't get out of hand. At least, it put a little spice into meetings that could get pretty dull.

The next year, Bill and his inerrantist friends, as they were now known, were back and trying to get the same issue on the floor. They lost again to skillful parliamentary maneuvering. Was something going on here?

I began reading Bill's paper, which he published sporadically and seemed to be little more than a paste-up of sensational articles with perjorative, get-the-liberals' editorials by Bill. I couldn't accept his premise that many professors—including some whom he named in our seminaries—believed portions of the Bible, including Genesis 1-11, to be other than historical fact. My Old Testament profs at New Orleans, J. Wash Watts and J. Hardee Kennedy certainly had not held parts of the Old Testament to be mere "faith" history. Yet, Bill kept pecking away with sensational stories of problems in agencies and charges that some professors didn't believe all of the Bible to be true. To establish the latter, he printed answers to letters from some teachers he had written who refused to answer such questions as, "Do you believe Adam and Eve were flesh and blood people just like us?"

I noticed that most reporters skipped the pre-convention special interest sessions and arrived just before the convention was to start. A denominational editor suggested that I come early before the next convention and attend the Pastors' Conference which he said "has a tradition of setting candidates up to be nominated for president of the convention. The Pastors' Conference," he added, "has been taken over by the inerrantists."

In 1977, I took his advice and heard W.A. Criswell, pastor, of the First Baptist Church of Dallas, the largest church in the denomination, declare, "From beginning to ending, there is not a word or syllable or revelation in the Word of God that has contradicted, or ever will contradict, any true, substantiated scientific fact."

And Adrian Rogers, pastor of the Bellevue Baptist Church of Memphis, second largest church in the SBC, state, "If Genesis 3 is a myth, John 3:16 is a farce."

And Sam Cathey, an evangelist from Oklahoma, who termed himself "a Southern Baptist from my front bumper to my tailight," suggest that those who can't subscribe to inerrancy should "just get out. . . and as you go, don't take any of our churches with you." [1]

The pastors then elected Bailey Smith, a super-church pastor from Oklahoma, as their next president, succeeding Jerry Vines of Georgia.

When the convention opened, Vines was nominated by Adrian Rogers to be president of the SBC. He lost in a runoff to Jimmy Allen, the candidate for "unity amidst diversity," the code phrase adopted by those who were afraid of the doctrinal uniformity being pushed by the inerrantist camp.

The biggest hassle that year came over a motion asking that the salaries of denominational executives be reported in the denominational media. After the motion was narrowly defeated, I asked an editor of a state denominational paper if he knew what the agency heads made. "Sure," he grinned, "but I'm not allowed to publish the figures. I'll tell you and you can do what you wish with the information." Citing a "reliable source" (the editor), I reported the salary range in several agencies. [2]

By 1979, it was obvious to the most indifferent reporter at the SBC that the denomination was divided and in trouble over the question of truth in Scripture. That year, in Houston, the conservatives, as Bill Powell and his friends called themselves, elected Adrian Rogers of Memphis to the SBC presidency. Powell told reporters in the press room that Rogers would use his appointive powers to name people to the Committee on Committees who believed the whole Bible to be historically true.

Writers who did not toil in the denominational vineyards became educated in the way the Southern Baptist democratic system worked. One afternoon, I proudly displayed my expertise to a *Newsweek* writer who was covering the SBC for the first time.

"Here's how the power flows," I said with the air of an expert. "Autonomous churches contribute money to the Cooperative Program unified budget which is apportioned among agencies by the Executive Committee. The churches send messengers, not delegates, to the annual convention who elect a president. The president appoints several committees, the most important of which is the Committee on Committees. It's composed of two members from each cooperating state convention. At the next Southern Baptist Convention, the Committee on Committees presents a Committee on Boards, two from each state, for election. The year following, the

Committee on Boards nominates a percentage of trustees for each seminary and agency to replace those whose terms have expired. The messengers can reject these nominees, but I've never heard of this happening. The new trustees join other trustees in setting policy and electing administrators to run the agencies. Adrian Rogers was elected this year. If Bill Powell is correct, in three years, Adrian's influence will begin showing up on boards of trustees."

I looked at the new writer and grinned. "Get it?"

She mumbled, "I think so," and shuffled off.

"Moderates," calling themselves "denominational loyalists", soon became visible with their intent to turn back the conservative challenge. By the cheers or moans from denominational editors in the press room and upraised hand votes at the agency tables in front of the platform, it seemed obvious that the moderates had strong support from denominational employees. Friends in agencies confided that this was so and that they wished Bill Powell and his cohorts would go away and let mainline Southern Baptists get on with their work.

At age 49, I was now working on a Ph.D. in mass communications at the University of Tennessee in Knoxville. As a free-lance writer with a family, I couldn't afford to spend much time with denominational affairs. The best I could do was cover the annual convention for *Christianity Today*. Still, I sensed the controversy was approaching the crisis point when in 1980 at St. Louis the conservatives elected Bailey Smith, former president of the Pastors' Conference to succeed Adrian Rogers as Convention president. Behind Smith was a long line of prominent conservative pastors, waiting in the wings for denominational office.

That fall, I turned down an attractive offer to teach journalism at a Baptist university, opting to continue as a free-lance religion writer. The following spring, I accepted a part-time position as writer-in-residence at Hannibal-LaGrange College in Mark Twain's home town of Hannibal, Missouri. Here, I would be in an academic environment, lead seminars in journalism, and could continue a writing and speaking ministry.

Larry Lewis, president of Hannibal-LaGrange, urged me to write an "informational booklet" about the controversy in the SBC. "You know the situation about as well as anyone. Tell both sides and let readers decide."

I began gathering files and notes from a decade of reporting on the SBC,—stacks of Baptist Press dispatches; hundreds of pages of transcribed taped interviews with every president of the SBC since 1975, and some presidents prior to that, leaders in the conservative movement, astute moderates, and denominational employees. There were books, journals, and hundreds of clippings—an enormous mass of information, much of which had been gathered in my year-by-year coverage of the annual SBC business meeting called *a convention.*

I soon realized that the story called for a book and began querying contacts at book publishers. "Too hot for us," responded an old friend who is vice-president and editor-in-chief of one of the largest and most prestigious evangelical houses in the country, "I don't doubt that it will sell," he added, "but we can't afford to get involved in a fuss in a denomination as big as the Southern Baptist Convention."

The top editor at another publishing house wrote back to say they would publish the book. A few weeks later he called to say, "Sorry, but I've been vetoed by the people upstairs. They're scared of it."

Finally, a small, new publisher—Criterion Publications—in Texas, offered to print and promote the book. The founders of this company are identified with the conservative movement, and for this reason I was reluctant to have them do it. I agree with SBC conservatives on inspiration of Scripture, but I feared that objectors would say the book was a project for the Texas conservatives.

Larry Lewis, president of the college where I am writer-in-residence and a leader among the conservatives, had urged only that I write a history of the conflict as "you've seen it happen." Lewis never insisted that I follow any particular slant. And for the record, I did not do the book on "college time."

I realize that some—not many, I hope—in my denomination will be displeased at the candor of the book. They may feel that such a book will erode the confidence of laity in the religious institutions they support. The truth is, much confidence has already been lost among those who cannot understand what the squabble is all about, and why so many SBC leaders should be so exercised over a "preachers' quarrel."

I am not a particularly brave person. I dislike personal conflict. I want everyone to like what I write. Yet, I believe an honest airing of the history and issues in the controversy can help clear the air. The future of America's largest evangelical church body may depend upon how Southern Baptist church "messengers" vote during the next one or two annual conventions. I am convinced that what we will become and the impact we will make upon the nation and world for Christ depends largely upon how we will deal with the grave crisis which now threatens to rend us asunder.

But, I am not naive enough to think that this small account will serve to solve the critical problems and bring reconciliation. It is simply presented as the contribution of one observer, among many, in the journalistic fraternity, who cares.

REFERENCES

1   James C. Hefley: "Southern Baptists: Tension and Togetherness," *Christianity Today,* July 29, 1977, pp. 32, 33.

2   Ibid.

2 THE CONTENDERS AND THE CRISIS

The party labeling in the Southern Baptist Convention is confusing and irritating to many laymen and not a few pastors. Andy Rainey, vented his feelings in a "guest opinion" for the Mississippi *Baptist Record* titled, "You preachers shut up and listen to a layman for a change!" Rainey declared:

I'm fed up to my Adam's apple with all this gobbledy-goop from you preachers, classifying each other a liberal, conservative, moderate, ultra-liberal, ultra-conservative. Don't you know that what you may consider liberal views may be moderate to me or what I might consider moderate views may be conservative to someone else? Who gave you the right to classify anyone except yourself? [1]

Such scolding will not do away with the labels which have invaded the SBC, all of Christendom, and indeed all organizational entities. In government and religion, party labels range across the spectrum from "far left" to "far right," with "conservative" held to be right of center and moderate slightly to the left. Labels are now carelessly thrown about in our present denominational imbroglio, so that one man's "far right" may be another's "moderate." "Ultra-orthodox" may be appropriate for some Southern Baptists on the right and "liberal" for some on the left. Personalities have become so identified that in the SBC one man's "bell-ringer" may be another's "ding-a-ling."

But in broad definition and function there are only two parties with a large swing vote between. According to an editor's note released by Baptist Press, February 21, 1986, the official denominational news service has adopted the terms "fundamental-conservative" and "moderate-conservative" to identify the opposing sides in the SBC controversy. "These will replace the currently used terms 'conservative' and 'moderate.' " By way of explanation, the note said the terminology originated with Peace Committee Chairman Charles Fuller, who addressed the annual meeting of The Southern Baptist Press Association and supported the use of such terms. Some use the terms conservatives and liberals. Most describe the two groups, between which the denomination stands polarized, as simply conservatives and moderates. I prefer this designation.

These are not parties in the sense of formal membership. They represent large blocs of Southern Baptists who can generally be distinguished by differences, beliefs, affiliations, styles, and practices. Within each bloc is a core of activists seeking to enlist partisans and gather votes to attain clearly defined ideological and structural goals.

In this chapter, I will attempt to profile the parties by illuminating these differences.

The Peace Committee (about which more will be said later), elected in June, 1985, at Dallas, has announced that the most critical difference is in theology, something which has been steadfastly denied by many moderates.

The theological issue is confusing to many Southern Baptists because moderates and conservatives uniformly affirm the Baptist Faith and Message confession of 1963, the most recently adopted doctrinal statement for guidelines in institutions. The dispute centers on the nature of Biblical inspiration, yet all acknowledge the Bible to be authoritative and inspired, with the Biblical writers given freedom to express their own personalities in the writing. On the surface, it seems, as a former classmate of mine insists, "All Southern Baptists believe the Bible."

Conservatives disagree, saying moderates have misconstrued the meaning of a critical statement in the *Baptist Faith and Message*, "[The Bible] has God for its author, salvation for its end, and truth, without any mixture of error, for its matter . . ." [2] Moderates, conservatives claim, loudly affirm the *Baptist Faith and Message*, leaving untutored church members to think they believe all the Bible to be true, when actually they take the statement to mean only that the truth contained in the Bible is "without any mixture of error." They believe that only "faith truth" as revealed to the individual by the Holy Spirit, is fully authoritative, while the text which embodies this "truth" is subject to the errant limitations of fallible writers from a pre-scientific age. Moderates will say that where the Bible speaks to truth, it is without error though scientifically or historically it may indeed be incorrect.

Conservatives call themselves "inerrantists". They believe divine inspiration protected the Biblical writers from error of any form, historical, scientific, doctrinal, theological, or philosophical. Declares Memphis conservative Vaughn W. Denton, "Anyone who does NOT accept the Bible as infallible AND inerrant is a heretic and disbeliever! [3]

The next chapter will explore in more detail this truth that divides. Here we will give attention to other differences which are important in the dispute.

Heading the list is the critical question of the reason for unity: What binds a conglomerate of white and blue collar workers, Democrats and Republicans, Northerners and Southerners, ethnics and Anglos together? What is the *raison d' etre* for the unity of Southern Baptists?

Moderates, who assume that all Southern Baptists believe the Bible and are sufficiently sound in the doctrines that matter, say that the method and mission—realized in cooperative funding of agencies governed by duly elected trustees—provides the basis for "unity amidst diversity," a phrase which has become a code word among denominationalists. "We do not get together to check out each other's theology," declares Cecil Sherman. "We get together to do missions." [4]

Conservatives, who hold that many Southern Baptists in agencies and churches have drifted dangerously apart from Biblical truth, say the unity must be based on something more foundational. James T. "Jimmy" Draper, Jr., a former SBC president, asserts:

> There is no example in history of a church or a denomination which became more and more zealous for genuine biblical evangelism while at the same time becoming less biblical in its theology and moving away from the authority of Scripture. These two concepts are antithetical. The more biblical one is, the more he is interested in that which is biblical, that is, missions and evangelism. The less biblical one becomes, the more interested he becomes in the "social gospel." [5]

Conservatives declare that they fully support the convention method of cooperatively doing through agencies what local churches cannot do. But the foundation or reason for existence of the work is not the work itself, they say. It is the ideology or system of beliefs which undergirds and fires those who do the work, which rests upon an authoritative, inerrant Bible. "Who or what is the source of our authority?" asks Draper. "Is there a standard, a 'rule' which will be authoritative for God's people today?" 6 For Draper this authority is the Bible, inerrant in its original text.

Moderates agree that the source of authority is the Bible, though they do not believe an inerrant text is necessary. The rub comes with how diverse seminaries and other agencies can be in determining what is truth in the Bible. Moderates say it is not important whether teachers and other denominational employees hold to textual truth or message truth. Conservatives say if the text is errant, then the message can hardly be trusted.

It is not surprising that most denominational executives and teachers who have expressed themselves (and many have not) favor the moderates' position. Workers within a corporation tend to side with shareholders who are happy with the system. To date, none of the six seminary presidents have admitted (publicly, at least) to any doctrinal deviation in teaching in their institutions, though it is common knowledge that many professors do not hold to inerrancy. The moderates, and those they defend in denominational agencies, have stood united through seven years of conservative presidential victories at the annual convention.

Agency executives, teachers, and other key denominational employees have understandably kept personal views on the Bible truth question close to their vests. A few have "slipped" by answering Bill Powell's questions and found their "heresy" headlined in his journal. They have learned to be careful about what they write and say to reporters on the prowl.

Many agency executives, state and national, are known to take the moderate view on Scripture. They prefer to speak of Biblical inspiration in broad generalities. Many others, who believe in the inerrancy of the Biblical autographs, are reluctant to say so because they fear being ranked with the conservative party which is challenging the agencies on inerrancy and subsidiary issues. One executive—an inerrantists—told me, "It's enough that you know personally where I stand. Just don't quote me on anything."

Some refuse to be placed in either camp. As New Orleans Seminary president Landrum Leavell declares, "Controversy gets in the way of doing God's work. Frankly, there isn't either extreme that represents me. Theologically, I identify with the group on the far right. Denominationally, I identify with the group on the left. But neither group fully represents me." 7

While agency heads, with a few notable exceptions, are cautious, many pastors are not, especially those who feel secure within their churches. It is among these pastors that the differences in beliefs and ministerial styles are most obvious. Here are some generalizations which seem to apply.

Moderate pastors tend to be more active in denominational affairs by attending meetings and serving on committees and boards. Conservatives, until 1979, spent most of their energies in evangelism and building strong local churches. Conservatives are now paying more attention to the denomination. Moderates are striving to be more aggressive in their churches.

Most of the moderates and conservatives attended the same Southern Baptist schools. More moderates are seminary graduates than conservatives, although a growing number of conservative pastors are obtaining seminary doctorates. Some moderates have done graduate study at liberal Protestant schools. Some conservatives are also graduates of Luther Rice Seminary, which affirms Biblical inerrancy and places strong emphasis on development of administrative gifts in the pastorate.

Charles Stanley, who graduated from an SBC college and Southwestern seminary and took a doctorate in theology at Luther Rice, was honored as Luther Rice's alumnus of the year just before he was elected president of the Convention.

A growing number of conservatives, who attended Baptist colleges, attended independent Mid-America Seminary, which is now as fully accredited in theology as denominational seminaries. Many others studied at the Criswell Center for Biblical Studies, which is accredited with the prestigious Southern Association. Both Mid-America and the Criswell Center hold to inerrancy. Each of the three independent school presidents holds an earned denominational seminary doctorate.

In the local community, moderate pastors are more likely than conservatives to join clergy associations and work closely with mainline Protestant pastors, Catholic priests, and Jewish rabbis in inter-faith social ministries.

Conservatives tend to be more separatist and avoid associations with religious "liberals." Conservatives are more comfortable with Biblical inerrantists in other denominations and with workers in evangelical parachurch ministries such as Campus Crusade for Christ. Says Harold L. Fickett, Jr., "There is more fellowship between an Episcopalian and a Baptist who both accept the plenary (full or absolute) inspiration of the Scriptures than there is between two co-denominationalists who do not." [8]

Moderate preachers tend to gravitate to educated and affluent university-type Southern Baptist congregations where tolerance of diverse beliefs is a virtue. Conservative ministers are more likely to serve churches of the middle class. Moderate pastors feel at home in churches which are accommodating of theological and lifestyle diversity. Conservatives are in churches which expect their pastors to take strong stands on Biblical doctrine and perceived social evils.

Moderate and conservative pastors tend to prefer different forms of worship. Moderates tend to be more "high church" in liturgy and music while conservatives prefer the informality and spontaneity of the "old-time religion."

Distinct differences in preaching styles may be observed. Moderates are more apt to keep their congregations up on the latest ideas in psychology and social sciences. Verse-by-verse Biblical exposition is less important to them. They tend to be more vague on the "steps" of salvation than conservatives. They talk less about repentance than conservatives. They are less confrontational.

Conservatives probably spend more time in the Bible and preach with greater affirmation of authority than do moderates. W. A. Criswell and a number of other well-known conservatives follow the plan of preaching straight through the Bible. They tend to preach more in terms of blacks and whites than do moderates who often fall back into ambiguities. Conservatives spell out the "plan" of salvation in greater detail than moderates and give an evangelistic invitation at almost every service.

Conservative pastors tend to run a tighter ship in the local church than do moderates. Conservative pastors of large churches typically follow a corporate form of structure with the pastor as the unquestioned chief executive officer. Conservatives, and some moderate preachers also, dislike ruling "boards" of deacons and emphasize subjection of the diaconate to the pastor's leadership. Conservatives spend less time with committees; in fact, some practically ignore the traditional committee system in order to give more attention to church growth ministries.

Conservatives hold that the Scripture precludes ordination of women to the ministry, although most do not object to non-ordained women speaking from the pulpit. Women missionaries are always welcome. Conservative Charles Stanley, who staunchly opposes women's ordination, says he was converted under the preaching of a woman. Some conservatives have no problem with the ordination of women deacons or deaconesses, so long as the women officers are not in authority over men. Moderates generally are amenable to the ordination of women both to the ministry and to the diaconate. Some moderates are ardent promoters of women's ordination. Both conservatives and moderates, however, respect the autonomy of the local church on ordination.

Pastors of conservative churches that win large numbers of new converts each year insist on "standards" for church officers and Sunday School teachers. Typical requirements include attendance at the three major services, regular visitation of church prospects, tithing, and abstention from drinking and tobacco. Moderates, who tend to win far fewer people to Christ and church membership, dismiss this as legalism.

Conservative pastors pursue evangelism with two or more "revivals" each year. Many moderates have substituted low-key "retreats" and "religious emphasis weeks," during which few "decisions for Christ" are made.

Conservatives are more media wise than moderates and extend their preaching through radio and television. Conservatives tend to be more innovative and aggressive in church programs and ministries. Pastors of large conservative churches bring in "Christian" celebrities for testimonies in revivals and other special events. They are more apt to use show business techniques, such as special lighting in services, than moderates who chide conservatives for showy sensationalism.

Conservatives are more likely to sponsor innovative non-traditional mission programs, with some encouraging or allowing their churches to support members who feel called to serve in a non-Southern Baptist ministry. Moderates are more "orthodox" in working through denominational channels.

In sum, conservative pastors are generally more aggressive, energetic, and evangelistic at the local level than moderates. The result is seen in baptisms. I know of only one moderate pastor, William L. Self of Wieuca Road Church in Atlanta, who baptized more than 100 persons in 1984. Some prominent moderates baptized less than 20 each. One "First" church of over 2,000 members with a five-million-dollar plant, which probably holds the record in inviting moderate denominational personalities to speak, baptized five in a recent year. A large church, served by a leading moderate in an adjoining state, baptized ten. Moderates do not brag about low baptism-to-membership ratios. When the astounding differences are cited, they tend to give such excuses as, "We're not in the numbers game" or "we're building a strong fellowship." "Our church is in a slow growth area." Rarely will a moderate concede that preaching style, church programs, and theology might be factors.

According to conservative Paige Patterson, 22 of the top 25 churches in baptisms in the SBC for 1984 are led by pastors who are inerrantists, though not all of the pastors identify themselves with the conservative group. Moderates are glad to see conservative baptisms included in total yearly baptisms for the denomination, but when comparing churches, they prefer to talk about percentages in Cooperative Program giving where they tend to do better.

Many strong evangelistic churches pastored by conservatives do give smaller than average percentages of total budget to the Cooperative Program, but these proportions still rank ahead of many churches pastored by moderates. A few conservative churches which lead in baptisms give only token amounts to denominational ministries through the CP as the following table indicates.

TOP 25 IN NUMBER OF BAPTISMS, 1984

Church and pastor	Baptisms	Cooperative Program
1. Jacksonville First (Jacksonville, FL) Homer Lindsey Jr., Jerry Vines, co-pastors	1,183	$125,000
2. North Phoenix (Phoenix, AZ) Richard Jackson, pastor	1,073	$687,500
3. Del City First Southern (Del City, OK) Bailey Smith, pastor	1,006	$108,940
4. Dallas, First (Dallas, TX) W.A. Criswell, pastor	984	$474,946
5. Bellevue (Memphis, TN) Adrian Rogers, pastor	656	$329,725
6. Albuquerque First (Albuquerque, NM) (no pastor present that year)	650	$ 34,038
7. Sagemont (Houston, TX) John D. Morgan, pastor	568	$128,900
8. Fort Lauderdale First (Fort Launderdale, FL) O.S. Hawkins, pastor	558	$ 54,267
9. Houston First (Houston, TX) John Bisagno, pastor	523	$520,647
10. San Antonio First (San Antonio, TX) David Walker, pastor	519	$186,800
11. West Palm Beach First (West Palm Beach, FL) Jack Graham, pastor	460	$116,680
12. Graceland (New Albany, IN) (no pastor present that year)	396	$ 68,152
13. Westside (Jacksonville, FL) Harold Hudson, pastor	377	$ 14,250
14. Prestonwood (Dallas, TX) Bill Weber, pastor	375	$ 48,102
15. Fielder Road (Arlington, TX) William Everett, pastor	374	$264,194
16. Orlando First (Orlando, FL) Jim Henry, pastor	367	$626,532
17. Houston Second (Houston, TX) Edwin Young, pastor	354	$253,333
18. Cameron (Lawton, OK) Bobby Jones, pastor	352	$ 66,523

19. Castle Hills (San Antonio, TX) George Harris, pastor	331	$ 88,677
20. Fletcher Emanuel (Lumberton, TX) Richard A. Vaughn, pastor	310	$ 12,000
21. Green Acres (Warner Robins, GA) Terry Taylor, pastor	309	$ 81,565
22. Champion Forest (Houston, TX) Damon Shook, pastor	308	$290,167
23. Mount Pisgah (Austell, GA) James Rock, pastor	304	$ 37,498
24. Geyer Springs First (Little Rock, AR) Paul Sanders, pastor	303	$182,140
25. Cottage Hill (Mobile, AL) Fred Wolfe, pastor [9]	301	$ 76,955

The second table below shows the 25 largest church givers to denominational causes through the Cooperative Program. Many are pastored by men known to be active in the conservative movement. Note the number which are also on the list of leading churches in baptisms.

TOP 25 IN COOPERATIVE PROGRAM

Church and pastor	Cooperative Program	Baptisms
1. Midland First (Midland, TX) Daniel G. Vestal, pastor	$944,512	165
2. North Phoenix (Phoenix, AZ) Richard A. Jackson, pastor	687,500	1,073
3. Orlando First (Orlando, FL) James B. Henry, pastor	626,532	367
4. Amarillo First (Amarillo, TX) W. Winfred Moore, pastor	591,428	234
5. Broadmoor, (Shreveport, LA) John P. Sullivan, pastor	588,858	118
6. Tallowood (Houston, TX) Lester B. Collins, Jr., pastor	551,082	122
7. Houston First (Houston, TX) John R. Bisagno, pastor	520,647	523
8. Park Cities (Dallas, TX) James L. Pleitz, pastor	518,853	130
9. Dallas First (Dallas, TX) W. A. Criswell, pastor	474,946	984
10. Jackson First (Jackson, MS) Earl H. Craig, Jr., pastor	427,500	140
11. Wichita Falls First (Wichita Falls, TX) Morris H. Chapman, pastor	414,441	174
12. Lubbock First (Lubbock, TX) D. L. Lowrie, pastor	333,718	126
13. Immanuel (Little Rock, AR) Charles Barfield, pastor	330,299	052
14. Bellevue (Memphis, TN) Adrian Rogers, pastor	329,725	656
15. Olive (Pensacola, FL) Jerry Passmore, pastor	318,528	151

16. Euless First (Euless, TX)	311,497	277
James T. Draper, Jr., pastor		
17. Broadmoor (Jackson, MS)	309,541	052
David R. Grant, pastor		
18. Pampa First (Pampa, TX)	297,082	131
Claude W. Cone, pastor		
19. Bossier City First (Bossier City, LA)	296,938	225
Fred Lowery, pastor		
20. Champion Forest (Houston, TX)	290,167	308
Damon Shook, pastor		
21. Lake Jackson First (Lake Jackson, TX)	287,005	068
John A. Hatch, pastor		
22. Wieuca Road (Atlanta, GA)	285,200	107
William L. Self, pastor		
23. Shreveport First (Shreveport, LA)	273,382	043
William E. Hull, pastor		
24. Grand Avenue (Ft. Smith, AR)	273,108	185
James W. Bryant, pastor		
25. Mountain Brook (Birmingham, AL)	265,281	027
James C. Moebes, pastor [10]		

For closer comparisons of moderates and conservatives in baptisms and stewardship let us look at the 1984 records of three churches pastored by moderates and three by conservatives in the Long Run (Louisville) Association of Kentucky. In the column under baptisms, the first figure is for 1984, the figures in parenthesis on the top line in each entry are for 1982 and on the bottom line for 1979.[11]

Churches with conservative pastors	Baptisms	Membership	Budget	Cooperative Program
Ninth and 0 (middle class, city)	208 (116) (143)	4515	$1,037,000	$24,000
Valley View (middle class suburban)	68 (147) (113)	2265	$1,078,000*	$59,000
Highview (middle class, suburban)	141 (166) (163)	4344	$2,258,203*	$42,000
Churches with moderate pastors				
Deer Park (middle class, city)	9 (13) (6)	951	$294,492	$25,791
Broadway (suburban, upper middle class)	10 (14) (5)	1351	$398,122	$63,336
Crescent Hill (city, upper middle class)	9 (37) (10)	1445	$428,857**	$41,000**

* Building program costs included
** 1984 budget and CP figures not available. 1982 amounts listed.

Ratios of membership to baptisms and Cooperative Program giving make interesting comparisons. In 1984 the conservative churches in Louisville averaged approximately one baptism for every 28 members, while moderates averaged one for 138 members. Comparisons for per-member-average in Cooperative Program giving are inverse to the above. Conservatives averaged $11.44 per member while moderates (1982 figure is used for Crescent Hill Church) gave $33.79, almost three times as much. Yet when total Cooperative Program dollars for the three conservative congregations and the three moderate churches are compared the figures are much closer, with $125,000 coming from the conservatives against $130,127 from moderates. The reason is that conservatives grow larger churches which in dollar amounts of Cooperative Program giving come close to moderates who give larger per-member averages. In this respect there is little difference in giving, while a vast gap exists in baptism comparisons.

One of the conservative-led congregations in Louisville, Ninth and 0, is pastored by LaVerne Butler who has led Kentucky Baptists in baptisms for 10 of the past 17 years. Butler, who calls himself "a fundamentalist with a small f——not a fighting fundamentalist," has long been prominent in the conservative movement. Crescent Hill Church, adjacent to Southern Seminary, includes many seminary faculty and students in membership. It has a history of moderate pastors. A former pastor, John Claypool, recently left the SBC for the Episcopalian priesthood. Another moderate church in the Louisville comparison, Deer Park, also has strong ties to Southern Seminary. Deer Park is a resource center for Southern Baptist active in the nuclear freeze movement.

Many moderates favor a nuclear freeze, "peace with justice," and leftist "liberation" movements in Latin America. Activists in the SBC conservative party are more rightist in national policy. They favor "peace with strength" and support a strong line against the Marxists in Nicaragua and elsewhere. They tend to ally with such leaders of the so-called religious right as Jerry Falwell, Frankie Schaeffer, James Kennedy, Tim LaHaye, and Pat Robertson. Charles Stanley and two former SBC presidents, James T. Draper, Jr. and Adrian Rogers serve on the executive board of the American Coalition for Traditional Values (ACTV), which is chaired by LaHaye. Bailey Smith, another former SBC president in the conservative camp, is a member of ACTV's board of governors. The ACTV measures political candidates by ten "basic concerns," including a constitutional amendment to prohibit abortion (heading the list); a public school prayer amendment; tuition tax credits for parents; a strong national defense; and opposition to homosexual rights, pornography and "misguided" welfare programs. While most Southern Baptist conservatives may not be formally aligned with ACTV, the Moral Majority, and other "new right" socio-politico groups, they tend to share some or all of the above concerns. Not surprisingly, many, if not almost all, SBC conservatives supported Reagan-Bush, while moderates preferred Mondale-Ferraro in the 1984 presidential election.

Many moderates, on the other hand, feel a fraternal spirit with Jim Wallis, the Berrigans, Ted Kennedy, Gary Hart and others on the left in American politics and socio-moral controversies.

Moderate John Buchanan, a former Congressman and Southern Baptist minister from Alabama, for example, is an official with Norman Lear's People For the American Way, which spends millions fighting conservative efforts to restore "traditional moral values" in public school textbooks. Moderate James Dunn, Executive Director of the Baptist Joint Committee for Public Affairs, which represents the SBC and several small Baptist denominations in Washington, was a long time board member of Lear's lobby until forced by pressures from SBC conservatives to resign. The Cooperative Program funds four fifths of the Baptist Joint Committee's budget. Another agency head, Foy Valentine, Executive Director of the Christian Life Commission, has also shown sympathy with some trendy liberal causes, as indicated by some of the personalities invited to address Christian Life Commission forums. Both Dunn and Valentine, on separation of church and state grounds, oppose and are reluctant to promote conservative-backed resolutions passed at the SBC calling for constitutional amendments on school prayer and to prohibit abortion.

The contrasting alignments of SBC conservatives and moderates on national social, moral, and political issues are documented in a recent study by Furman University political scientist James L. Guth, who presented his findings at the Midwest Political Science Association in Chicago in April, 1985. In Guth's study, 66 percent of almost 1,000 SBC pastors returning a survey distributed to a random sample classified themselves Republican. Four years before in a similar poll Guth found only 29 percent professing Republican affiliation. Seventy percent of the SBC ministers who were now Republicans responding to the 1985 poll "strongly agreed" that the Bible is inerrant, 88 percent opposed the Equal Rights Amendment, 56 percent felt women should not be ordained; 78 percent favored the Moral Majority, and 98 percent preferred President Reagan. The minority identifying themselves as Democrats and non-inerrantists tended to hold opposite positions on the above issues. The percentage who classified themselves as Democrats fell from 41 percent in 1980 to 25 percent in 1984.

Professor Guth thinks it "clear" that the people who have moved within the SBC have turned to the conservative side. "The Southern Baptist Convention has always had the sort of problem it is facing now, but this time the fundamentalist faction is better organized," he says. [12]

Some SBC moderates see an ominous linkage between certain leading conservatives in the denomination and on the national scene. Moderate Paul Simmons, an ethics professor at Southern Seminary, for example, finds a parallel between the "current authoritarian trend" in conservative religious circles of America and the failure of the German church to speak out against Hitler . . . Now people there [in Germany] have little confidence in the church." [13]

Such pronouncements infuriate SBC conservatives, especially when coming from a seminary professor. The conservatives deny that any such parallel could exist.

Not surprisingly each faction in the SBC blames the other for the controversy. Moderates charge the crisis has been engendered by a political grab for power engineered by Paige Patterson, president of the Criswell Center for Biblical Studies in Dallas, and Paul Pressler, a Texas Appeals Court judge from Houston, along with a coterie of supportive "super-church" pastors. Southern Seminary President Roy Honeycutt declared in his 1984 convocation address: "The crisis facing Southern Baptists . . . is political. However much [the conservative] political machine may use biblical and theological smoke screens, this is the issue: Our convention is being wrenched apart by an unprecedented political crisis engineered by Dr. [Paige] Patterson and Judge Pressler." [14]

Conservatives say they are only trying to turn the denomination back from a liberal drift to its historical, Biblical moorings. Paige Patterson replies to Honeycutt's charge: "To say that we're trying to gain power implies that some other group has been in power, and it has countenanced a departure from historic Baptist beliefs in some of our institutions." [15]

Strong words from both sides. If moderates and conservatives are so far apart, what can they agree on? They are together on many long-cherished doctrines and principles of Baptists, including the primacy of Scripture; the Incarnation, virgin birth, deity, atoning death, and bodily resurrection of Christ; the priesthood of the individual believer; the autonomy of the local church; and a free church in a free society.

They are also agreed that the present crisis is very grave. Before the 1985 Dallas convention, Bailey Smith knew "of nobody who can bring us together because the issues are so deep and strong." Cecil Sherman, one of the most outspoken moderates, had "given up hope" for a reconciliation.[16] This was said before the appointment of the Peace Committee at Dallas. Sherman now serves on that committee along with many fellow moderates, vocal conservatives, and middle roaders.

Most Southern Baptists probably still think the controversy is a "preacher's quarrel" which could be settled by compromise. Most who do understand some of the issues have probably not yet taken public stands. Here is the great middle, the swing vote in every election. They are now studying the spoken differences, and praying for personal direction and the future of the denomination they love. The following chapters will hopefully give them and open-minded believers in other church bodies some enlightenment. The Southern Baptist Convention is not unique in the differences faced by many church bodies today.

REFERENCES

1   "Guest Opinion," Vol. 8, No. 8, p. 2.

2   *The Baptist Faith and Message*, published by the Sunday School Board of the Southern Baptist Convention, 1963.

3   "Letters to the Editor," *Baptist and Reflector*, April 17, 1985, p. 3.

4   Charlie Warren: "J. Sullivan Evaluates Current State of SBC," *Baptist and Reflector*, April 17, 1985, p. 3.

5   James T. Draper, Jr.: *Authority: The Critical Issue for Southern Baptists*, Fleming H. Revell, Co., Old Tappan, N.J., 1984, p. 96.

6   Ibid., p. 9.

7   Landrum Leavell: *The Vision*, Spring, 1985, p. 9.

8   Harold L. Fickett, jr.: *A Layman's Guide to Baptist Beliefs*, Zondervan Publishing House, Grand Rapids, Michigan, 1965, p. 14.

9   Listings as reported in *The Baptist Standard Daily*, Southern Baptist Convention Edition, June 11, 1985, p. 6.

10   Ibid.

11   Figures from *Directory* of Long Run Baptist Association of Kentucky.

12   James L. Guth: "Southern Baptist Ministers Shifting to Republicans," *The Southern Baptist Educator*, July-August, 1985, p. 16.

13   Michael Duduit: "Southern Ethicists Warn of Threat to Churches," *Baptist and Reflector*, October 31, 1984, p. 3.

14   Roy L. Honeycutt: Convocation Address. Southern Baptist Theological Seminary, 1984.

15   Paige Patterson, as also cited in Reference 11, Chapter 6.

16   Jack Sanford: "Sanford's Perspectives," *Western Recorder*, April 16, 1985, p. 2.

3 THE 'TRUTH' THAT DIVIDES

Next to the Bible, a little 19-page booklet with an orange cover is the most controversial writing among Southern Baptists. It is not the sayings of any "chairman," but the work of a 24-member committee, building upon the efforts of previous committees and published by the Baptist Sunday School Board. As the most widely used statement of faith in the SBC, it is must reading for many denominational employees, for it spells out what most Southern Baptists expect them to believe.

This is the *Baptist Faith and Message*, adopted by the Southern Baptist Convention in 1925 and reaffirmed on May 9, 1963. In ecclesiastical parlance it is a confession, not a creed. Confessions, as the committee states in the introduction, "are only guides in interpretation, having no authority over the conscience." The "sole authority" for Southern Baptists is the Bible.

Significant changes were made by the committee as they worked from a statement adopted by the SBC in 1925, to arrive at the one adopted in 1963. Southwestern Seminary Professor L. Russ Bush and Mid-America Seminary Professor Tom J. Nettles, formerly of Southwestern when they co-authored *Baptists and the Bible*, explain:

> In the first sentence a phrase was added that describes the Bible as being "the record of God's revelation of Himself to man." For most Baptists this simply affirms the obvious fact that the Bible tells of God's revelatory activity as such activity was historically manifested. In other words, to take one example, God actually spoke to Moses in a burning bush. The historical event was the moment of direct revelation. The Bible, then, is the record of that historical event. Some scholars, however, have suggested that a human

"record" is one step removed from the divine revelation itself; and thus, they suggest, the Bible is likely to be characterized by human error just so long as it provides a generally trustworthy account of the theological "matter" that was revealed. This subtle distinction did introduce an element of ambiguity into the statement ["It is a perfect treasure of divine instruction. It has God for its author, salvation for its end, and truth, without any mixture of error for its matter,"] which was welcomed by some. The next two sentences were seen by other Baptists as being an adequate safeguard against this more liberal interpretation. However, if one takes the word "matter" to be a reference only to the theological content (as opposed, for example, to all historical affirmations), then this article makes no claim at all for biblical infallibility in its traditional sense. The claim is only for "religious truthfulness," not total truthfulness. If, on the other hand, one understands the term "matter" to mean the properly interpreted meaning of the text (including facts and explanations), then the confessional statement clearly does affirm the traditional position on biblical infallibility. The article, worded in this way, does not exclude either group of interpreters from affirming the confessional statement.[1]

Most moderates and conservatives appear to agree that "matter" can be interpreted either way. The dilemma comes over how the *Baptist Faith and Message* is to be applied to denominational employees, particularly the ambigious phrase on page 7, "It [the Bible] has . . . truth, without any mixture of error, for its matter." Here is the friction point around which great billows of semantical smoke swirl: Is the Bible text inerrant or is only the theological message of the text, as perceived by the reader under the guidance of the Holy Spirit, without error?

Moderates claim that conservatives want to "creedalize" all Southern Baptists and make textual inerrancy a test of fellowship. Baylor University president Herbert Reynolds declares, " . . . The fundamentalists say, 'If you do not see this book as we see it, then you're not a first-rate Christian. You are not really qualified to have fellowship with the rest of us because you are not sufficiently orthodox.' "[2]

Conservatives retort that no one can creedalize autonomous churches, but that teachers, editors, and other key denominational employees, whose salaries are paid by all Southern Baptists, must affirm the *Baptist Faith and Message*, or some other acceptable doctrinal statement which declares the whole Bible to be absolute truth. "We can put the controversy to bed overnight," says Paige Patterson, "if our agency heads will guarantee that no one will be hired who does not believe in the accuracy and complete truthfulness of the Bible." [3]

Most denominational employees are required by their agencies to affirm and/or sign the *Baptist Faith and Message*, which includes the disputed phrase about truth. In a 1979 survey, Walter Shurden found that five of the six SBC seminaries require their faculty to subscribe to the *Baptist Faith and Message*. The sixth, Southern, asks faculty to sign an "Abstract of Principles," in use since 1859 and written by Basil Manly, Jr. who believed in the "plenary (full or absolute)" inspiration of the Scriptures. The Home Mission Board has adopted the *Baptist Faith and Message* but does not require employees to sign. The Foreign Mission Board asks missionary candidates two questions: "Are you familiar with the content of the *Baptist Faith and Message*? Are you in agreement?" The Sunday School Board requires employees "in certain designated positions" to sign the *Baptist Faith and Message*. The Annuity Board takes the *Baptist Faith and Message* as "guidelines" but does not require employees to sign. None of six Commissions (Brotherhood, Christian Life, Education, Historical, Radio and Television, and Stewardship) require employees to affirm the *Baptist Faith and Message*. Only seven of the 31 state conventions responding to Shurden's survey had offically adopted the 1963 Confession.[4] Presumably, the remaining state conventions and the six SBC Commissions require affirmation to an earlier or similar statement of faith.

Judge Paul Pressler calls the *Baptist Faith and Message* a "splendid" doctrinal statement. The SBC doesn't need more creeds or confessions, he says, but "more integrity" on the part of signatories to the *Baptist Faith and Message*.[5] Pressler, Patterson, and other conservatives think many denominational employees are deceiving untutored Southern Baptists by "playing" word games in affirming an interpretation of the *Baptist Faith and Message* which most members of the denomination do not accept.

Bemoans an agitated W.A. Criswell, "They believe the Bible is only inspired in spots and they are inspired to spot the spots." [6]

Moderates freely admit to believing that the truth contained in the Bible is the faith message which God revealed through errant writers. "It's clear to me," says Wayne Ward, professor of Christian theology at Southern Seminary, "that the message of the Bible . . . has truth without mixture of error for its matter. That means its substance. Its content. Its message. What it is about." [7]

Compare Ward's statement, which is representative of moderates, with former SBC president Jimmy Draper's position on Biblical infalliblity and inerrancy: "We simply mean that, in the original autographs, every word is inspired of God. . . . Infallible is . . . that which cannot lead astray or be deceived. Inerrant means without error . . . The terminology is flexible . . . Choose "true", or "accurate", or whatever word conveys the same idea." [8]

There are conservatives and moderates on Biblical truth in every mainline Protestant denomination. Taking the SBC as a locus, let us first attempt to clearly understand what each side does and does not mean by truth and inspiration. To paraphrase English statesman Edmund Burke: "Much of the mischiefs that vex the world arises from the misuse of words."

Conservatives do not hold that the Bible was dictated by God, as a business executive might dictate to a secretary, but that God used each writer's intelligence, memories, emotions, and literary skills and spoke in historical and cultural contexts to both immediate needs and future concerns. Conservatives also recognize that the Biblical writers sometimes acted as editors in drawing from previous written and oral accounts. They agree with the classic inerrantist, L. Gaussen that "Scripture is entirely the word of man, and Scripture is entirely the word of God." [9] But, as the Word of God, the text, however written and under whatever circumstances, was protected from error by God.

The biblical writers became inerrant and infallible only when writing under inspiration, say conservatives. Draper thinks it "quite likely that the Apostle Paul believed that the earth was flat," but "Paul was never called upon to comment on the shape of the earth. Therefore, it does not make any difference what he believed about it." What is important is that Paul and other Biblical authors were not "allowed to introduce error into what they did write, and that is what we believe happened through divine inspiration." [10]

Conservatives believe that only the originals are inspired. For those who chide, "Why be concerned about the inerrancy of a text we do not have?", conservatives point to the mass of ancient Biblical manuscript evidence extant in the form of versions, translations, and copies, plus multitudinous quotations in the writings of the early church fathers. Over 15,000 partial and complete New Testament manuscripts, in Greek, Syrian, Latin and other languages, are preserved, with almost complete texts reaching back to the fourth century and some portions dated before. This massive and well-attested evidence, conservatives say, has forced many liberal scholars to concede that the Gospels and Epistles were written much closer to the actual events than was once believed. Conservatives note that the late and revered A.T. Robertson, Southern Baptists' preeminent Greek scholar, estimated that only one thousandth of the entire New Testament text is in dispute between the oldest manuscripts and the King James text of the 17th century, with no major doctrine being affected.[11] Conservatives further assert that archaeology—in particular the discovery of the Dead Sea Scrolls (1947)—has pushed back the once accepted age of the oldest Old Testament manuscripts hundreds of years.

Conservatives are not literalists in ruling out metaphors and other literary figures of speech. "It is just as destructive of Biblical truth," says Draper, "to take a figurative passage literally as it is to take a literal passage figuratively or allegorically. Either will destroy the intended meaning of Scripture." Draper cites Jesus' statements, "This is my body . . . This is my blood," as examples.[12]

Conservatives further say that inerrancy is not violated by approximations such as the use of round numbers, loose quotations (as when a New Testament writer quotes from the Old Testament), inexact repetitions in parallel Gospel accounts, and grammatical and linguistic non-conformities to "acceptable" standards of our times. Literary vehicles and grammar are always relative to the period when used.

History and science, as descriptions of reality, are not contradicted in the Bible, conservatives say, although they concede that some differences do exist between Biblical accounts and some current interpretations of history and science. French scholar Jacques Ellul (not a Biblical inerrantist) states, "The problem is that our scientific controls are variable; what was considered an error 50 years ago might be considered true today. Science may change; God never lies to me." [13] Conservatives do not take the Bible as a text on any physical or social science, however when it speaks about any science, they affirm that it speaks correctly.

As to what moderates believe and do not believe about the Bible, here we must be careful in generalizing. There is no standard definition of inspiration among moderates, which conservatives say is part of the problem. Some who call themselves moderates believe the text is inerrant in the original, but since we do not have the autographs, and are not likely to find any, then we must accept and deal with errant translations. These are not moderates, but conservatives in their approach to Scripture, even though they may position themselves in the moderate camp. The real moderates believe—as contradictory as it may sound—that Biblical authority is not dependent upon inerrant originals, but upon the message which God gave through chosen writers, whose work, even under inspiration, was subject to misconceptions of science and history at the time.

Some SBC conservatives describe moderates as "liberals," but only in the sense of alleging that they believe the Bible to be errant. No SBC conservative of respect accuses denominational moderates in general of classic liberalism: denying the divine authority of Scripture; the sinfulness and lostness of man; the deity, virgin birth, atonement, and bodily resurrection of Christ; salvation by grace through faith; Heaven and Hell; and eternal security in Christ.

Conservatives, however, do note that some Baptist colleges hire non-Baptists to teach. Some of these, and possibly a few Baptist teachers, conservatives think, are less than orthodox evangelicals.

Some moderates hold that the only essential doctrine is the divinity of Christ. Moderate Cecil Sherman, a "biblicist" of his "own mix," says rejection of Christ's divinity is the only candid reason "singled out in Scripture" for exclusion of a teacher from an SBC school. A teacher, for example, who might be led by Scripture to not believe in the virgin birth, Sherman says, should not be fired. "[The virgin birth] is in two Gospels, but not in two others," he notes. "Did Mark and John make a mistake by forgetting to list it? If the virgin birth is desperately important, [Mark and John] must have erred." [14]

Some moderates see the cross more in terms of a moral atonement than a substitutionary sacrifice for man's sins. Where conservatives define evangelism as proclaiming that Christ died in our place as a sin offering, these moderates may mean, while speaking of Jesus dying for us, that we should make Jesus our Lord and teacher. Says Draper, "I am very much afraid that we [conservatives] do not agree with some of our brethren as to what evangelism and missions are." [15]

Moderates, along with some agency heads, use "authoritative," "sufficient," "fully inspired," and "infallible in purpose" to describe Scripture. These terms keep appearing in stated views of inspiration. For example, Milton Ferguson, president of Midwestern Seminary, declares, "I believe the Bible is fully inspired, reliable, sufficient, and authoritative for God's redemptive purposes. I affirm what the Bible says about itself." [16]

"Biblical authority is no problem for me," says Southern Seminary's Roy Honeycutt, who agrees with SBC theologian E.Y. Mullins that "infallibility is determined in light of purpose." Honeycutt speaks "of the inspiration of a prophet or apostle, . . . in the context that he's writing at his best and his finest in a unique way with insight he would not normally have apart from the Spirit of God." [17] Honeycutt has taken a strong stand against the inerrantist "political party."

Ferguson and Honeycutt use some terms acceptable to conservatives. But they have not gone on record as affirming textual inerrancy. New Orleans Seminary President Landrum Leavell has no such qualms. "Do I believe in inerrancy? Yes, absolutely. I was preaching the Bible was inerrant before these boys [conservative pastors] ever got ordained." [18]

Terminology about the Bible is one thing; applying it to Biblical passages is another. Deacon Smith at Crossroads Baptist Church may nod approvingly at such terms as "fully inspired" and "authoritative." But let him read or hear a seminary president or professor speak of contradictions in the Gospel accounts or say that certain Bible characters are only symbolic or representative figures and his dander may rise. Consequently, agency heads and teachers who may hold such positions tend to speak carefully when preaching or in interviews with reporters.

Genesis 1-11 is a major battleground between moderates, who tend to see primeval Bible characters as representative and/or mythical persons, and conservatives, who identify them in the same historical reality as George Washington. I asked Honeycutt if he saw the personalities in early Genesis as "flesh-and blood people with addresses." His reply is fairly typical of many moderates.

> I think the early chapters of Genesis deal with ultimate truth . . . You have some historical material, but when you get into ultimate beginnings just like the ultimate end [in Revelation], well, Genesis 1 is certainly in that framework of basically figurative language. I see the whole of Genesis 2 and 3 as fundamentally a statement about our rebellion against God. I see [the Fall] as representative. It happened to all of us. I see the narratives in personal dimension. I read Cain and Abel in terms of personalities.[19]

Randall Lolley, president of Southeastern Seminary, said in answer to the same question:

> My personal conviction is that the first chapters of Genesis are authentic—literal, although I don't have an [explanation] of literal. To say they are real history is not enough. I think they are supra-historical, above history, holy history. I believe there was a man named Noah, men named Cain and Abel; there are references in Scripture to these specificities, whether they were absolutely persons with names and addresses or not, I don't know. I'll have to wait until glory to find that out.[20]

Neither answer is satisfactory to conservatives who would like their agency heads to be less ambiguous.

There are other hot points of contention. Many moderates take Jonah as a parable and Job as a poem. Some date Old Testament prophetical books—Daniel, for example, beyond the events foretold. Some think that certain miracles were actually propitious natural events, seen in retrospect as supernatural by untrained observers or by later historians as mighty acts of God. Some use redaction criticism, about which more will be said later, to find "the Word of God within the words" of Biblical text.

Here is an example of the interpretation of a miracle by Eric Rust, uttered while professor of Christian philosophy at Southern Seminary.

> The miracle or wonder was not characterized by being unusual or abnormal, for even normal happenings could be wonders. What characterized a miracle was that the divine activity was especially evident in it to the man of faith and that it significantly furthered the accomplishment of the kingly power of God in redemptive mercy.[21]

In a later writing, after his retirement from Southern, Rust applies this philosophy to the "miraculous" crossing of the Red Sea by the freed Hebrew slaves.

> . . . In one sense, what occurred might be dismissed as a natural phenomenon. A strong wind drove back the waters and provided a way of escape over the dry seabed. Its cessation made possible the return of the waters and the drowning of the Egyptians. But the miracle was not just a wind driving back waters from a reedy lake and marsh. More was involved. The miracle was its occurrence at the time it did. It happened at the time when Israel needed it and when Moses was present to point to the divine presence of God. The miracle was God **using a natural happening** [emphasis mine] to deliver his people and so guiding them and the forces of nature that they fulfilled his liberating purpose. This was no mere chance occurrence of nature. It was a mighty act of the Lord. The historical happening became a revelatory act. It was a salvific event in which the Hebrew people were redeemed and recognized the greatness of their God.[22]

Rust's former New Testament colleague at Southern, Frank Stagg, provides an excellent illustration of how moderates use redaction criticism to determine the Word within or behind the text. A redactor is one who edits or revises. The example is part of a larger article by Stagg for *Folio*, a newsletter for Southern Baptist Women in Ministry, in which the author attempts to show how "flawed" interpretation of the "rib story" in Genesis 2:18-23 has served "to denigrate women or subordinate them to men."

> Isolated, the rib story does subordinate woman to man; but we do not have this story in isolation! We have it only as it appears in Genesis as a whole. There are at least two creation stories in Genesis, the rib story in Chapter Two being developed by a newer story in 1:1-2:4a, echoed in 5:1. The story in Chapter One is free of any subordination of male or female to the other and this story overrides and gives new perspective to the rib story . . . Significantly, there is no trace that Jesus ever referred to the rib story. He built upon the egalitarian story in Chapter One . . .[23]

Many more examples could be given to illustrate the broad differences between SBC conservatives and moderates on the nature of Biblical truth.

In sum, conservatives hold the text to be inerrant truth, while moderates ascribe truth to the message emanating from the text, and in conjunction with other passages as disclosed by the Holy Spirit.

Which position is Biblical? Which is the view of the church fathers, the Protestant Reformers, and our Baptist founders?

Conservatives and moderates both appeal to Scripture and quote such familiar texts as 2 Timothy 3:16, "All Scripture is given by inspiration [literally "God-breathed"] . . .;" 2 Peter 1:21, ". . . holy men of old spoke as they were moved (carried along) by the Holy Spirit;" John 10:35, ". . . Scripture cannot be broken;" John 17:17, ". . . thy word is truth;" and Matthew 5:17,18, ". . . till heaven and earth pass, one jot or one tittle shall in no wise pass from the law, till all be fulfilled." Moderates note that the term inerrancy is not mentioned in any of these passages, nor elsewhere in the Bible. Conservatives say inerrancy is assumed by the Biblical writers. Conservatives ask, "How can God 'breathe' error?" And, "If God's word is truth, how can it be errant?"

Both look to Jesus for support. Conservatives say if Adam, Noah, and Jonah were mythological or representative figures, then Jesus erred, for he spoke of them as actual people. Moderates say Jesus spoke of Old Testament characters as they were understood in his day. Moderates further say that the Living Word fulfills and stands above the written Word which is to be interpreted in the light of Christ's ethic and love. Conservatives say that the authority of Jesus is linked to the authority of the written Word, which declares Him to us. The arguments continue ad infinitum, with both acclaiming the Bible to be authoritative.

Most SBC moderates and even classic liberals in other denominations concede that church history until the 19th century belongs to inerrantists. Kirsop Lake, a liberal New Testament scholar at the University of Chicago, wrote in *The Religion of Yesterday and Tomorrow (1926)*:

> How many were there, for instance, in Christian churches in the 18th century who doubted the infallible inspiration of all Scripture? A few, perhaps, but very few. No, the fundamentalist may be wrong; I think that he is. But it is we who have departed from the tradition, not he, and I am sorry for the fate of anyone who tries to argue with a fundamentalist on the basis of authority. The Bible and the *corpus theologicum* is on the fundamentalist side.[24]

The evidence, as Kirsop Lake concedes, is beyond serious question.

Clement of Rome (about 90 A.D.) said "The Scriptures are the true words of the Holy Spirit." [25]

Augustine (354-430): ". . . Not one of [the Biblical authors] has erred." [26]

Calvin (1509-64): A "testimony of the Holy Spirit" who dictated the whole content of the Bible.[27]

The objection is made that the Reformers and the early Protestant creeds and confessions did not use the term inerrancy. While that is true, conservatives argue convincingly that they assumed inerrancy; indeed the doctrine was not questioned until after medieval times. H.E. Dana, whose hermeneutics text has been studied by thousands of SBC seminarians, declared of the Augsburg Confession (1530), the earliest formal declaration of Protestant faith, "[Inerrancy] without doubt presupposes the Medieval theory of mechanical inspiration." [28]

Dana notes that the later Westminister Confession (1648) "gives the fullest and most complete statement of the Protestant view of scripture as the inspired and infallible word of God which has ever appeared." [29] The Westminister Confession became the standard for Presbyterians, Congregationalists, and many Baptists in both England and America.

Baptists do not claim to be Protestants in the sense of splitting away from the Catholic Church. But Baptists built upon previous Protestant statements of faith in writing their own. Like Protestants, almost all of our Baptist pioneers held to an inerrant Bible. For example, John Smyth, founder of the first Baptist church on English soil, declared in 1608, "The holy Scriptures viz. the Originals Hebrew and Greek are given by Divine Inspiration and in their first donation were without error moste perfect and theerefore Canonicall." [30]

The seminal synthesis of the beliefs of our Baptist forefathers on inspiration is L. Russ Bush and Tom J. Nettles' *Baptists and the Bible* (Moody Press, 1980). Their compilation, from historical documents, solidly establishes that Biblical inerrancy, as defined by SBC conservatives today, is the belief of our heritage.

The writings of the founders of Southern Baptist institutions are veined with references to Biblical authority and inerrancy.

J.M. Frost, founder of the Sunday School Board, stated, "We accept the Scriptures as an all-sufficient and infallible rule of faith and practice, and insist upon the absolute inerrancy and sole authority of the Word of God." [31]

B.H. Carroll, founder of Southwestern Seminary, in his book on Biblical inspiration, declared,

> If the words [of the Bible] are not inspired, how am I to know how much to reject, and how to find out whether anything is from God? When you hear the silly talk that the Bible "contains" the word of God and is not the word of God, you hear a fool's talk.[32]

As to embellishments of events in the life of Jesus by Gospel writers (which many moderates allege), Carroll said,

> There were no shorthand reporters in those days, and there is not a man on earth who could, after a lapse of 50 years, recall *verbatim et literatim* what Christ said, and yet John, without a shadow of hesitancy, goes on and gives page after page of what Christ said . . . Inspiration in that case was exercised in awakening the memory so that John could reproduce these great orations of Christ.[33]

James P. Boyce, who chaired the committee to organize Southern, the SBC's oldest seminary, held views on inspiration similar to Carroll. Boyce said the Bible "often gives underlying evidence that its authors knew truths of science that could not have been known to the science of that day." [34] Boyce believed Adam and Eve were historical figures and that their existence was necessary to the doctrines of the unity of the race, the dignity of mankind, and the universal sinfulness of man. Boyce insisted on the "adoption of a declaration of doctrine" by those "who assume the various professorships . . . No professor," he said, "should be . . . at liberty to modify the truth, which has been placed [in the seminaries] to inculcate." [35]

Basil Manly, Jr. was one of the first four professors at Southern and the first president of the Sunday School Board. Manly said that an uninspired Bible would "furnish no infallible standard of truth." He held to "the doctrine . . . commonly styled Plenary Inspiration, or full inspiration, meaning that the Bible as a whole is the Word of God, so that in every part of Scripture there is both infallible truth and divine authority." 36

SBC moderates readily concede that Carroll, Boyce, Manly, and many other theological pioneers were, in effect, inerrantists. Moderates take their comfort from theologians E.Y. Mullins and A. H. Strong.

Mullins, who wrote articles for *The Fundamentals* which served as a defense against liberalism, presided over Southern Seminary for 28 years and the SBC from 1921-1924. Mullins noted in *The Christian Religion in its Doctrinal Expression* (1917) that no theory of inspiration explains everything, neither the "plenary, verbal theory" of inspiration which "holds that every word of Scripture was selected by the Holy Spirit and dictated to the writer," nor the "theory of dynamical inspiration" which "maintains that the thought rather than the language was inspired," so "that men were enabled to declare truth unmixed with error, but permitted to convey their ideas in forms of their own selection." 37

A statement by Mullins that the supreme source of the knowledge of God is "the revelation of God in and through Jesus Christ" is often quoted by moderates who say that Jesus is the standard to judge truth in the Bible. Mullins never intended that. For him the "historical facts on which Christianity rests" are contained in the Scriptures.38

Moderates have a much stronger ancestor in A. H. Strong, a Northern Baptist theologian whose *Systematic Theology* and other works have been widely studied in SBC seminaries. Strong, who held to the dynamic theory, never cited any actual errors in the Bible, yet he said inspiration did "not guarantee the inerrancy of Scripture in every historical and scientific detail," but made the Bible "infallible" in "its purpose of communicating moral and religious truth" 39 "Infallible in purpose" is often used by Southern Baptist moderates today, while conservatives say the text is also infallible.

Strong partially accepted theories of higher criticism which called for rationalistic revisions of miracles and prophecies in the Old Testament. His contemporary, Crawford H. Toy, professor of Old Testament at Southern Seminary, went much further and asserted the Bible could not be reconciled with science in some areas, and therefore the Bible must be in error. Though Toy insisted that he had "always taught . . . in accordance with, and not contrary to" the seminary's Abstract of Principles (still used today), he was asked to resign in 1879.40 James P. Boyce, Toy's colleague and close friend, escorted him to the railroad station where Boyce reportedly raised his right arm and lamented, "Oh, Toy, I would freely give that arm to be cut off if you could be where you were five years ago, and stay there." [41]

Toy was engaged to marry the celebrated missionary Lottie Moon when she was to come home from furlough the next year. Years later, in reflecting on why she broke the engagement, Miss Moon told a relative,. . . "God had first claim on my life, and since the two conflicted, there could be no question about the result." [42]

Toy moved on to Harvard, which had long before fallen away from evangelical orthodoxy, and ultimately became a Unitarian.

Toy and many other churchmen were caught up in the currents of rationalism and higher criticism which were sweeping Europe and America at the time. This movement is so relevant to the Southern Baptist controversy today that we should step back and briefly sketch its development.

Radical questioning of the Bible as a supernatural book grew out of the humanistic climate produced by the Renaissance and was reinforced by German philosophy, French romanticism, and Western materialism and scientism. People became less mindful of the supernatural and the authority of the Bible as a source book and standard for life.

Directions in Western philosophy paved the way for rejection of the Bible as an historical and objective revelation of God. For Immanuel Kant (1724-1804), man's free will and immanent perception of right gave him power to develop morality within. George W. F. Hegel (1770-1831) saw God as manifesting himself in history through a process of reconciliation and contradictions, which Hegel labeled thesis and antithesis. Hegel said these opposites were always coming together and forming a new reconciliation or synthesis which led ever upward in a philosophical evolution. There was no absolute right or wrong, black or white, but only an amalgam of gray becoming better with every synthesis. Only the God above the processes was absolute. Friedrich D.E. Schleiermacher (1768-1834), the third member of the great philosophic triad, looked at man subjectively and made feelings the matrix in which religious consciousness was formed. Other thinkers influenced and were influenced by these three. Albercht Ritschl (1822-1899), for example, turned Schleiermacher's religious feeling into the social consciousness of dependence on religion. Religion, including Christianity, became in effect both the creation and necessity of man.

Romanticism rejected the Biblical doctrine of sin and affirmed the innate goodness of man. Sparked by Jean Jacques Rousseau, romanticism, which said man had been corrupted by ownership of property, spawned the libertarian and egalitarian theories which led to the French Revolution and helped prepare the seedbed for Marxism.

Romanticism also spurned materialism and scientism, brought on by the Industrial Revolution and the lionizing of scientific inventions in the press. The pursuit of a higher standard of living and an almost worshipful attitude of many Westerners toward science made the supernatural less needful and theories undermining the authority of Scripture less unsettling.

Johann G. Eichhorn (1752-1827) was the first to lay down the precept that the Bible should be subjected to criticism in terms of a human book. Jean Astrauc (1684-1766), a French doctor, had already decided that two creation accounts were in Genesis because of the use of the Hebrew *Elohim* for God in some places and *Yahweh* in others.

Such segmenting of the Old Testament reached an apex in the latter part of the 19th century with the Graf-Wellhausen documentary hypothesis, which denied the unity of the Pentateuch (the first five books of the Bible) and its Mosaic authorship. Later critics divided Isaiah, advanced prophecies, and relegated miracles to natural events perceived by the credulous who wanted to believe. The underpinning of critical thought was that all nature and history are locked in a closed system and there could not have been any intervention by a god from without. Darwin's new theory of evolution from lower to higher life forms, through natural selection and survival of the fittest, slipped smoothly into this philsophic frame.

German higher criticism and Darwinian evolution swept across the Atlantic and slammed into Protestant seminaries and divinity schools with hurricane force. Citadels once firm in supernatural faith began falling. Presbyterians lost Union and Princeton seminaries. Northern Baptists surrendered the University of Chicago Divinity School. Preachers, philosophers, politicians, and industrialists proclaimed the coming of a kingdom of ethical righteousness by social and political reform.

World War I delivered a hard punch to the utopian liberals. They quickly recovered, calling it "the war to end all wars." Then the League of Nations, in which they had placed their hopes, failed. The Great Depression, World War II, and the disclosure of the Holocaust, in which some of Germany's brightest minds participated, shattered dreams of an earthly utopia.

Liberal theology was dead in the water, with denominations decimated by membership loss and seminaries depleted of students for lack of purpose.

A new "theology of crisis," posing as a new orthodoxy, proposed to blend the best of the old and the new. The "mighty acts of God" would be resurrected from Reformation theology and grounded in a view of the Bible compatible with modern science. Trumpeted by Barth, Brunner, the brothers Niebuhr, and many others, neo-orthodoxy accepted the contradictions of human existence (man, for example, is both believer and unbeliever, obedient and disobedient, child of death and of eternal life) and called for a leap of existential faith to the God beyond reason, the Ground of all Being, and the truly Other.

Seminarians, including Southern Baptists, pored over the works of the great neo-orthodox lamplighters, and sloganized, "Love thy Barth with all thy heart and thy Neibuhr as thyself." The Bible was acclaimed the "reliable and fully authoritative guide," but still a fall ible book which became the Word of God to Every Man by illumination of the Spirit. As such, it was to be studied with the best tools of historical criticism.

So higher criticism remained to gather strength in denominations which had long been resistant of outside influences. Chief among these was the Southern Baptist Convention.

While battles between fundamentalists and modernists had raged in the North, the conservative SBC had been fighting over evolution. In 1921, J. Frank Norris swung his "broad ax" at a Baylor University sociology professor who reportedly denied Genesis history and advocated evolution. The Baptist General Convention of Texas exonerated Baylor in a committee investigation, then the professor departed in peace. It was a procedural game which everyone understood. A loud protest erupted over a professor. A denominational committee investigated and cleared the school. The administration discreetly advised the faculty member to look elsewhere for employment.

Protests against evolution kept popping up across the South. Norris came to every Southern Baptist Convention and pitched a tent near the Convention hall to damn the "liberals." An alarmed committee of Baptist educators warned the 1922 Convention in Jacksonville, Florida that "great care should be exercised lest, by innuendo and nebulous criticism, the minds of the people be weaned away from loyalty to their schools."

At the same time, the committee urged SBC schools "not to use" textbooks "calculated to undermine the faith of the students in the Bible." [43]

Convention president E.Y. Mullins then made three points "clear" in his presidential sermon:

First, we will not tolerate in our denominational schools
any departure from the great fundamentals of the faith in
the name of science falsely so-called. Second, we will not
be unjust to our teachers, nor curtail unduly their God-
given right to investigate truth in the realm of science.
Firm faith and free research is our noble Baptist ideal.
Third, we will be loyal to every fact which is established in
any realm of research, just as we are loyal to the supreme
fact of Christ, His virgin birth, His sinless life, His atoning
death, His resurrection and present reign." [44]

Pressures mounted for the SBC to adopt a binding doctrinal
statement for denominational institutions. A committee was appointed,
with Mullins as chairman, to report to the 1925 Convention in Memphis.

This was the year of the Scopes Trial and passions were running
high. Fearing a crackdown, the Baptist educators' association urged
schools to "avoid alliance with either Fundamentalism or Modernism."
The educators also declared that the "Bible cannot be taken literally
and never was meant to be." [45]

T. T. Martin from Mississippi, one of the chief critics of
"liberalism" in the schools, then proposed that the SBC divide. "Let
all who endorse . . . this stand taken by the Southern Baptist
Educational Association go into one convention; let all who reject
and repudiate this action go into the other convention." He warned
of "fearful division and strife" if this were not done.[46]

The Convention averted a possible split by adopting the Confession
of Faith presented by the Mullins committee. The document
included a revision of the 1833 New Hampshire Confession, a preface
on the meaning of confessions, and a concluding word on science
and religion taken from Mullins' statement on the two spheres at the
1923 Convention.

The New Hampshire article on the Bible was accepted with the
statement that the Bible has "truth, without mixture of error, for its
matter." One important phrase was omitted. The 1833 article
declared the Bible to be the "supreme standard of Christian
union . . ." "Of Christian union" was dropped in 1925.

An added preface included the qualification that the Confession
was "not to be used to hamper freedom of thought or investigation in
[non-religious] realms of life."

Some felt a sentence in the section on science and religion, "Man
was created by the special act of God as recorded in Scripture," did
not go far enough. In a strike against evolution," Committee member
C.P. Stealey sought to add, "This creative activity was separate and
distinct from any other work of God and was not conditioned upon

antecedent changes in previously created forms of life." His motion failed and the Confession was adopted. But the next year, SBC President George MacDaniel declared in his closing address, "This Convention accepts Genesis as teaching that man was the special creation of God, and rejects every theory, evolution or other, which teaches that man orginated in, or came by way of, a lower animal ancestry." Louisiana's M.E. Dodd moved that MacDaniel's statement be adopted as the sentiment of the convention and the creation-evolution issue be dropped from further discussion. The motion passed unanimously.

The SBC, at the convention level, averted major clashes over evolution and Biblical "truth" until the early 1960s, although skirmishes continued in some Baptist state conventions and colleges.

The most notable and volatile local uprising came at Georgia's Mercer University in 1939, a presage of later battles over the Bible in the larger arena. Mercer's top student scholar led a group of ministerial students in charging the Bible teacher, John D. Freeman, with teaching that Adam and Eve were mythical, Christ's death was not necessary for salvation, the Bible contradicted itself, and Biblical writers were shackled to the superstitions of their times.

A "committee of inquiry" held a hearing in a crowded college chapel, at which the leader of the student protestors stated his case and defense witnesses testified for the professor. The committee dismissed the meeting late in the afternoon, and the leader of the rebellion and his supporters emerged to face a rock-throwing mob of fraternity men, angry at the accusations against the professor. The Macon police had to be called to quell the riot.

The Georgia Baptist editor refused to print the charges of the ministerial students in the state Baptist paper. Mercer president Spright Dowell thought J. Frank Norris was behind the trouble and sought to expel the student "prosecutor". Dowell backed down only when a trustee suggested that the student might sue. The student was then graduated with scholastic honors. As had happened earlier at Baylor, Professor Freeman was cited by the inquiry committee for "mistakes" and was quietly permitted to resign. Norris had never visited the campus, but had provided encouragement to the students in publications.

Because of the way the incident had been handled, the student prosecutor left Southern Baptists over the incident and, after a few months at J. Frank Norris' "seminary" in Fort Worth, went to China as an independent Baptist missionary. When World War II came on, he attempted to enlist in the American forces as a chaplain, but was persuaded to accept a commission as an intelligence officer with the privilege of preaching wherever he traveled. He became one of the

most heroic figures in the China war theater and was recommended
for medals up to the Congressional Medal of Honor.

Then, ten days after the war ended, he was mysteriously killed by
Chinese Communists. An official investigation by the Allied com-
mander fixed the blame on Mao Tse Tung's revolutionaries. But the
report was "covered up" by U.S. diplomats sympathetic to Mao and
his "agrarian reformers," as they were then known. His parents were
told that their son had been killed by stray bullets fired by Chinese
"irregulars." His recommendations for medals became lost in the
military pipeline. Years later, the truth became known and a newly-
formed anti-Communist political organization took the young
preacher and war hero's name.[47] Few Southern Baptists are aware of
this incident involving the Mercer student by the name of John Birch.

It is an irony of history that John Birch's closest scholastic
competitor at Mercer was Chauncey R. Daley, who supported
Professor Freeman. Daley later was appointed editor of Kentucky
Baptists' *Western Recorder* and, after retirement, became a leading
ideologue of SBC moderates. Known for his candor, Daley went to
the root of the conservatives' complaint in a recent tape-recorded
lecture to a class at Southern Seminary:

> Doctrinally or inerrancy wise, the poison [conservatives]
> claim is Biblical criticism. That's what they are
> after . . . When the seminaries started teaching Biblical
> criticism and started talking about documentary
> hypothesis and other conclusions, that's when the poison
> started. When I came to [Southern] Seminary [in the
> 1940s], I can remember only one professor who stood
> up strongly for the Mosaic authorship of the
> Pentateuch. . . . The seminaries have been moving in
> that direction. . . If you want the Mosaic authorship of
> the Pentateuch, the historicity of the first eleven chapters
> of Genesis, and Job and Jonah as historical figures, go to
> Mid-America [an independent seminary founded by former
> SBC professors who hold to inerrancy].[48]

Few Southern Baptists knew higher criticism was moving into
denominational seminaries at the time. Professors who held the neo-
orthodox view on Biblical inspiration were largely restricted to
Southern, and they were extremely cautious about expressing
opinions on the sensitive issue. SBC historian, E. Glenn Hinson,
another ideologue of moderates, says "the majority" of Southern
Baptists were "still biblical literalists or near-literalists" and that as
recently as 1953, "historical critical interpretation had barely gotten
started, even in Southern Baptist seminaries."[49]

Conservatives have no difficulty with some types of Biblical criticism. Textual or "lower" criticism, which seeks to determine the text closest to the originals, is accepted by all. Literary criticism, which examines literary styles and methods—poetry, parable, allegory, etc.—of passages and books, is utilized by inerrantist scholars. Source criticism, which looks at the author's written sources, poses no real problem. Form criticism, which considers the oral stage in back of the writing, is acceptable to those who recognize that many Bible accounts were oral history before they were written.

Redaction criticism, as illustrated earlier, is troublesome and controversial among conservatives. The redactionist assumes that an editing process preceded the actual writing of much, if not most, of the Bible. The best known assumption is that Matthew, Mark, and Luke used other sources in writing their biographies of Jesus. The critic attempts to dig into the literary process, to discover, for example, why only Matthew told about the wise men. This presents no difficulty to the scholar who assumes that inerrancy and infallibility occurred at the moment of writing, whether the Biblical author was using his own remembrance, the memory of others, or a special revelation from God. The thin line of danger in redaction criticism comes, in the view of conservatives, when the investigator begins to assume that the text is not trustworthy.[50]

The ultimate transgression, from the conservative point of view, comes when the redactionist decides that large sections or even certain books should be removed from the Bible and replaced with "more desirable" material from the same time period.

T.C. Smith, for example, departed Southern Seminary in 1958, after suggesting that questions of the Biblical canon be reopened with some portions of the traditional text excised and other material added. Smith moved to Furman University in South Carolina, which presumably could accomodate his more radical redactionism.

Conservatives fear redactionists, in their search for "higher truth," will lead students to assumptions which could send some over the "edge" and into unacceptable liberalism and rationalism. Warns Jimmy Draper, "Every generation of students tends to take the teachings of its professors further than the professors themselves." [51]

Southern Seminary president Roy Honeycutt thinks conservative fear of higher critical study in seminaries is unwarranted. Honeycutt concedes that the "development hypothesis" once argued that Moses couldn't have written the Pentateuch. He sees "all kinds of evidences to the contrary" and thinks that Moses wrote at least some of the first five books traditionally assigned to Israel's lawgiver.[52]

In the dispute which now threatens to divide the SBC, the conservatives take a stand, beyond which they will not go, in critical assumptions about the Bible. They take the whole text, in the originals, to be inerrant and harmonious with natural truth, however difficult some parts of the Bible may be to understand or to reconcile with some current assumptions and theories of science and history.

Moderates leave themselves open to subjectivism by acclaiming that Scripture is only authoritative in "infallibility of purpose," "truth of the message," "truth as illumined by the Spirit," and other characterizations which do not demand textual inerrancy. Some moderates think denominational teachers should not be hindered by any parameters of a confession or creed beyond their faith in Christ. Cecil Sherman stated in the SBC's Christian Life Commission's *Light*:

> In the present day, we see colleges and seminary professors assailed. Whether they are right or wrong is not the primary question, [but] have they come to their conclusions by seeking the mind of Christ as revealed in the Scriptures? If they have, we may disagree with them, but they have functioned as Baptists. On these grounds alone should these Baptists be evaluated. And they should be praised for inquiring into the Scriptures rather than sandbagging them from behind a wall of tradition.[53]

SBC conservatives take a much more restricted view of Scripture and doctrine. For them, the truth of inerrant Scripture is not to be disputed, or to be reconciled with passing theories of science and philosophy, but to be held and proclaimed. Moderates are more change minded. They believe that great pillars of doctrine and revelation do not change, but that interpretations in the light of changing knowledge do. The text is fallible. The truth as different generations perceive it is infallible.

Conservatives and moderates do agree on the translation and meaning of Scripture at many points. Both find variations in Gospel accounts of many events in the life of Jesus, for example. Conservatives say the differences are not contradictory, but that the problem is in our limited understanding of the text and historical situation. Moderates say contradictions are possible, if not probable, because God disclosed his revelation through fallible authors. The revelation—the message God intended—is infallible. Thus the great difference between the two opposing factions in the controversy that threatens to split the Southern Baptist Convention is in the assumptive approach taken to the nature and inspiration of Scripture.

For many years, most conservatives were slow to see the great difference between themselves and those who take the neo-orthodox position on Scripture. Moderates (they did not call themselves that then) became impatient with the slowness of the denomination to move into 20th century thought and theology, as they perceived it. Finally, in the 1960s, they decided the time had come to "educate" Southern Baptist preachers with commentaries taking the new approach. The new ideas, published by the Sunday School Board's Broadman Press, stirred up a veritable hornet's nest. Conservatives fought back and the war began which engulfs the Southern Baptist Convention today.

REFERENCES

1   L. Russ Bush and Tom J. Nettles: *Baptists and the Bible*, Moody Press, Chicago, 1980, pp. 390-91.

2   "Baylor President Denounces SBC 'College of Cardinals,' " *Baptist and Reflector*, December 17, 1984, p. 2.

3   Tape recording of speech to pastors' group, Pleasant Valley, Missouri, March, 1985.

4   Walter B. Shurden: "Southern Baptist Responses to the 1925 and 1963 Confessions," *Review and Expositor*, Published by the Faculty of Southern Baptist Theological Seminary, Winter, 1979, pp. 69-84.

5   "An Interview with Judge Paul Pressler," Special Issue of *The Theological Educator*, Published by the Faculty of New Orleans Baptist Theological Seminary, 1985.

6   Interview, Hannibal, Missouri, 1985.

7   From a taped lecture at a Continuing Theological Education Conference, December 10, 1975, cited in William A. Powell's, *The SBC Issue & Question?*, Baptist Missionary Service, Buchanan, Georgia, p. 104.

8   James T. Draper, Jr.: *Authority: The Critical Issue for Southern Baptists*, Fleming H. Revell, Co., Old Tappan, J. J., 1984, p. 90.

9   L. Gaussen: *The Inspiration of the Holy Scriptures*, Moody Press, Chicago, 1949, p. 50.

10   James T. Draper, Jr.: *Authority: The Critical Issue for Southern Baptists*, p. 85.

11   James C. Hefley, *What's So Great About the Bible*, Revised and Expanded Edition, David C. Cook Publishing Co., Elgin, Illinois, 1973, p. 59.

12   James T. Draper, Jr.: *Authority: The Critical Issue for Southern Baptists*, p. 86.

13   David W. Gill: "Jacques Ellul: Answers from a Man Who Asks Hard Questions," *Christianity Today*, April 20, 1984, p. 18.

14   Interview, Southern Baptist Convention, Pittsburgh, June, 1983.

15   op. cit. Draper, p. 98.

16   Interview, Southern Baptist Convention, Dallas, June, 1985.

17   David Simpson: "Personal Interview with Dr. Roy L. Honeycutt, President, Southern Seminary," *Indiana Baptist*, November 20, 1984, pp. 2, 3, 8.

18   Interview, Southern Baptist Convention, Dallas, June, 1985.

19   Interview, Southern Baptist Convention, Dallas, June, 1985.

20   Interview, Southern Baptist Convention, Dallas, June, 1985.

21   "Biblical Faith and Modern Science," *Review and Expositor*, Published by the Faculty of Southern Baptist Theological Seminary, Spring, 1974, pp. 229-242.

22 *Advanced Bible Study*, Baptist Sunday School Board, Nashville, Tennessee, October—December, 1981, pp. 29, 30.

23 "Hermeneutics and Women," *Folio*, Published by Women in Ministry, Summer, 1985, pp. 1, 8.

24 op. cit. William A. Powell, *The SBC Issue & ?*, p. 34.

25 op. cit. James C. Hefley, *What's So Great About the Bible*, pp. 21.

26 Ibid. p. 22.

27 op. cit. J.L. Neve, *A History of Christian Thought*, Muhlenberg Press, Philadelphia, Vol. 1, 1946, p. 288.

28 H.E. Dana: *Searching the Scriptures*, Central Seminary Press, Kansas City, 1946, p. 96.

29 Ibid. p. 10.

30 James Leo Garrett, Jr.: "Biblical Authority According to Baptist Confessions of Faith," *Review and Expositor*, Winter, 1979, pp. 43-54.

31 op. cit. L. Russ Bush and Tom J. Nettles, *Baptists and the Bible*, Moody Press, 1980, p. 19.

32 *Inspiration of the Bible* (J.B. Cranfill, Editor), First Published in 1930 and Reprinted in 1980 by Thomas Nelson Publishers, Nashville, 1980, p. 20.

33 Ibid. p. 22.

34 op. cit. Bush and Nettles, p. 209.

35 Ibid. 206.

36 Ibid. 212 ff.

37 Judson Press, Valley Forge, Pa., pp. 143-44.

38 op. cit. Mullins, pp. 41, 47.

39 op. cit. Bush and Nettles, p. 264.

40 Ibid. p. 233.

41 William W. Barnes: *The Southern Baptist Convention 1845-1953*, Broadman Press, Nashville, 1954, p. 136.

42 op. cit. Bush and Nettles, p. 227.

43 Walter B. Shurden: *Not a Silent People*, Broadman Press, Nashville, 1972, p. 94.

44 *Southern Baptist Convention Annual*, 1922, pp. 35, 36.

45 op. cit. Shurden, *Not a Silent People*, p. 96.

46 Ibid. p. 97.

47 See James and Marti Hefley, *The Secret File on John Birch*, Tyndale House Publishers, 1980.

48 The two independent and conservative publications which quoted extensively from and offered the tape of Daley's talk for sale were the *Southern Baptist Advocate* and *Baptists' United News*, both in February, 1985 issues. Daley expressed his feelings about such use of the tape in the moderate periodical, *The Call*, March, 1985: "The desperation of the Southern Baptist fundamentalist faction is revealed in the sale and use of a retired editor's classroom discussion of ethics in Southern Baptist political life. The presentation was an honest revelation of Southern Baptist presidential politics before and after capture of the convention political process by the fundamentalist faction in 1979. [The lecture] was conducted with full awareness of the presence of Pressler-Patterson spies in the class; therefore, it is not suprising a tape ended up in the war room in Dallas. . . Those interested are encouraged to secure the tape, but it's not worth the $5 advertised in the fundamentalist [*Advocate*] publication." Quotations in this book are taken directly from a copy of the tape.

49 Glenn E. Hinson: "Eric Charles Rust, Apostle to an Age of Science and Technology," in *Science, Faith, and Revelation. An Approach to Christian Philosophy* (Bob E. Patterson, Editor), Broadman Press, Nashville, 1979, p. 24.

50 See "Redaction Criticism: Is It Worth the Risk?" *Christianity Today*, October 18, 1985.

51 op. cit. Draper, *Authority: The Critical Issue for Southern Baptists*, p. 21.

52 op. cit. David Simpson, "Personal Interview . . . "

53 May, 1983.

4 How the Conservatives Came to Power

In July of 1961 the Sunday School Board's Broadman Press began shipping to Baptist Book Stores the first of 4,000 copies of an innocent looking tan book with *The Message of Genesis* engraved in purple letters on the spine. It was a book that would become a time bomb to disrupt the unity of the SBC and set the stage for the crisis which is shaking the denomination today.

Author Ralph H. Elliott, a professor at Midwestern Seminary in Kansas City, plainly declared the stories of Adam and Eve, Cain and Abel, Noah and the Flood, the Tower of Babel, and some events in the life of Abraham to be non-historical and error-prone. "These stories," he said, "are what Alan Richardson called parables—'parables of nature and man in order to convey deep historical insight.' " [1] It was not important, Elliott continued, that the Biblical writer should now or then use poor grammar, poor science, or even poor history in reporting God's act. The important thing is the fact that the divinely inspired writer presents the act itself with clarity and truth. Error in literary vehicle does not necessarily mean error in message or the essential purpose of God.[2]

Elliott was simply taking the approach of neo-orthodox crisis theology which focused on "great acts of God" revealed in the Biblical text and subject to the errant perceptions and limitations of fallible writers in their times. The Sunday School Board apparently took the bold step in publishing Elliott's book in response to pressure for more recognition of the views of the neo-orthodox wing of the denomination. In so doing, they ignited fires of protest that would keep burning long past the controversy over Elliott's book.

K. Owen White, influential conservative pastor of First Baptist

Church, Houston, called the book "death in the pot . . . liberalism, pure and simple," a "sort of rationalistic criticism [which] can lead [us] only to . . . disintegration as a great New Testament denomination." [3] Sixteen of the 28 SBC state editors joined White and other pastors in criticizing the book.[4]

The two institutions directly affected dug in their heels. Trustees of the Sunday School Board urged Broadman to continue publishing a diversity of theological views. The Midwestern Seminary Board affirmed Elliott a "loyal servant of Southern Baptists . . ." [5]

If the two agencies thought the clamor would die, they were wrong. An informal group of conservatives met the following March to consider "the current theological crisis within the denomination." Baptist Press reported that their "apparent immediate objective" was to get conservative men elected to the Midwestern Seminary Board. Critics called the idea Ku Klux Klanism.[6]

The Elliott issue dominated the 1962 San Francisco convention. Church messengers supported unanimously, by standing vote, a motion by K. Owen White, reaffirming "faith in the entire Bible as the authoritative, authentic, infallible Word of God." Another White motion passed by a large majority expressing "abiding and unchanging objection to the dissemination of theological views in any of our seminaries which would undermine such faith in the historical accuracy and doctrinal integrity of the Bible. . . " This motion further called on trustees to "remedy at once those situations where such views now threaten our historic position." [7]

In deference to the trustee system, motions were defeated instructing the Sunday School Board to stop publishing the Elliott book and to recall all copies in distribution. The administrator of the Board did this anyway. A committee of Midwestern trustees met with Elliott and obtained a commitment that he would go easy on the higher-critical method. But when they asked him not to republish his controversial book with another publisher, he refused. The trustees then fired him for insubordination. This action pleased almost no one. Conservatives slammed Midwestern trustees for failing to deal with the theological issue. Moderates scalded the seminary board for doing Elliot a grave injustice in not clearing him of charges of heresy.

Elliott took a church in the Northern Baptist Convention. His defenders were unhappy with his treatment by the Midwestern trustees. If Elliott is "a heretic," said Kentucky editor C.R. Daley, "then he is one of many . . . Professors in all our seminaries know that Elliott is in the same stream of thinking with most of them, and is more in the center than some of them." [8]

Herschel Hobbs, pastor of First Baptist Church, Oklahoma City, had been elected SBC president. He conferred with the worried Porter Routh, then Executive Secretary-Treasurer of the Executive Committee. Both feared a division over the Bible issue unless stronger common ground could be established between the inerrantist and neo-orthodox camps. Routh came up with the idea of having a committee, chaired by Hobbs and with state convention presidents serving as members, to formulate a new confession of faith for presentation at the next year's convention in Kansas City. Hopefully, by then, passions would have cooled and all could unite behind the statement of faith. Routh's suggestion was presented as a motion and accepted by a virtually unanimous vote.

In submitting the *Baptist Faith and Message Confession* the committee plowed little new ground beyond previous confessions. They lifted intact from the 1925 Confession the phrase "The Bible has . . . truth, without any mixture of error," as applied to the Bible. Conservatives, as before, took this to mean inerrancy of the Biblical autographs.

Then, in a bow to moderates, the committee declared, "The criterion by which the Bible is to be interpreted is Jesus Christ." And they added a new introduction which stated, "Confessions are only guides in interpretation." With assurances from denominational media that the SBC was back on track, and that liberalism would not be tolerated, most Southern Baptists apparently believed the problem had been solved.

Other fracases put the battle over the Bible on the back burner for the next five years. Baylor alumni, upset by Harry Truman's salty language, pressured the university to cancel plans for awarding the Southern Baptist president an honorary doctorate. No one appeared to notice or care that Truman's theology was more Unitarian than Baptist.

Students at many Southern Baptist schools joined civil rights activists in protesting racial discrimination. W.A. Criswell, pastor of the largest church in the denomination, confessed that he had been wrong in opposing integration. First Baptist Church of Dallas would henceforth be open to all races. Many churches quietly changed their policies, while many others remained defiant.

Worried executives at the Sunday School Board consulted secretly with sociologists from the Massachusetts Institute of Technology and the University of Iowa on how to effect attitude change in the SBC toward integration. Board president James L. Sullivan recalled later how they were advised not to take the sledge-hammer approach which had driven thousands of members out of some mainline denominations. "They told us," Sullivan said, "that a revolution couldn't be effected by coercion, but only by educational process . . . We decided to take their advice and make a general approach: God created all mankind. God had a purpose for every life. As Christians, we could do no less than help each person discover their divine purpose and to reach their highest level of potential. We didn't deal directly with race, because we wanted to hang on to our people. We couldn't publicize our purposes. The segregationists would have blocked us.⁹

The plan, supported by other agencies, helped guide Southern Baptists through the civil rights crisis.

Meanwhile, the greater conflict over the nature of Bible truth and authority continued to seethe. *The Baptist Faith and Message* had helped, but many conservatives felt that some agency employees were applying "truth . . . without any mixture of error" to the message and not the text of Scripture.

Conservatives continued to be elected to the Convention presidency. K. Owen White had succeeded Herschel Hobbs in 1964. Hobbs personally affirmed inerrancy, but was no boat rocker. White took a stronger personal stand, but had no great influence on agencies. Wayne DeHoney and H. Franklin Paschall respectively followed White, with each elected to two one-year terms. Both were establishment men, who could overlook neo-orthodoxy, but neither were believed to personally hold the position that only the message of Scripture was infallible. Then, in 1969, came W.A. Criswell, the man many conservatives considered as their model in the pastorate. Not coincidentally, Broadman published that year Criswell's *Why I Preach That the Bible Is Literally True*. This infuriated moderates who were still resentful over the treatment of Elliott and his book.

Criswell accused no specific persons or institutions, but he minced no words in assailing the neo-orthodox view on Biblical truth. SBC moderates cherished the statement in the *Baptist Faith and Message* that Jesus is the "criterion by which the Bible is to be interpreted." Criswell thundered, "If we accept the teaching of Jesus Christ, we must accept the whole Bible, for Jesus Christ had set his stamp of authority upon the entire Book." ¹⁰ Moderates said the Biblical text was bound to the scientific ignorance of the writers' times. Criswell declared, "There is no contradiction in the Bible to any fact of science."

Moderates held Genesis 1-11 to be non-literal "faith history." In the context of discussing early Genesis, Criswell said "no small part of our problem [in seeing errors] lies in our stupidity."

Moderates were enamored with higher criticism in scholarly study. Criswell said, "higher criticism is often turned into channels of blasphemy and defamation because of the presuppositions of the men who are thus studying the Word of God." [11]

As for the dynamic or "thought" theory of inspiration, Criswell asserted,

> Thoughts are wedded to words as necessarily as soul to body. As for thoughts being inspired apart from the words which give them expression, you might as well talk of a tune without notes or a sum without figures. No such theory of inspiration is intelligible. It is as illogical as it is worthless. [12]

Then in a direct assault on crisis theology, Criswell declared,

> The divine origin of the Scriptures is now disputed in the name of scholarship, science, and religion. This is being done by those who profess to be friends and champions of the Word of God. Much of the learning and theological activity of the present hour is dedicated to the attempt to discredit and destroy the authenticity and authority of God's Word. The result of this is that thousands of nominal Christians are plunged into seas of doubt. Many of those who are paid to stand in our pulpits and defend the truth of God are now the very ones who are engaged in sowing the seeds of unbelief and destroying the faith of those to whom they minister. [13]

It was plain to all who he had in mind. Many members of the Association of Baptist Professors of Religion (ABPR) saw Criswell's book, which was being promoted heavily by Broadman and the Sunday School Board, as an attack on academic freedom. At their 1969 meeting the ABPR adopted a resolution brought by Robert Alley and W.C. Smith of the University of Richmond critical of the publicity given the book. At their next meeting, held in the First Baptist Church of Atlanta, ABPR president T.C. Smith charged that he and other professors had been intimidated by Criswell for their previous resolution critical of Criswell's book. At the same meeting, Smith repeated his call (for which he allegedly had left Southern Seminary 12 years before) that the books in the Biblical canon be reconsidered in the light of modern scholarship.

Conservative winds were blowing strongly at the 1969 convention in New Orleans where W.A. Criswell was elected president. On the eve of the convention the Sunday School Board announced that time-honored Training Union was giving way to a new membership training course called *Quest*. When the change was presented for a vote, a pastor asked if the planners knew that *Quest* was the name of an intimate deodorant for women. Uproarious laughter swept the hall. When he could be heard again, the pastor asked that the magazine be killed. "We aren't questing for anything," he shouted. "We've found the truth."

Editors had been so confident of the new periodical's acceptance that they had printed thousands of copies for shipment to churches. When *Quest* was put to rest by rambunctious messengers, these had to be destroyed.

Conservatives at the 1969 New Orleans convention also served notice again that agencies were to be watchdogs of doctrine. A motion passed stating,

> That this convention call to the attention . . . of agencies [the *Baptist Faith and Message*] and vigorously urge the elected trustees responsible for these agencies to be diligent in seeing that the programs assigned to them by the convention be carried out in a manner consistent with and not contrary to the convention's aforesaid statement of faith.

Planning for a new 12-volume *Broadman Commentary* series had been going on at the Sunday School Board for several years. The first volume was to cover Genesis and Exodus. Bob Mowery, a member of the planning committee and pastor of Park Avenue Church in Nashville, objected when Clifton J. Allen, then editorial secretary of the Board, announced that G. Henton Davies was to author the Genesis section. In recalling the discussion, Mowery wrote,

> [Davies] was known to be more liberal than the average Southern Baptist. I said, "Dr. Allen, Southern Baptists went through the trauma of the Elliott controversy. Why do you want to take us through the same thing again with a liberal commentary on Genesis? Dr. Allen replied, "Southern Baptists have come a long way since the Elliott controversy." Landrum Leavell, who at that time was a pastor and a member of the committee, spoke up, "Dr. Allen, if you think Southern Baptists are going to swallow a liberal line on the Bible, you don't know Southern Baptists." [14]

Allen apparently didn't "know" Southern Baptists. The brouhaha over *Quest* was mild compared to the uproar over the Genesis commentary in the Broadman Bible Commentary series, released in October following the New Orleans convention. J. Terry Young, editor of *The California Southern Baptist* praised the Sunday School Board for publishing "this significant set," adding in the greatest understatement of the year, "We don't know who will get to read the first copy off the press, but we confidently expect that he will find something in it with which he disagrees." [15]

Davies, a British Baptist scholar, took virtually the same non-historical tack on the first 11 chapters as had Elliott. But it was his interpretation of Abraham's proposed sacrifice of Isaac that drew the most fire. Davies said the patriarch had been mistaken about hearing God's command to sacrifice the boy. The idea, he said, came as "the climax of the psychology of [Abraham's] life." [16]

W. Ross Edwards, conservative editor of Missouri Baptist's *Word and Way* wondered,

> why some theologians do not emphasize the truths of the Bible without raising doubts . . . The writings of Dr. Davies are not suitable for an army marching forth to victory. He sounds more like a drummer boy beating a retreat . . . We believe that Southern Baptists cannot grow spiritually on a diet like Dr. Davies offers. I'm not prepared to "eat it." How about you? [17]

Venerable J. Wash Watts, an Old Testament scholar at New Orleans Seminary, said Davies' interpretation of the episode "casts dark doubt on the word of the Bible." Watts asked rhetorically, "Can Southern Baptists remain loyal to their confession of faith in the inspiration of the Bible and promote a treatment that abuses it as this one does?" [18]

However, Kentucky editor C.R. Daley argued that the argument was "the same old story of literalism versus nonliteralism." [19] One could disagree with Davies' interpretation without charging him with denying divine inspiration, Daley said.

Ross Edwards would not "eat" his colleague's reasoning. Edwards and several other aroused conservatives set up an "Affirming the Bible Conference" for May 30, 1970, to precede the Southern Baptist Convention meeting that year in Denver. Moderates were caught unprepared. In 1968 they had organized an E.Y. Mullins Fellowship to meet before the annual convention. Interest lagged and they had planned no meeting in Denver.[20]

The "Affirming the Bible Conference" gathered a wide cross-section of establishment Southern Baptists, with two former SBC presidents, Ramsey Pollard and K. Owen White, and one future president, Jimmy Allen, on the program.

Mild-mannered Joe Odle, editor of the Mississippi *Baptist Record*, stoked the fires for conservative protests at the upcoming convention. Odle's address on "The Bible and Baptist Leadership" was all the more influential because it came from a long-time denominational insider. The Mississippian declared,

> There is appearing, in some of the literature, materials

which are raising questions in the minds of a large seg-
ment of the Southern Baptist constituency. A rumbling is
being heard that will not be silenced . . . No amount of
reassurance from leaders has been able to stop it, nor can
we expect it to ebb as long as objectionable materials continue to appear.

Odle was alarmed over specific trends in convention publishing:

1. A "tendency to allow questions of Biblical criticism to creep
into curriculum materials."

2. A trend in "moving away from the positive doctrinal stand"
which the SBC "has espoused during its entire history." Odle was
"not nitpicking, but . . . concerned." He asked,

Have we become so weak doctrinally, that we cannot even
say this is what Baptists believe about God, this is what
Baptists believe about sin, man, etc.? If we do not have a
doctrinal position on these great central truths, then what
excuse do we have for existence as a denomination?

3. An "overemphasis on social action, with resultant danger of
neglect of the central spiritual message."

4. A "tendency to so emphasize the intellectual approach, instead
of a Biblical one, that the material all too often fails to meet the
spiritual needs of the people."

Odle called these trends "the 'uncertain sounds' which so many
are hearing" from agencies. "When we distill them to their basic
meaning we find that in almost every case the issue is the Bible and
the Bible message." Odle then referred to the 1969 convention
motion addressed to trustees:

Note the words "vigorously," "diligent," "see to," "consistent with and not contrary to." I do not know how a statement could be stronger, and this instruction is addressed
to the trustees of every Southern Baptist board, agency,
and institution.

"I am of the opinion," Odle continued, that great numbers of
Southern Baptists would seriously question whether the convention's
instructions were followed in the publication of some of the
materials which have been mentioned." Odle asked further,

Why is this happening? . . . Trustees, executives, editors,
and writers [may] feel that even though they accept some
of the more liberal theological views, that their position
actually is conservative, and that they are carrying out the
will of the convention. If this is their thinking, then I
believe that their interpretation or definition of conservatism is quite different from that of many Southern

Baptists. It may be, however, that these men who have the responsibility for the agencies and for the literature they produce, feel that the convention is wrong in what it is requesting, and that their more liberal view is the correct one. They feel that their position is what Baptists need to have, so they are publishing these materials with their point of view, despite the instruction of the convention.

After arguing that distinctive doctrines make Baptists, Odle recalled hearing a conservative pastor in Nashville in another denomination address a conference of SBC evangelism leaders:

He said, "I should like to take each of you by the nape of the neck and shake you, and say . . . , 'Act while you have the votes. Get rid of liberalism while you can. If you do not, the day will come when the situation will be like it is in my denomination. There the liberals can vote the conservatives out any day that they wish.'" [21]

The 1970 Denver convention turned out to be one of the most rancorous on record. Conservative messenger Gwin T. Turner of California was ready with a motion stating,

that because the new . . . *Broadman Commentary* is out of keeping with the beliefs of the vast majority of Southern Baptist pastors and people, this convention requests the Sunday School Board to withdraw Volume 1 from further distribution and that it be rewritten with due consideration of the conservative viewpoint.[22]

Striking a managerial stance for "unity amidst diversity", Sunday School Board head James L. Sullivan defended publication of the commentary by saying no Broadman book had ever been intended to express the official SBC position on anything and that the Board's policy was to produce books for different segments of the denomination. Clifton J. Allen, general editor of the commentary, urged messengers to permit the Board to pass on to the next generation a heritage of the open mind and open Bible. Their pleas went unheeded. Turner's motion passed by almost a three-fourths majority.

The Sunday School Board then asked Davies and Roy Honeycutt, author of the commentary on Exodus in the volume, to revise their material. This was not satisfactory to many conservatives. At the 1971 convention in St. Louis they pushed through a motion instructing the Sunday School Board to replace Davies with another writer. The Board assigned Clyde Francisco, a professor at Southern Seminary, to do Genesis. Francisco accepted, while making it clear that he did not reject the work of Davies, a man for whose doctrinal integrity he had great respect. Then in an apparent settlement with

Davies, the Board authorized a British publisher to reprint and sell the old commentary in England and several other countries outside the United States. Conservatives were infuriated when they found out about the deal.

Conservatives could only look back over the past decade in frustration. They had won almost every vote on the Bible issue at the Southern Baptist Convention, but it seemed little had been accomplished with the agencies, particularly the Sunday School Board and Midwestern Seminary. Elliott had not been discharged for teaching that the Biblical text was errant, but for taking his book to another publisher. The Sunday School Board had stood by its position of publishing books by both inerrantists and errantists. In reviewing the "tragic" decade, conservative Bill Powell would later reflect that nothing had changed: " . . . the generals are running the SBC while the troops are financing it."

Rumors ran strong that unless the perceived liberal trend was halted, some conservative pastors intended to take their churches out of the SBC. Alarmed at this possible loss and the need to educate the grass roots on the movement away from inerrancy, along with other perceived liberal trends, conservative leaders felt the time had come to start a publication that would voice their concerns. They met in the First Baptist Church of Atlanta in 1973, the same church where the ABPR had convened three years before to denounce W.A. Criswell.

First Baptist Church of Atlanta had undergone some changes. Roy McClain, the pastor when the moderate ABPR met there, had departed, a victim of racial strife. Charles Stanley, McClain's assistant, became interim pastor and developed a following among those who liked his strong conservatism and Bible exposition. When the pulpit committee declined to recommend Stanley as McClain's successor, Stanley's supporters called for a vote by the congregation. Stanley won. Ironically, Stanley had attended the University of Richmond, where T.C. Smith, the ABPR president who had proposed reopening the canon, now taught. Stanley, who was not raised a Southern Baptist, would later allege that one of his professors at Richmond had denied the resurrection of Christ.

Moving quickly to consolidate his leadership and get the church moving ahead, Stanley persuaded a majority of church members to vote to adopt "standards" requiring deacons and Sunday School teachers to tithe, visit church prospects, and be loyal to services. Thirty-six deacons resigned in protest and transferred their membership to Second Ponce de Leon Baptist, where the more accomodating Russell Dilday was pastor.

The conservatives, who met in Stanley's church, incorporated under the name Baptist Faith and Message Fellowship, in respect to the confession which declared the Bible to be "truth, without any mixture of error for its matter." They voted to start *The Southern Baptist Journal* and named as editor, William A. "Bill" Powell, a veteran Home Mission Board worker. A specialist in surveys, bus evangelism, and starting new churches, Powell was well-known to many conservative leaders. But he had not been conspicuous in the previous Genesis controversies.

Powell now took center stage as he came out swinging in the Baptist Faith and Message Fellowship's *Journal*, quoting from books of "liberal" professors and printing letters to denominational teachers and executives, asking them if they believed Adam and Eve, Cain and Abel, Noah and Jonah, and other Biblical characters to be historical personages. He printed yeas, neas, evasive, and sarcastic answers, and he cited those who refused to reply.

In his first issue of the *Southern Baptist Journal*, Powell reprinted an article from the December, 1970, *Baptist Program* by William Hull, then dean of theology at Southern Seminary, titled, "Shall We Call the Bible Infallible?" Hull said he wrote against the background of protests at the 1970 Denver convention and the "Affirming the Bible Conference" against "liberals" in the SBC. Hull, who declared the Bible to have errors—"its dates do not always agree," for one thing—said the doctrine of infallibility of Scripture caused division in churches, was not taught in the Bible, and was not practical for three reasons: (1) No original copies of the Bible have survived. (2) Even if there were a perfect text, it would need to be translated. (3) Even if "we did have a perfect text rendered in a perfect translation, we would be far from an infallible Bible because it would still have to be explained by fallible interpreters."

Powell recalled that at SBC conventions in 1971 and '72, motions had been made requesting that the *Baptist Program* print an article "expressing the Southern Baptist position on the infallibility of the Bible," to counter Hull's article. The magazine, then edited by W.C. Fields, had not.

Powell believed Southern Baptists to be "the greatest people in the world," but he said, "We have a cancer in our denomination. This cancer is that a small handful [of teachers, writers, and leaders] believe that the Bible contains serious errors. This cancer will destroy our great denomination unless it is removed." Still he assured readers, "There will be enough Baptists to rise up and help remove these liberals from our payrolls and places of leadership."

Powell kept hammering away at the theology dean. Hull resigned two years later, in 1975, to become pastor of First Baptist Church,

Shreveport, Louisiana. The seminary denied that he was leaving because of protests over his article on infallibility. Powell did "not ever plan to take credit for Dr. Hull leaving the seminary," though "many rejoice that Hull will no longer be in position to influence many young students." However, the reprinting of the article by Powell, followed by editorial comments and continued criticism, in the *Southern Baptist Journal* must have made Hull uncomfortable.[24]

In the past, Powell said, many conservatives had been "satisfied simply to take a stand. But we . . . must take action! The liberals are taking control while the conservatives are only taking a stand." [25]

SBC moderates and denominational leaders began to pay more attention to Powell's *Journal* though he published it only as funds were available, and sometimes several months went by without an issue. When it did appear, the paper stock was of poor quality, the layout uneven, and the content mostly reprints of sermons by conservatives and the editor's nettlesome correspondence, with editorials spotted throughout the paper.

Moderates tried to ignore his citations which were stirring up a storm among some pastors and laymen. Criticism centered on the name of the tabloid, How dare a jackleg bunch of fundamentalists take the name Baptist Faith and Message Fellowship and call their rag *"The" Southern Baptist Journal*? Who gave them such authority? Then agencies began receiving inquiries and accusations from churches, demanding to know if the reports in the *Journal* were true. Pastors and laymen also began popping up at denominational meetings with bothersome objections and introducing troublesome resolutions calling for adherence of agencies to the *Baptist Faith and Message* on Bible truth. The snickering and sniping by some moderates turned to gnashing of teeth.

Powell then embarrassed his board by reporting indiscretions of some denominational leaders. The most notorious was a prayer by a prominent North Carolina pastor, Randall Lolley, at the opening of a brewery.

Lolley explained in a statement to Powell that he had gone to a luncheon at the new brewery and offered a prayer at the invitation of a neighbor. "As it turned out," Lolley stated, "my prayer was called an 'invocation,' but was surely never in any case considered by [my neighbor] or by me as a prayer of dedication for that brewery." Powell printed Lolley's rejoinder in the the *Journal*. Lolley became president of Southeastern Seminary and Powell made the reporting of the prayer an annual event. It was such muckraking, along with other "personal attacks," which caused most of the Baptist Faith and

Message Fellowship's founding board to resign. Powell found more board members and continued.

More than anyone else in the conservative camp, the patient, plodding, and often painful Powell kept the Bible issue prominent during the middle and late 1970s. By his demanding and nagging letters to targeted individuals (which most learned not to answer) and by publication of revelatory remarks from the writings of some teachers and agency executives, Powell kept Southern Baptists aware that many in their denomination did not believe in an inerrant and infallible Biblical text. The stories and editorials in his tabloid were cumulative, consonant, and relatively constant (depending on when he had the money to publish), and they stirred more waters than the troubled SBC establishment would ever admit.

Except for an occasional jibe, the denominational press largely ignored Powell's allegations of liberalism. Occasionally, however, an SBC moderate in a denominational post said something that made alarming headlines beyond Powell's *Journal* and helped the conservative cause immensely. Conservatives had the Richmond (Virginia) *News Leader* to thank, and not the denominational press, for a report on theologian Robert Alley, head of the religion department at the University of Richmond. He was quoted as saying in the local First Unitarian Church,

> I see Jesus as really a Jew. I don't imagine for a moment that he would have had the audacity to claim the deity for himself. I think the [Bible] passages where he talks about the Son of God are later additions—what the church said about him.[26]

Alley, who had taught at the Virginia Baptist school for 15 years, did nothing more than take the redactionism of higher criticism a step further than many others who considered parts of the Gospels to be interpolations by the early church. But because he denied that Jesus had believed himself to be God, the story crackled across the SBC kingdom. Alley never repudiated the remarks, which were picked up by Baptist Press after being reported in the Richmond paper. Despite a deluge of protests, the president of the Virginia Baptist school merely moved him to another department where he would be less conspicuous. The story soon died in the denominational press, but Powell puffed and repeated the piece for all the mileage he could get.

Neo-orthodoxy and historical criticism continued to grow in the SBC despite stern reproofs and get-tough motions by conservatives at the annual convention, along with Bill Powell's drumbeat of liberalism, liberalism, and more liberalism in SBC agencies. By 1976, some SBC moderates and others who trumpeted "unity amidst diversity" were seeing the conservative threat as more than a small Norris-like cloud in the sky. What if a militant conservative should get elected SBC president? What if he used his appointive powers to stack the Committee on Committees with other militant conservatives, who in turn would select an action-minded Committee on Boards, who the next year would nominate a slate of get-tough trustees to agency boards, with the convention quietly accepting the nominations as they almost always had in times past. A string of such presidents could turn the denomination upside down so it would never be the same. The possibility was worrisome and some of the keepers of the old order became concerned.

They looked around to see who might be most likely to get elected and start the dreaded offensive. Kentucky Editor C.R. Daley, in his class lecture at Southern Seminary on denominational ethics, recalled their fear of Adrian Rogers, one of the original organizers of the Baptist Faith and Message Fellowship, and what they did to head off his rise to the presidency.

> Some of us saw the rising star out of Memphis named Adrian Rogers—in my mind, the most brilliant of this group, the one who poses the gravest threat to the Southern Baptist Convention. It was obvious he was to be the king. It was obvious to some of us that he wasn't the kind of king we wanted. So in 1976, when it seemed to be his time, some of us who are editors began to write and talk about the kind of leadership we needed. The kind of leader that most of us felt we needed was a fellow like Dr. Sullivan, . . . recently retired as president of the Sunday School Board. It was with my mind on him that I described in [editorials], paragraph after paragraph, the kind of leader we needed for the convention. This was [also] done by other [editors]. Dr. Sullivan was nominated. He was elected. He was used by some of us to head off Adrian Rogers.
>
> When [Sullivan] refused to be nominated for a second term there was a scrambling and out of that scrambling emerged Dr. Jimmy Allen . . . the first who openly asked to be supported for convention president. It was not an inerrancy candidate who was the first one who actually went out seeking votes. Representatives in most of the states, chosen by Allen on the basis of his knowledge, were called and asked to support Jimmy Allen. When asked why he wanted to be president, Allen would reply,

"It's to be me or Adrian Rogers, which do you want?" [27]

Allen was a known conservative in theology who had spoken at the "Affirming the Bible Conference" in Denver. But he was a tolerant conservative who believed in "unity amidst diversity." He was a man who could stave off the threat of a perceived conservative militant to the presidency.

Enter Paul Pressler, a Texas Appeals Court Judge, deacon, and Sunday School teacher in the Second Baptist Church of Houston, a man destined to play perhaps the key role in the conservative advance to the power position.

Pressler, a fifth-generation Southern Baptist, knew something about the decadent influence of liberal theology. As a student at Phillips Exeter, an Ivy League prep school, he had seen

> a church there . . . that was on its last leg because theological liberalism had killed it. I came on down to Princeton University and saw a university that, again, had been founded by believers to train people in the Word of God, which was then completely secular and humanistic and was undermining the basic truths of the gospel.[28]

Returning to Texas, Pressler "found the same type of liberalism [neo-orthodoxy] that I had known in the East, and that was the first awakening to me that we had problems in the Southern Baptist Convention." [29] Pressler said that the

> acuteness of the problem came to me when some students, who had trusted in the Lord through a Bible study which I had here in Houston, had gone to Baylor University and called me and told me that they were being very much confused, and asked that I come to Waco and meet with them, and study the Word with them and see their textbooks and listen to what had been going on in class . . . So I went up there. Coming back from Waco that night after reading *People of the Covenant* where it talks about the errors in Daniel, where it talks about the historical inaccuracies, and the other things that were in the book that was written by the one who would soon become chairman of the Baylor Religion Department, and who was teaching the same thing along with the rest of the faculty members in the class, according to these students, I felt that I was not going to sit around any longer, and help finance the destruction of the faith of my young people. Something had to be done.[30]

The Elliott controversy prompted Pressler to write a pamphlet called *A Message to Southern Baptists* in which he stated his concern about "liberalism" in SBC schools. His concern led to meeting other conservatives, including Paige Patterson, who would become the leading ideologist in the conservative push to power.

Patterson was another Texas Baptist blueblood. His father had served for over a decade as Executive Director of the Baptist General Convention of Texas. Patterson would subsequently earn a doctorate of theology at New Orleans Seminary, become associate pastor to W. A. Criswell, and be named president of the new Criswell Center for Biblical Studies.

During the 1960s and '70s, Patterson studied theology and Baptist history. He observed the protest over *The Message of Genesis* and the *Broadman Commentary*. He wondered how "a [conservative] theological direction established by Boyce, Robertson, Mullins, Carroll, and Scarborough could reverse itself so quickly?" [31] As he began asking questions, he began to experience

> denominational pressures in new ways. Sometimes threatened, sometimes ostracized by the "establishment," I soon learned the coercive potentials of a burgeoning bureaucratic denomination. The perils of bucking the tide were reinforced whenever an apparently threatening but sincere question was ventured. [32]

Patterson saw a "clear liberal drift" in which the SBC was "repeating the deadly errors of our brethren [English, Canadian, and American (Northern) Baptists who had through neo-orthodox theology lost their evangelistic fervor]." And he perceived a growing "centralization" in his denomination, borne along by a "modern, super-corporate convention structure." [33]

Pressler and Patterson met for the first time at New Orleans Seminary where Pressler and his wife, Nancy, had come for a Bible conference. A fellow deacon had told Pressler that he should meet a red-haired graduate student at the seminary named Paige Patterson "who thinks as you do." Pressler recalls,

> One night about ten-thirty, we knocked on the Pattersons' door. We went downtown for coffee and donuts at the Cafe du Monde. I guess you could say it was there where the Pressler-Patterson coalition was born. We talked about what could be done to turn Southern Baptists back to belief in an inerrant Bible. [34]

Pressler and Patterson studied recent history to determine why agencies had not been responsive to convention resolutions and a confession of faith which, in the Texans' minds, called for affirmation of inerrancy by agencies. The problem, they decided, lay with trustees who for various reasons would not act. The solution was then to get trustees who would. That could only be done by electing a string of conservative presidents who would appoint persons of firmness and purpose to the Committee on Committees and start the ball rolling towards control of agencies.

W.A. Criswell admitted that with all of his strong talk against "liberal influences," he had failed in his stewardship as president. He would later confess:

> I dallied on my appointments until finally Porter Routh [then Executive-Secretary of the Executive Committee] called and reminded me. I told him, "You know the Convention better than I do. Give me a list of the people you think best qualified to serve." I don't know who Porter consulted, but he submitted the names and I approved them. I regret now that I was unwittingly a part of the process that permitted our Convention to reach the place where we have men in our seminaries who deny the truth of parts of the Bible.[35]

Pressler and Patterson began accepting invitations to speak to conservative groups, mostly pastors' conferences. "We've been fighting battles without knowing what the war is all about," they said.

Then they explained how "Bible-believing" conservatives could start winning the war by getting messengers from their churches—up to ten per church, depending on membership and Cooperative Program giving—to the next convention and help elect a president who would act.

In 1977, before Pressler and Patterson launched their campaign, the popular Jimmy Allen was elected president. That year, the conservative vote divided between Jerry Vines, a pastor from Rome, Georgia, and Richard Jackson, who served a large congregation in Phoenix. Adrian Rogers was not nominated. Vines outpolled Jackson then lost to Allen in a runoff. Allen was elected to a customary second one-year term in 1978. Pressler, Patterson, and allies set their sights on the 1979 convention in Houston.

By spring before the June session, the Houston judge and the Dallas theologian had spoken to "rallies" of conservatives in 15 states urging them to get out the vote and bring the maximum number of messengers allowed for their churches to the convention. Although Pressler and Patterson did not vocally endorse anyone, it was understood that Adrian Rogers of Memphis was the best conservative prospect for election. Rogers was pastor of the SBC's second largest church, Bellevue Baptist in Memphis. He was young, attractive, and a compelling evangelistic preacher. He was an unquestioned conservative who had aided in the development of independent Mid-America Seminary which had met in Bellevue Church before purchasing a vacant synagogue a block away. Mid-America stood solidly for inerrancy. Adrian Rogers' popularity had been demonstrated by being elected president of the pre-convention conservative-dominated Pastors' Conference, a staging area for a number of previous presidents. Rogers, the man moderates and their compatriots in agencies feared, was the man for the conservatives. He had not yet given his consent, but they believed he would answer the call when it came.

Denominational editors and executives had now caught on to what was happening. Most denounced the rallies as "political," Oklahoma Editor Jack L. Gritz declared:

> Such maneuvering . . . is an insult to the intelligence, integrity, and ability of the messengers who will be coming . . . to the Houston convention . . . This group should never be permitted to take over the elected posts and organizational structure of the convention . . . When I get to Houston, as soon as I find out who the clique's candidates are—regardless of who—then I shall vote for someone else.[36]

The Texans made no apologies for their pre-convention campaign. As Pressler said later:

> . . . *We have to communicate. The Baptist press had constantly misrepresented our intentions, . . . our motivations, [and] . . . what we have been doing and so we have to have a method of getting behind the Baptist Press in order to let people know what is actually going on.*[37]

At the Pastors' Conference preceding the Houston Convention, Adrian Rogers turned up the thermostat. Every Baptist church with an excellent track record in baptisms, he said, "is a conservative, Bible-believing church" with a pastor who "believes in the inerrant, infallible Word of God. Inerrancy is not the only ingredient, but it is the basic ingredient." [38]

Evangelist James Robison warned that if Southern Baptists tolerate liberalism, "we will be guilty of the death of the convention. Without the Bible you have no message . . . no evangelism." [39]

But it was W. A. Criswell who evoked the loudest cheers when he told the mostly conservative gathering of almost 10,000 pastors, "We will have a great time here if for no other reason than to elect Adrian Rogers as our president." [40]

Still, Rogers was not eager to enter the arena. In fact, he adamantly refused when asked by some conservatives about six o'clock on Monday evening. Later that night, Miss Bertha Smith, a retired missionary whom he greatly admired, told him that she felt God had impressed her that he should run for the office of president. Then his wife, Joyce, who had been very opposed to his running, told him that God was changing her heart on the matter. After discussing this in their room, Rogers went downstairs about 11:30 p.m. to take a walk and pray about the decision. When he exited the elevator on the first floor, he ran into two leading conservative friends who were coming from opposite directions. He told them of his new uncertainty. The three of them returned to Rogers' room where they prayed with he and his wife until the Memphis pastor sensed a "clear direction" from God to run at 2:30 a.m., the morning the convention was to open. The election of president was on tap for that afternoon. Rogers later told reporters, "God came down in tears of joy as I was praying with two friends [Paige Patterson and Jerry Vines]."

As time for election of officers approached, agency executives warned of possible division. William M. Pinson, Jr., president of Golden Gate Seminary, said the 1979 convention "may mark the most serious crisis" in the denomination "since the financial crisis of the Depression. Our vital signs are weak. Our institutions are under attack from within. It troubles me in my gut." [41]

John Newport, vice-president for academic affairs of Southwestern Seminary, conceded inerrancy to be a "legitimate issue" but criticized those who impose 20th century science "on a book God ordained to be written centuries ago." [42] Lame duck President Jimmy Allen asked the SBC Executive Committee to kneel and pray that the denomination might not be diverted from its mission task.

Six men were nominated. Moderates hoped Rogers could at least be forced into a runoff. They were counting on support from agency employees (up to eight percent of the local church messengers) and others who did not want a party of theological uniformity on inerrancy to come to power.

When the popular Rogers won handily on the first ballot against his five opponents, there were gasps from stunned messengers, then whoops and applause from supporters. Grim-faced moderates groaned while high above the convention floor inerrantist leaders embraced in sky boxes—executive suites loaned by business friends of Judge Pressler—congratulating one another.

When reports of "Texas-style" politics arose, angry moderates cried foul. A pastor said he had seen one man voting eleven ballots in the presidential election. A registration clerk reported finding unmarked books of ballots with only those designated for the presidential vote missing. Votes on succeeding issues indicated that many messengers had voted in the president's race and then left. A later investigation showed no "massive" wrongdoing with voting irregularities involving only 284 persons. Conservative leaders denied encouraging improper registrations, while admitting privately that some might have erred because they had never attended a convention before and did not know the rules.

The biggest howl came when someone discovered that Judge Pressler had registered as a messenger from a church where he, even though a layman, had served as interim pastor and held only honorary membership. Pressler had been advised by a leading pastor not involved in the conservative movement that this was "the way it was done." When he discovered that this was being questioned, he tried to turn in his credentials. The attack lost its steam when it was discovered that some seminary professors had apparently registered in exactly the same way. In defense of the pre-convention campaign, Pressler declared,

> I've always felt Southern Baptists are 90 percent Bible-believing people, and that our institutions should be responsive to the will of the people. We were just trying to get Southern Baptists to . . . let their institutions know how they felt. Our activities were not unprecedented. The ten percent has been organized and reorganized. Look at the boards and you'll find they represent a very small fraction of our people. The 90 percent have never been organized at all. [43]

Moderates had shocked conservative messengers with two commentaries in the 1960s. Criswell had upset moderates with his *Why I Preach That the Bible Is Literally True* in 1969. Now came conservative Harold Lindsell's well-documented thunderbolt, *The Bible in the Balance*, timed by Zondervan Publishing House for introduction at a press conference at the fateful Houston convention.

Lindsell, Editor Emeritus of *Christianity Today* and a respected Bible scholar across denominational lines, was then president of the Baptist Faith and Message Fellowship. A leading, lifelong Southern Baptist theologian who had never been able to participate in Southern Baptist denominational life, the Wheaton, Illinois resident was termed a "carpetbagger" by some moderates. Lindsell pulled no punches in his press conference. He said his new book covered the "battle for the Bible" (title of a previous book) in many denominations, but the longest chapter was titled "The Southern Baptist Convention Moving Towards a Crisis."

Unlike Criswell, Lindsell named names and quoted excerpts from the writings of some SBC seminary teachers to "prove" their denial of inerrancy and deviation from doctrines which he said ran "counter to traditional Baptist standards." Lindsell also included results of a thesis survey by a Southern Seminary student indicating a decline in orthodoxy as students progressed through studies there.[44] Lindsell noted that the thesis had been read and approved by a faculty committee. Holding up his book to show the table of results, Lindsell declared, "If I were the president of this seminary, I would demand an investigation by an impartial committee." The seminary's president, Duke McCall, came back with his own press conference, at which he denied Lindsell's charges that some of his faculty were liberal, hinting that Lindsell might be losing his powers [becoming senile] in thinking so." When reporters relayed this to the book's author, Lindsell suggested that McCall was incompetent if he didn't know some of his professors were teaching liberalism and that he lacked moral standards if he did know and failed to have them fired. The exchange between the two respected theologians was not one of the high marks of the convention.

Zondervan, Lindsell's publisher, had hoped for a big splash at the convention, but the Sunday School Board's Baptist Book Store exhibit refused to display the controversial book. Bill Powell hawked copies on the sidewalk and distributed free ones to reporters in the newsroom. The attempted ban by the official exhibit and the controversy between Lindsell and McCall gave the book a giant sendoff.

Moderates were still reeling over Rogers' election when conservative Larry Lewis, then pastor of the largest SBC church in Missouri, offered a resolution calling for "doctrinal integrity" in SBC agencies. The resolution was patterned after a measure passed the previous year by the Missouri Baptist Convention calling "for academic responsibility and doctrinal integrity" in Missouri Baptist schools and exhorting trustees to employ only teachers who believe

> in the inerrancy of the original [Bible] manuscripts, the existence of a personal devil and a literal Hell, the actual existence of a primeval couple named Adam and Eve, the literal occurrence of the miracles as recorded in the Bible, the virgin birth and bodily resurrection, and the personal return of the Lord Jesus.[45]

Before Lewis' resolution was to be voted upon, Wayne Dehoney, a past SBC president with close ties to Southern Seminary, introduced a motion reaffirming the Bible to be "truth, without any mixture of error." Adrian Rogers came to the podium where Jimmy Allen was presiding and asked that Dehoney be "more specific in what he means by 'the Bible is truth, without any mixture of error, . . . If [he] means the truth of the Bible is true, that's nonsensical. The truth of everything is true." [46]

Dehoney pulled Rogers aside for a brief conference, then returned to the podium and asked Allen again for permission to speak. My interpretation and Adrian's," Dehoney said, "is that in the original autographs God's revelation was perfect and without error— doctrinally, historically, scientifically, and philosophically . . . . I bring that and ask you to support it." [47]

Hearing this, Larry Lewis said he could "cheerfully" withdraw his resolution for "doctrinal integrity."

Herschel Hobbs, who had chaired the Baptist Faith and Message Committee, supported "the Dehoney motion and the position of our president-elect, Adrian Rogers." Hobbs then said,

> I've received many letters asking what the committee meant by the Bible is truth, without any mixture of error—if that included the entire Bible or just the part that is truth. Obviously we had reference to the original manuscripts, but we accept [them] by faith, not by sight . . . The committee understood and so recommended to this convention [in 1963], and the convention adopted it understanding [truth, without any mixture of error] to include the whole Bible. [48]

With Hobbs' explanation, Dehoney's motion was voted upon and accepted by a sizable majority.

As a reporter at the 1979 convention, I happened to be in the press room and was not aware of the discussion and voting on Dehoney's measure until Larry Lewis and a group of Missouri conservatives walked in chortling about a "great victory."

"You elected Adrian Rogers," I said.

"Yes, and we won another victory," Lewis declared. "We finally got the convention on record that 'truth, without any mixture of error' means the whole Bible. It was part of the Dehoney motion that passed."

I quickly scanned the latest Baptist Press report of actions in the convention hall. "There's nothing here about that," I noted.

Lewis dropped a tape of the proceedings next to the tape recorder beside my typewriter. "Baptist Press didn't tell the whole story. Play this."

I typed from the tape the interpretation accepted by the convention and showed the transcript to the Baptist Press news director. "We pulled the man assigned to cover Dehoney's motion off to do another story," he explained. "The guy who covered for him didn't get all the details."

"Well, you've got them here," I said, trying to be helpful.

"I think we'll let it pass. The folks in the churches don't care about such detail."

"You'd better believe they care. I suggest you put it in the next report." He shrugged off the idea and walked away.

So the interpretation as stated by Rogers, Dehoney, and Hobbs and accepted by a majority of the messengers did not go into the denominational media net. Nor was it inserted in the convention annual which reports official actions. It did appear in my story from which some of the denominational papers subsequently quoted.[49] Once again conservatives won a majority vote on a resolution calling for agencies to respond on the Bible issue. Once again they failed to get the action sought.

But the conservatives had elected Adrian Rogers to the presidency, the man most feared by concerned moderates and denominationalists. Denominational editors quizzed him intensely in the traditional press conference that followed the presidential election.

Did he belong to the "Pressler-Patterson" political faction?

I don't belong to Paige Patterson, Judge Pressler, or anybody. I belong to the Lord Jesus Christ."

Did he favor a "witch hunt" of "liberals" in SBC seminaries? "No, but I will support an investigation by a fair and balanced committee. I am not against anyone or anything except the devil and sin. But I'll always be in favor of any [seminary professor] being replaced when it is proven by his admission that he doesn't believe the Bible to be the Word of God." [50]

Conservatives left Houston cheered by Adrian Rogers' declarations. Judge Pressler was pleased, but he urged them not to claim victory. Adrian Rogers had been elected for only one year. They had won only the first battle. They had to start preparing immediately for 1980 in St. Louis. A line of presidents, Pressler reminded, would be needed to appoint "good" people to the Committee on Committees, who in turn would nominate a Committee on Boards, who would nominate responsive trustees, who would bring balky agencies back to the "faith of our fathers." [51]

As for moderates, a key denominational employee was looking two years ahead to Los Angeles, when Rogers would be ineligible for candidacy. . . "We'll have an advantage there," he said. "The inerrantists cannot afford to bring as many supporters to L.A.. Institutional people are on expense accounts and will be there in force." [52]

REFERENCES

1   Ralph H. Elliott: *The Message of Genesis*, Broadman Press, Nashville, 1961, p. 15.

2   Ibid. p. 14.

3   Walter B. Shurden: *Not a Silent People*, Broadman Press, Nashville, 1972, p. 106.

4   Ibid. pp. 107, 108.

5   Ibid. p. 106.

6   Ibid. p. 108.

7   *Southern Baptist Convention Annual*, 1962, pp. 65, 68.

8   James C. Hefley: "The Historic Shift in America's Largest Protestant Denomination," *Christianity Today*, August 5, 1983, pp. 38-41. Much information from this printed article and my larger manuscript is contained in this chapter.

9   Personal Interview, 1977. This interview and other details on how the *Sunday School Board* met the racial crisis are included in James and Marti Hefley's *The Church That Produced a President*, Wyden Books, New York, 1977. The book was written on the occasion of Jimmy Carter's election to the presidency of the United States. See pp. 153-155 for specific information on how the Sunday School Board "educated" the SBC constituency on civil rights.

10   W.A. Criswell: *Why I Preach That the Bible is Literally True*, Broadman, 1969, p. 19.

11   Ibid. p. 47.

12   Ibid. p. 43.

13   Ibid. p. 78.

14   Bob Mowrey: "The Current Controversy Among Southern Baptists—Power Politics or Theological Division?" *The Sword of the Lord*, May 17, 1985, p. 3. Mowrey says that when he was a student at Southern Seminary, "I only had one professor who would come out and publicly state that he believed in the historicity of the first twelve chapters of Genesis. Recently a student at our Southeastern Theological Seminary called and read my title clear. He accused me of being out of step with Southern Baptists because, he said, "I don't have any professors at Southeastern who believe that Genesis 1 to 12 is to be taken literally and historically."

15   op. cit. Shurden, *Not a Silent People*, pp. 111, 112.

16   G. Henton Davies: "Genesis," Vol. 1, *The Broadman Bible Commentary*, Broadman Press, Nashville, Tenn. 1969, p. 198.

17   W. Ross Edwards: "Witnessing to the Truth, Editorial," *Word and Way*, January 8, 1970, p. 2.

18   op. cit. Shurden, *Not a Silent People*, pp. 113, 114.

19   Ibid. p. 114.

20   "Mullins Fellowship Plans No Meeting in Denver," *Word and Way*, May 28, 1970, p. 7.

21   Odle's entire address is printed in William A. Powell's *The SBC Issue & ?*, Baptist Missionary Service, Buchanan, Ga., pp. 158-173.

22   *Southern Baptist Convention Annual*, 1970, p. 63.

23   op. cit. William A. Powell, *The SBC Issue & ?*, p. 128.

24   Ibid. pp. 22, 23. For Powell's discussion on Dean Hull see pp. 114, 115, 228, 229, 241, 242. Hull's article is also reprinted by Powell in his book, pp. 230-241.

25 Ibid. p. 24.

26 Baptist Press, December 14, 1977 (Dispatch to media).

27 C.R. Daley: Lecture and Discussion on Denominational Ethics at Southern Seminary. Class on Ministerial Ethics Taught by Henlee Barnett. 8:00 a.m., July 20, 1984. For more information on dissemination of this lecture and discussion see reference 48 at end of Chapter Three in this book.

28 "An Interview With Judge Paul Pressler," in "The Controversy in the Southern Baptist Convention," a special issue of *The Theological Educator*, Published by the Faculty of New Orleans Baptist Theological Seminary, 1985, pp. 15-24.

29 Ibid. p. 16.

30 Ibid. pp. 17, 18. Judge Pressler also recounted this experience in a personal interview with me.

31 "Stalemate, The Controversy in the Southern Baptist Convention," Ibid. pp. 3-10.

32 Ibid. p. 4.

33 Ibid. p. 7.

34 Personal Interview, Houston, TX., June, 1979.

35 Personal Interview, Hannibal, Mo., May, 1985.

36 James C. Hefley: "Southern Baptists Turn Toward Inerrancy," *Moody Monthly* September, 1979, pp. 126-134.

37 "An Interview With Judge Paul Pressler," as cited above in *The Theological Educator*, p. 18.

38-42 James C. Hefley: "Southern Baptists Turn Towards Inerrancy," as cited above.

43 Personal Interview, Houston, Tx., June, 1979. The information on alleged irregular voting by "some seminary professors" was not made known by me until March, 1986.

44 Harold Lindsell: *The Bible in the Balance*, Zondervan Publishing House, Grand Rapids, Michigan, p. 173. Lindsell refers to Noel Wesley Hollyfield, *A Sociological Analysis of the Degrees of "Christian Orthodoxy" Among Selected Students in the Southern Baptist Theological Seminary*, 1976. The uncopyrighted thesis was later copied without permission from the author and sold by William A. Powell, not to make money, Powell says, but to "awaken" Southern Baptists to what was happening at Southern Seminary.

45 The background behind Lewis' resolution on doctrinal integrity is as follows: About a year before the Houston convention, conservative pastors in Missouri became upset over a story in the *Kansas City Star* which quoted a Bible professor at one of the four state Baptist colleges as saying he did not believe in a personal devil. Fred Powell, one of the pastors, called a meeting of the concerned pastors. Some wanted to bring a motion at the upcoming Missouri Baptist Convention to have the teacher fired. Lewis argued, "This is not the way we do things in Southern Baptist life. We cannot sit in a forum here and determine whether a teacher is guilty or not guilty of doctrinal inconsistency. We have to trust the trustees to do that. We [in the Missouri State Convention] do have a right, but also a responsibility to give direction and guidelines to trustees."

While the pastors continued discussing the issue, Lewis penned a "doctrinal integrity" resolution on the back of an envelope which "exhorted" trustees of the four colleges to hire only those and continue employment of only those who believed the Bible "in the original autographs to be the inerrant Word of God," in a primeval couple named Adam and Eve, that the Biblical miracles literally happened, that historical accounts in the Bible were true, and that Jesus was the virgin born, resurrected Son of God." Lewis presented this to the pastors and they accepted it and agreed to support it when introduced at their upcoming state convention.

When introduced, the resolution was referred to the Resolutions Committee which reported it out to be voted upon by Missouri messengers as a reaffirmation of the *Baptist Faith and Message*. Lewis then spoke from the floor and moved to substitute his resolution as an amendment. After an hour-and-half discussion, the doctrinal integrity resolution as an amendment was voted on and accepted by a large majority.

After the state convention the Missouri conservative pastors felt there should be a follow-up on the colleges. They began meeting about once every two months at the Bonanza Steak House in Columbia, Mo. At each meeting, a member of the group who was a trustee at one of the four colleges reported on what progress was being made to implement the resolution at his respective college. The professor who had been quoted in the *Star* subsequently retired and two Bible professors at another Missouri Baptist college went elsewhere.

46-48   From a personal interview with Larry Lewis who provided a tape recording of convention proceedings, Houston, TX., June, 1979.

49   James C. Hefley: "Southern Baptists Turn Towards Inerrancy," as cited above.

50   Press Conference, Southern Baptist Convention, Houston, TX., June, 1979.

51, 52   Conversations at the close of the Southern Baptist Convention, Houston, TX., June, 1979.

5 HOW THE CONSERVATIVES KEPT WINNING

Several denominational leaders were standing in the lobby of a Houston hotel discussing the election of Adrian Rogers. "Oh, it'll pass; it's the same old Norris stuff," they told themselves. Suddenly a young church history professor from Southern Seminary began shouting, "Fire! Fire!"

One of the old heads tried to reassure him. "Walter [Shurden], you just aren't old enough to remember; we've seen it before; we'll see it again; don't get too excited about it." [1]

In the memory of Shurden's elders, the SBC had survived J. Frank Norris, fights over evolution, the Great Depression, racial integration, and Genesis, plus the election of firebrand inerrantists K. Owen White and W. A. Criswell, both of whom had been cooperative in their committee appointments. It would surely weather Judge Pressler, Paige Patterson, and Adrian Rogers. Rogers would probably get the customary second one-year term at the next convention in St. Louis. Their wisdom was to be patient until 1981 when the "uncooperative" Tennesseean would be ineligible for nomination again. A strong denominational man could then be elected who would support "unity amidst diversity" and reverse any trend in committee appointments which Rogers might have started. So they reasoned.

Judge Pressler, Paige Patterson, and their conservative compatriots had the long haul in mind. Carrying writings of "liberal" denominationalists, they hit the hustings, speaking to groups of laity and pastors, reading quotes that appeared to demonstrate deviation from traditional beliefs.

Down in Georgia, Bill Powell kept pressure on with the Baptist Faith and Message Fellowship's *Southern Baptist Journal*. Powell was now trying to unseat the popular Jack Harwell, who had exercised great courage during the struggle over integration, from his post as editor of Georgia Baptists' *Christian Index*. Five years before Powell had arranged for a friend who subscribed to the *Index* to write and ask Harwell for his beliefs on the Bible and Adam and Eve. Harwell, not suspecting the plot, was "always happy to answer any of my readers." He candidly stated that he believed the Bible to be the Word of God, but did not "use the word infallible because the Bible is written by men." Harwell noted that the *Baptist Faith and Message* statement says "truth is not mixed with error but it does not say that the Bible is not mixed with error." Harwell could "cite many, many instances where a literal, absolute, blind acceptance of the Bible without an understanding of human nature leads to all types of contradictions." Harwell also did "not believe that Adam and Eve were one man and one woman," but that "the terms Adam and Eve represent mankind and womankind."

Powell began circulating copies of Harwell's letter without the editor's permission, an action which some conservatives did not approve. Confronted by possible court action, Powell stopped.[2] But, through the years, Powell kept urging that something be done about the editor. "Most Southern Baptists," Powell said, "will choose to believe what God says in His Bible rather than some new theories that Dr. Harwell learned from some of our liberal Southern Baptist teachers and leaders."[3]

After Adrian Rogers' election in Houston, Powell felt the time had come to strike and so he and his allies made plans to introduce a motion at the upcoming Georgia Baptist Convention to have Harwell dismissed. Moving rapidly to protect Harwell and keep the problem off the convention's official agenda, the Georgia Executive Committee asked its administrative sub-committee to meet with the directors of the *Index*. They were to bring a report back to the Executive Committee on the charges against Harwell's doctrinal beliefs resulting from circulation of the five-year-old private letter.

The newspaper's directors and the administrative sub-committee reported that Harwell had reaffirmed his "acceptance of and adherence to the *Baptist Faith and Message* statement" which had been adopted by the SBC and the Georgia Baptist Convention. The Executive Committee then reported to the state convention messengers that since Harwell had reaffirmed the *Baptist Faith and Message*, the committee had voted that he "continue his services as editor." The committee further expressed appreciation "for Harwell's professional ability," but added that the paper was "to reflect the spirit and theological position of Georgia and Southern

Baptists." The editor was "responsible for editorial expression," the committee said, but it was "understood that at times the editor's thinking and statements may not be in harmony with Baptists and other leaders in Southern Baptist life."

The skillful handling of the problem by the Georgia Executive Committee paid off. The convention approved a motion by a margin of four to one, expressing "our full confidence in the personal and professional integrity of the Editor." Messengers sustained a ruling that motions to fire Harwell were out of order.[4] The committee and parliamentary actions and the vote proved that the conservatives did not have the power in Georgia that they had at the national convention.

The Pressler-Patterson "information" campaign was now getting greater attention across the SBC. Southern Seminary President Duke McCall, who had been stung by allegations of heresy among his faculty, compared the "takeover" attempt by the Texans to the recent overthrow of the Baptist president of Liberia. McCall likened possible success of the inerrantist group to a "communist" revolution, and said a Pressler-Patterson triumph would spell the end of free elections in annual conventions. Control of agencies by the "inerrantist faction," McCall warned, could cause many churches on the eastern seaboard [where Baptists are reportedly more liberal] to withdraw Cooperative Program support. One way to avoid this, he suggested, would be to shift appointment of the Committee on Committees to state conventions.[5] Objectors said this would be a step towards establishing a connectional church in violation of the denominational constitution.

Pressler, Patterson and supportive conservatives now had at least a skeleton organization in every state convention. Patterson made no apologies for this in an interview with Toby Druin, associate editor of the Texas *Baptist Standard*. "The issue is still truth," he said. "Is the Bible in fact totally and completely true? Are we really in substance reduplicating the faith of our founding fathers. . . ?"

Patterson was of the persuasion that most Baptists still "held such beliefs." He was also convinced that "a very large contingency in significant denominational posts" did, in fact, no longer hold the Bible to be without error.

Patterson "was perfectly happy" with the 1963 *Baptist Faith and Message*, because "it says the Bible contains truth without mixture of error . . . "Let's admit what it means, which, of course, both Herschel Hobbs and Wayne Dehoney did at the Houston convention."

"Eternal vigilance," Patterson declared, is "the price of a God-honoring denomination. The real question is: Do you help anybody by pretending that serious disease is not present?"

Nor did Patterson have apologies for going to laymen. "Many pastors," he declared, "lack the courage to deal with the problem. We have found that when a layman has [the Bible problem] put in front of him, and he looks at it, he says, 'Oh, my goodness.' He is not trying to go to a new pastorate."

Laymen, Patterson further observed, "also control the money. And apparently that is the only thing some [denominational] folks understand." As for allegations of politics, Patterson recalled it was "no secret" that "Jimmy Allen publicly politicked for the office of president . . . We are not running a candidate. We are concerned Baptists, and if that is politics, then what state paper editors do when they write is also politics. [The editor] is giving his viewpoint, and he has an entree to the people that even pastors don't have." 6

Amidst mounting condemnations by denominational papers of the conservative "political machine", a few members of First Baptist Church, Dallas, became bothered by Paige Patterson's "political activities" and urged Pastor Criswell to rein in his young associate. Patterson agreed to spend more time at home.

Adrian Rogers, in response to allegations by the editors, denied that he had ever been a part of any political machine. He was, however, using his presidential appointment powers to put persons on committees who believed in the integrity of Scripture. Then he announced that he wanted to spend more time with his church and family and would not be a candidate in 1980.

Rogers' withdrawal, coming only a month before the 1980 St. Louis convention, insured a wide open convention, a year before moderates felt the chance would come to elect a president who would be supportive of theological diversity. Individual moderates began hurriedly looking around for candidates.

Judge Pressler continued devoting most of his free time to speaking for the conservative cause. He came to the 1980 St. Louis convention with "no candidate," but could enthusiastically support, among others, the fiery Bailey Smith.

Smith, pastor of the 14,000-member First Southern Baptist Church in Del City, Oklahoma and president of the Oklahoma Baptist Convention, had averaged baptizing over 1,000 persons during each of the past six years. Also a past president of the Pastor's Conference, he believed "Jonah was a literal person swallowed by a literal fish and was in a literal mess." 7

But his church gave only two percent to the Cooperative Program. Still, he was nominated at St. Louis, along with five others. One of the five was Richard Jackson, an avowed inerrantist, from Phoenix, who had a baptismal record that compared favorably with Smith's, and whose church gave generously to denominational causes.

Many conservatives were planning to vote for Jackson when a rumor swept the hotels that he had made a deal with moderates and denominational leaders anxious to restore calm. When the ballots were counted, the computer gave Smith a clear majority over all five opponents. In his early forties, he was the youngest president in the history of the Southern Baptist Convention, and, in the view of many moderates and denominational men, the most militant among prominent conservative pastors.

Conservatives had been introducing and passing resolutions for over two decades calling for agency compliance with Biblical infallibility and/or inerrancy and getting little response. Agencies had ignored Hobbs' and Dehoney's 1979 interpretation that "truth, without any mixture of error" meant textual inerrancy. Energized by Bailey Smith's victory, conservatives introduced an even stronger resolution in 1980 at St. Louis, demanding,

> That . . . trustees of seminaries and other institutions affiliated with or supported by the Southern Baptist Convention . . . only employ, and continue the employment of faculty members and professional staff who believe in the divine inspiration of the whole Bible, the infallibility of the original manuscripts, and that the Bible is truth without any error.[8]

Herschel Hobbs quickly objected that "infallibility" would be "too strong" on the seminaries." He asked that the resolution be amended to have trustees "see that teaching in seminaries is done in conformity with "abstracts of principles and the 1963 *Baptist Faith and Message* statement.[9] This would protect Southern Seminary which did not have 'infallibility" in the Abstract which faculty were required to sign. On a hand vote, Hobbs' amendment failed decisively, with the group of about 40 denominational agency heads and state editors sitting at tables before the podium voting unanimously for it.

If not before, it was now clear to the conservative majority that the institutional leadership was solidly opposed to the requirement that Biblical infallibility be affirmed in agencies. The original resolution calling for this was then voted upon and passed by a substantial majority, with the agency heads and state editors at the tables raising hands in dissent.

Altogether, the St. Louis convention enacted 50 resolutions, including one calling for "appropriate [Federal] legislation and/or a constitutional amendment prohibiting abortion except to save the life of the mother." This resolution was clearly intended as a solid rebuke to foot-dragging by the Christian Life Commission on the abortion issue. The great majority of denominational executives and editors visible at the front tables voted against the strong anti-abortion resolution, as they also opposed a successful resolution opposing ratification of the Equal Rights Amendment.

Conservatives had again proven they could get out the vote to elect their choice as president at the national level. They had also pushed through a raft of resolutions, many of which were directly aimed at trustees and agencies which had paid slight heed to similar actions in the past. Now it was clearer than ever to conservative strategists that mere resolutions and motions could not reverse the perceived "liberal drift," no matter how great the majorities voting for agency compliance. Change could only be effected by electing trustees who would make agency executives pull in the theological fences. This meant, as Paul Pressler kept repeating, that they had to continue electing presidents who would move in the desired direction with committee appointments. Judge Pressler was highly encouraged by St. Louis. "The tide is now moving our way," exulted Judge Pressler.[10]

Worried moderates and denominational executives checked Adrian Rogers' committee appointments and saw names that had been linked to the conservative get-out-the-vote campaign. Now they could clearly see the "fire" of which Walter Shurden had warned the year before. The most important of the committees, the Committee on Committees, would present a Committee on Boards at Los Angeles, where Bailey Smith would name his Committee on Committees. Another year down the pike and the "conservative party's" Committee on Boards, resulting from Rogers' election, would present their first trustee nominees to replace trustees rotating off agency boards. A year later, the Committee on Boards, stemming from Bailey Smith's appointments, would deliver a list. Somewhere, somehow, the conservative juggernaut had to be stopped before the "take-over" group, as moderates were now calling inerrantists, took control of agencies.

Moderates had initially been encouraged by Adrian Rogers' withdrawal. Some now wondered out loud if it had not been planned, so conservatives could elect a man eligible to serve two years, thereby making a comeback for moderates and status quo-minded denominational employees more difficult in 1981. "We've got to get organized," worried moderates said. "We've got to convince people that this is serious."

In September of 1980, Judge Pressler spoke to a rally of conservatives at the Old Forest Road Baptist Church in Lynchburg, Virginia. Pressler stressed as he had to other groups, "We have been fighting battles without knowing what the war is all about. We have not been effective because we have not gotten to the root of the problem." Then he said, "The lifeblood of the Southern Baptist Convention is the trustees. We need to go for the jugular—we need to go for trustees."

Unknown to Pressler, an agency employee who wrote for Baptist Press was in the audience. Within days stories began appearing in state convention papers quoting Pressler as "going for the jugular." The expression became a code word, symbolizing Pressler as the chief villain in a movement which moderates charged was bent on destroying the denomination. It would be repeated thousands of times in denominational periodicals, church newsletters, and pastors' meetings.

Pressler was unable to get denominational editors to print his explanation of the word. "I was not referring to an actual, literal jugular vein of anybody or anything," he said in an interview. "I wish I could teach Baptist newswriters the use of metaphorical expressions in the English language. I was only trying to show the source of strength and power, where the lifeblood of Southern Baptists lies." [11]

Moderate Cecil Sherman, then pastor of First Baptist Church, Asheville, North Carolina, claims the expression galvanized him into action. Cecil and his brother, Bill, a pastor in Nashville, with many denominational employees in his church, along with Kenneth Chafin, then a pastor in Houston, rallied about a score of fellow moderates to a meeting in Gatlinburg, Tennessee to plot strategy for reversing "fundamentalist" gains. In a sort of tit for tat with "going-for-the-jugular", the meeting earned them the title, "The Gatlinburg Gang."

The "denominational loyalists," as they preferred to be known, felt that agency heads needed to use their influence more. Duke McCall had spoken plainly enough. Grady Cothen, president of the Sunday School Board, had indirectly criticized conservatives in the Board's newsletter, *Facts and Trends*. But every agency head, they declared, should join in countering the threat of the "take-over" group.

Members of the Gatlinburg group pleaded with denominational executives, saying in effect, "we're the best friends you've got. Don't leave us to fight the battles alone." None of the agency people made any solid promises.

Moderates got a boost when Bailey Smith remarked at a Dallas rally for "traditional values" that God "doesn't hear the prayers of Jews" or anyone else who doesn't accept Jesus as Messiah. With national presidential politics at a high pitch, the statement became front page news. SBC moderates jumped on the bandwagon condemning Smith for intolerance.

Seizing the initiative, the persuasive Smith met with leading rabbis and explained his personal conviction that Jesus was the only way of salvation. Then he offered his hand of friendship in causes on which Baptist and Jews could agree. By such bold action, Smith defused the issue for the upcoming annual SBC business session in Los Angeles.

On another front, attention turned to debates on inerrancy. In February, 1981, Paige Patterson and Cecil Sherman squared off before the Pastors' Conference of the Catawba River Baptist Association in North Carolina. Patterson maintained that the Bible was historically true in the autographs and that his position of plenary, verbal inspiration had been held by the SBC founders. Sherman acclaimed the "authority" of Scripture, which, he said, did not protect the "human" writers of the Bible from errors and contradictions." Taking a classic neo-orthodox stance, Sherman said he was "concerned with the message of the Bible, not the inerrancy." He saw contradictory pictures of God in Scripture: "In parts of the Old Testament, we have a tribal God, vindictive and cruel, low and mean, while the picture of God in Jesus is lofty and beautiful."

God's character, Sherman said, remains the same, "but our perception of His character is changing." 12

The Sherman-Patterson debate went unreported in the denominational press—"our budget couldn't afford it," Baptist Press News Director Dan Martin said.13 A second debate received major coverage in both secular and religious papers.

So many reporters were covering the Los Angeles convention that the Religious Newswriters of America scheduled their annual meeting in Los Angeles the weekend before the convention. They invited Paige Patterson and Kenneth Chafin to debate the proposition: "Belief in Biblical inerrancy is crucial for the survival of Southern Baptists as an evangelistic force." Patterson affirmed the statement; Chafin argued against it.

Chafin sharply attacked the motives and methods of conservatives (something Sherman had not done in his tout with Patterson), calling their effort, "a naked, ruthless reach for personal power that acts in ways that say any means are justified."

Those claiming SBC agencies harbor liberals, he added, show "vast, monumental ignorance."

Patterson called Chafin's denial "only so much window dressing; the facts speak otherwise."

When Chafin said conservatives made him "angry," Patterson

countered, "It's the moderate fringe that has the ugliest things to say."

Many observers felt Patterson won support by sticking to issues, while Chafin digressed with attacks on the motives of the conservatives.

The mellowness and camaraderie of past conventions was absent at Los Angeles where a sharp competitiveness prevailed. Denominational editors had come prepared for a "blood-letting," a "shootout," an "angry, knock-down battle" that would "produce a split or further polarization." [14] Tennessee Editor Alvin Shackleford warned, "The hope for healing looks dim. [We] cannot survive without . . . the trust and confidence that love produces in one another." [15]

In hopes of staving off the predicted fire and fury, convention planners scheduled and heavily promoted special prayer sessions for forgiveness and unity.

Arriving messengers were greeted by the headline in the *Los Angeles Herald Examiner*, "Southern Baptist Schism: Raising Cain vs. Praising Jesus." Moderates continued to maintain that they were only trying to preserve unity and keep the SBC in the center by opposing the "take-over" party of the "ultra-conservative right." They broke the tradition of not opposing an incumbent president for a second term by backing Abner McCall, then president of Baylor University, against Bailey Smith. Said Ralph Langley in nominating McCall,

> Some of our Baptists play best in right field, some play best in left. I think I play best in center field as do most of you. Abner McCall can be the manager and coach for us all. Come back to the middle with McCall, a latter-day Lincoln who can unify this convention and bring us to the middle. [16]

Bailey Smith still won by a 60-40 majority and indicated that the central difference was still over the Bible. "If you start saying part of the Bible is true and part is not," he argued, "then who can tell what is and is not?"

Then Smith eased tensions by saying "inerrancy should not be used as a club to hit people over the head." [17]

The conservatives, however, were by no means ready to compromise. Larry Lewis, for one, was determined to get on the record that the *Baptist Faith and Message* meant that the whole Bible was truth without error. That interpretation, as agreed upon by Rogers, Wayne Dehoney, and Herschel Hobbs, had been accepted by a majority of the messengers at the Houston convention, but had not been recorded in convention minutes or in convention dispatches by Baptist Press.

Lewis shared this intent with Rogers, President Smith, and Jimmy Draper. Lewis and Draper then met with Hobbs, who had chaired the committee that drafted the *Baptist Faith and Message* and who had already introduced a motion that the convention reaffirm the *Baptist Faith and Message* statement on Scripture being "truth, without mixture of error." They asked Hobbs if he would once again interpret what the committee had in mind about there being no error in Scripture.

Hobbs was willing. When his motion came up, he first made what seemed to be a bow to moderates and others who objected to the *Baptist Faith and Message* being made binding on agencies. Hobbs said,

> When the Convention voted to set up a committee to do the study that resulted in this [*Baptist Faith and Message*] statement, it said that the product **shall** serve as information to the churches and **may**—notice the difference—not shall, **may** serve as guidelines for agencies of the Convention.

Then for the conservatives, Hobbs declared,

> Now, the other one thing that I want to say is this. I was asked a question many times—I was asked it this morning—concerning the first paragraph [of the motion] that defines the Holy Bible: "which has truth without any mixture of error for its matter." Now I'm reading from the King James version—2 Timothy 3:16—"all scripture is given by inspiration of God." The Greek New Testament reads, "all,"—without the definite article—and that means every single part of the whole is God-breathed. And a God of truth does not breathe error."

Lewis asked if Hobbs' resolution would in any way nullify or negate the resolution on doctrinal integrity accepted in St. Louis in 1980. Hobbs said it would not and could "corroborate" the previous resolution. Lewis then said he was satisfied.

Adrian Rogers came to the podium and said with a broad smile, "Praise God! We can all agree on this. Mr. President [Smith], I would like to ask that by common consent this convention agree that these remarks [by Hobbs] be recorded in the official minutes."

Smith, who was presiding, and Hobbs concurred. The vote was taken and the motion—to quote from the minutes—"passed by an enthusiastic standing vote." [18]

Once more, the convention had taken a strong stand on inerrancy. Once more, judging from past history, conservatives did not expect the bureaucracies—without direction from trustees— to take the motion seriously. They would continue to interpret the *Baptist Faith and Message* as previously, and they would note that neither the *Baptist Faith and Message* nor any other confession was binding. The conservatives recognized this; still they were happy to at last have Hobbs' interpretation put on the convention record.

It had been two years since Adrian Rogers' election had put him in a position to name a Committee on Committees which had started the ball rolling toward the first conservative trustee nominations. The first fruits, in the form of over 100 trustee nominations, were announced at Los Angeles. Moderates found them "unrepresentative." Against strenuous objections from conservatives that the convention should not try to do the work of a committee, moderates began submitting substitute nominees from the floor. They succeeded in knocking ten conservatives from the list. This was small consolation since they could expect another slate the next year, another the next, and continuing as long as conservatives kept winning the presidency.

The denominational press had found few good things to say about the conservatives during the year. Conservatives made themselves available to other press in an attempt to get their views better known. In an interview, Larry Lewis explained the conservative stance on creedalism, doctrinal standards, and institutional conformity.

"None of us want a wholesale purging of our institutions," he said. Irreparable harm is done when a professor must be terminated, especially if he has tenure. It creates an unhealthy spirit of dissension at the institution.

"We do want trustees to take a closer look at new teachers. I would like for them to look at doctrinal integrity, as we do in ordaining ministers. This isn't the creedalism of which we are accused," Lewis maintained, explaining,

> Creedalism would be an effort to force a doctrinal position on persons joining a local church. A few members of my church have some weird doctrinal ideas, but I don't think they should be removed for that. But I cannot consent to someone teaching Sunday School who does not believe the Bible is the infallible Word of God. You cannot maintain the doctrinal integrity of a church if you just allow anything or everything. The same is true of the teachers and editors of our denomination.[19]

Tensions relaxed after Los Angeles. Contending pastors had to be about the work of their churches. Denominational executives had other fish to fry. Under the leadership of Jimmy Allen, the Radio and Television Commission had launched a bold new initiative in telecommunications via satellites. Seminaries, despite the theological clouds some were under, had record enrollments. The unified budget for convention agencies in 1982 was set to top $100 million for the first time in SBC history.

Paige Patterson had the Criswell Center for Biblical Studies to run, but continued to speak widely for the conservative cause. The chief objector to his activities from First Baptist Church, Dallas, had transferred to another congregation. Judge Pressler kept accepting every speaking invitation he could fit into his schedule. The denominational papers followed his travels from state to state, reporting what he said in many instances, with countering quotes from moderates. Denominational media could count on Pressler pulling no punches about the issues as he saw them. On one occasion, he likened the feeling among conservatives to that of a homeowner who finds robbers stealing everything he owns. "When he protests, and asks them to stop, he's called the troublemaker," Pressler said.[20]

To the surprise of many, Bailey Smith took a lower profile and avoided direct attacks, causing some moderates and agency people to think he might not be as partisan in his appointments as had been feared. For almost eleven months after L.A., things were pretty quiet. Then Baptist Press got the tape of a speech delivered by Adrian Rogers at the Rome, Georgia church pastored by his friend Jerry Vines. With barely a month to go before the New Orleans convention, the former SBC president's viewpoint on the state of the denomination stirred the controversy afresh in Baptist media.

The SBC, Rogers said, had started "with a moderately narrow theology," and while the denomination "always refused a written down, finely honed creed," there were common beliefs, such as "the inerrancy of the Scriptures, salvation by grace through faith, the priesthood of the believer, autonomy of the local church, baptism by immersion of believers only, the security of the believer . . ."

Alongside that "narrow theology," Rogers continued, the denomination "had a broad program" for many years. "Then somebody said about 1925, we need to narrow the program. So we got the Cooperative Program . . . Not only could we more or less believe the same things, but correspondingly and logically, we could support the same things."

After the "golden years" of church growth under a "narrow theology and a "narrow program," Rogers claimed,

> What we have now is a broad theology where everybody is saying we have unity in diversity. But the unity in diversity is only theological, not program wise. And somehow

the sin . . . in the SBC is not that you be aberrant in
your theology, but . . . that you be aberrant in your program, that you don't do the program just right, that you
fail to support everything. The question centers on what
we believe about the Word of God. If we can't believe that,
I believe it is the ultimate cancer that will destroy the
organism. There are two different schools of thought [in
the SBC]; there is a continental divide [between
us] . . . Either the Word of God is infallible or it's
fallible, it is inerrant or it is errant.

He charged that the denomination "has many professors who do
not believe the Bible is historically, philosophically, scientifically,
and theologically without error."

Some within the denomination, he continued, "would like to put a
steel band around our dollars. They say you do not have room to
wiggle program-wise, but we've got plenty of room on the other side
to wiggle theologically . . . I say, what is sauce for the goose is sauce
for the gander."

He thought the "best" solution "would be to go back and narrow
our theology again, so we can say everybody more or less believes
alike, everybody more or less supports [denominational agencies]
alike . . . Nobody's in a strait jacket." But, he added, "I sincerely
doubt that will ever happen . . . The Cooperative Program has
become a sacred cow . . ."

The "next best thing" is "that as we have widened the theology
correspondingly, we widen the program," to allow both freedom of
belief and freedom to support or decline to support various agencies
and programs in the denomination. "We could remove tension from
our Southern Baptist Convention, if we would relax our insistence of
Southern Baptists walking in lock-step program-wise." He said, "We
cannot put people in a strait-jacket program-wise and have an
unlimited freedom theologically."

The problem with interpretation of the disputed phrase in the
Baptist Faith and Message, he said, could be solved by changing the
Baptist Faith and Message from "the Bible has . . . truth . . ." to
" 'the Bible is truth, without any mixture of error.' " Even without
that change, the phrase carries the meaning of inerrancy, he said. By
inserting " 'is' " the average layman wouldn't see the difference but
"that is where the theological fur would fly." As matters stand, he
added, when denominational employees affirm the statement and
still believe the Bible is fallible, the "problem [becomes] not
theological, but ethical." [21]

Baptist Press asked six past SBC presidents if they thought the change in the *Baptist Faith and Message* proposed by former president Rogers was warranted. Owen Cooper, Carl E. Bates, Jimmy Allen, Herschel Hobbs, and Franklin Paschall all said the BFM was adequate as it stood. Only Jaroy Weber, president in 1975 and '76, thought the change to "the Bible 'is' truth, without any mixture of error" might be helpful.[22]

The "fur" flew over Rogers' description of the Cooperative Program as a "sacred cow." A wave of editorials and "letters to the editor" hit state papers questioning the loyalty of Rogers and his fellow conservatives to the SBC. All the old epithets were trotted out, "independent," "uncooperative," "ultra-conservative," and the like. Duke McCall, disapproving of what he had understood Rogers to say, called the Cooperative Program a "sacred how." McCall had previously suggested that some moderates might curtail their designations to the Cooperative Program. This apparently had been forgotten by SBC media. Rogers later explained at the New Orleans Convention that he did "not believe the Cooperative Program in itself [to be] a sacred cow. We have made of it a sacred cow."[23]

The flap over the sacredness of the Cooperative Program stirred the fires which some thought had abated after Los Angeles. The leaking of Bailey Smith's presidential address to the press a week before the 1982 convention was to open in the New Orleans Super Dome fueled the flames. Smith only knew that he had mailed the text to SBC offices in Nashville for printing. Someone with access had apparently sent it to Louis Moore, religion editor of the *Houston Chronicle*.

Some hoped that Smith might at least omit some of the most combative paragraphs in his delivery. He did not, declaring,

> It is inexcusable for a Southern Baptist to say he is a humanist and proud of it. It is inexcusable for Southern Baptists to pray for the opening of a brewery. It is inexcusable for a Southern Baptist to say Genesis is political rhetoric and not historical fact. It is inexcusable for a Southern Baptist to teach evolution in our schools. It is inexcusable that any Southern Baptist would social drink and have no shame about it.

He left no doubts that inerrancy was still the do-or-die issue.

> Somebody said to me, "Sure there was a day when preachers would preach the Bible as true from cover to cover, and sure that would do something to a community back then." Ladies and Gentlemen, I declare unto you that if ever the Bible was the holy, infallible, inerrant

Word of God, it is still the holy, infallible, inerrant Word
of God.[24]

Smith had apparently read Randall Lolley's famous brewery
prayer in the *Southern Baptist Journal* where Bill Powell had reprinted
it again. The reference in the presidential sermon to social drinking
apparently related to an allegation in the current *Journal* that Duke
McCall had a drinking problem. McCall, one of the SBC's most
distinguished elder statesmen and a champion of "unity amidst
diversity" had supposedly imbibed while on a trip to China.

An angry McCall, accompanied by one of his sons, strode into the
press room to set the matter right. McCall said he had been an
avowed enemy of alcohol all his life and had even served as president
of a temperance society. While in China, he and other Baptist
leaders were on a river boat excursion when he became dehydrated
and asked for water. "They gave me a choice between a dirty-looking
glass of tea and some Chinese beer," he explained. "Because of a
cardiac condition, I was under doctor's orders not to drink anything
with caffeine in it. I told my friends, 'I've never taken a drink before
in my life, but I've got to have some liquid.' I took a swallow of the
beer and it tasted so bad that I spit most of it out. Somehow I
survived and got back to where I could get something better to drink.
When I came home, I made a big joke out of it, and I suppose that
was where the rumor started that I had a drinking problem." McCall
said he was "deeply hurt," but would take no legal action. "I only
want to set the record straight." [25]

A petition had been circulated to "draft" Billy Graham for the
SBC presidency. Graham gave an evangelistic sermon in the Super
Dome where the convention was meeting. He had "always been
proud to be a Southern Baptist" (member of First Baptist Church,
Dallas), but asked that he not be nominated. Vice President George
Bush also gave a speech in which he defended the Religious Right,
bringing cheers from conservatives while moderates sat in stony
silence. For moderates it looked to be a long week.

Conservatives put their presidential hopes for a successor to
Bailey Smith on another star from the Pastors' Conference, Jimmy
Draper, pastor of First Baptist Church, Euless, Texas, a suburb of
Dallas. Draper, a former associate to W.A. Criswell, had a good
record in both baptisms and Cooperative Program giving. He was
also perceived to be a rock-hard inerrantist. Moderates backed Duke
McCall, nominated by Grady Cothen, soon-to-retire as president of
the Sunday School Board.

The entry of two "centrist" candidates, Perry Sanders and John
Sullivan, threw McCall and Draper into a runoff, with Draper winning

by a 57 to 43 percent majority. Some of McCall's vote might have been in sympathy for the ugly drinking story. Sullivan was then elected first vice president, raising moderate hopes that he might be a stronger presidential flag-bearer in a future election.

New Orleans marked the fourth straight conservative presidential triumph and the second presentation of conservative trustee nominations. Kenneth Chafin said he had "personally checked" two pastor nominees to the Sunday School Board and found that neither used Board literature in their churches. This was a sore spot for many loyal denominationalists, because, at a nearby hotel, an unofficial Baptist Literature Board was offering an alternative curriculum to that produced in Nashville.

Moderates offered an amendment calling for substitutions to the trustee nominees of the Committee on Boards. The two were defeated in a very close vote. Kenneth Chafin was challenging the nomination of a seminary trustee when Larry Lewis came to the platform and pulled Chafin aside. "Ken, we've got over a hundred nominees here. If you and your friends keep this up, we're going to have a real dogfight for the rest of the convention unless we reach some understanding. We can move the previous question and have the convention vote on your amendment for these three," Lewis said, "or we can refer your proposed substitutions back to the Committee on Boards where you will probably lose. Which would you rather do?"

Chafin wanted a vote. Lewis then said, "Okay, we [conservatives] will yield to you on the three you have challenged, and we'll then present the whole slate for a vote." The two joined in making the motion. The vote was taken. The three contested nominees were replaced. The report of nominees as amended was accepted. It was the best moderates could get in the crucial New Orleans election of trustees.26

The debate moved to resolutions. Moderates and some conservatives, with support from concerned Foreign Mission Board leaders, blocked a resolution that placed, in effect, God on Israel's side in the Mid-East conflict. Moderates also managed to get a hard-line resolution against abortion tabled. But they were unable to defeat two conservative resolutions directed at public schools. One called for support of the proposed Reagan amendment authorizing voluntary school prayer. Another backed the teaching of "scientific creationism" in public schools.

Larry Lewis feared that the tabling of the anti-abortion resolution might mislead the press to think that Southern Baptists were pro-choice on abortion. After having this confirmed by several newspaper representatives, Lewis came back in the afternoon session and reported what he had heard. He then made a motion that the convention reconsider its action on the abortion resolution. He included infanticide and euthanasia, along with abortion, and got a resolution passed, despite opposition from moderates.

The school prayer resolution aroused strong passions. "For once," said Atlanta's Charles Stanley, the SBC has "taken a firm, strong, positive, bold aggressive stand on a vital issue that affects not only this generation but generations to come."

James Dunn, Executive Director of the Baptist Joint Committee for Public Affairs, called the action an "incredible contradiction of our Baptist heritage." Dunn said his agency, three fourths supported by the SBC Cooperative Program in conjunction with several smaller U.S. Baptist denominations, would continue to fight the prayer amendment. Dunn had earlier aroused conservatives by calling President Reagan's proposed legislation, "despicable demagoguery." Dunn further accused Reagan of "playing petty politics with prayer." A motion to censure Dunn for these remarks was tabled in New Orleans. Dunn was later asked, in a press interview, if he was not bound to the vote of the convention. "I always do everything I can to work with the convention," he said, adding a familiar refrain of some denominational employees, "But you have to remember this [school prayer resolution] was passed by messengers making up one convention at one time. The next convention might change its mind."

Dunn's seeming intransigence against the resolution for a school prayer amendment brought deep rumbles from conservatives who had supported the resolution, and who vowed at a future convention to try and clip the Baptist Joint Committee on Public Affairs' $400,000 designation from the Cooperative Program.

Much of the convention at New Orleans was, as usual, given to reports of agencies, budgets, and numbers. In the latter category, it was reported that membership growth in ten southern states during the 1970s had not kept pace with population growth. Moderates said tensions raised by conservatives had diverted attention from evangelism and mission advance. Conservatives said that neo-orthodoxy, as fostered by moderates and harbored in agencies, was the major chilling factor.

The division ran through the last session of this fourth straight convention dominated by conservatives. They had won again simply by getting out the vote and working through the legalities of the system. A few more years of this and the challengers would be in position to start turning the agencies around. But they had to keep the pressure on.

Randall Lolley's "brewery prayer" and Duke McCall's alleged "drinking problem," as reported in *The Southern Baptist Journal* and alluded to in Bailey Smith's presidential address, had angered moderates and agency people and grieved the conservative leadership. The most touching moment of the convention came just before dismissal when Paige Patterson asked for a "point of personal privilege" and called Duke McCall to the podium. Raising an arm about the elder man's shoulder, Patterson said, "I want you to know how deeply sorry we are about the ugly story that was spread about you. I had nothing to do with it, I abhor such personal attacks, and yet I think I can speak for everyone at this convention, regardless of any theological disagreeements, and ask you to accept our deepest apology." [27]

With McCall graciously accepting the apology, the two men shook hands and, a few minutes later, the benediction was pronounced, marking the end of "the battle of New Orleans."

The denomination had enjoyed a lull after Los Angeles, and New Orleans was no different. Jimmy Draper pledged to "get Southern Baptists talking to each other, instead of about each other." He met with several leading moderates, asking their help in finding "common ground." They suggested that he share his appointive powers with leaders of state conventions, an idea which conservatives had rejected before.

The changes were urged by Cecil Sherman, Bill Sherman, and Ed Perry, pastor emeritus of Broadway Baptist Church of Louisville, Kentucky. The moderates' proposal as outlined in a September 17, 1982 Baptist Press release, called for state leaders—executive secretary, convention president and chairman of the executive board—to "nominate four names for each state's two positions on the committee on committees—two laypersons and two ordained persons—from which list the president . . . in consultation with the first and second vice presidents of the SBC, would choose one layman and one ordained person to be appointed to the two positions." The proposal also would require the president to seek and accept "one name . . . from each state for a list of nominees to the committee on resolutions, from which list the president . . . would choose the required number of names for the resolutions committee."

In rejecting the plan, Draper said he planned to consult with state convention leadership, his vice presidents and others, and added: "The only difference is I am choosing to do it rather than being required to do so by the bylaws."

Then Draper set moderates' ears ringing by telling SBC evangelism directors at a meeting in Puerto Rico, "The extreme theological stance of the left will absolutely kill evangelism." [28]

Still pushing dialogue, Draper set up a summit of moderate and conservative leaders in Irving, Texas, with agency heads invited to listen and contribute. Moderate Don Harbuck from Arkansas said "the judgmental spirit and exclusivistic posture of fundamentalism" was tearing the denomination apart. Paige Patterson disagreed and gave the agency heads a four-point proposal for peace.

Agencies, he said, should give conservatives parity with moderates in employment, especially in seminaries. Denominational employees who preferred not to use the term inerrancy should state "publicly, clearly, and unamibiguously" what they believe about the Bible and other essential doctrines. Students holding to inerrancy should not be ridiculed in classrooms. The Cooperative Program should be "restructured" to permit churches to give only to agencies whose programs they could in "good conscience" approve.

Moderates kept waiting for the agency heads to answer Patterson's "demands." Finally, Chafin announced he was throwing in the towel, because, until agencies are willing to fight for freedom, there is "absolutely nothing I or anyone can do to help them." The Irving summit marked a low point for moderates.

Draper kept his approach low key, stating that he was available to anyone who wanted to talk. In a circular letter to fellow moderates, Don Harbuck foresaw no credible oposition to the candidacy of Draper for a second term at the 1983 Pittsburgh convention, "despite the fact that he virtually disqualified many of us" in his speech to the evangelism directors. Cecil Sherman sent a sad letter to agency heads and denominational editors:

> Systematically, almost surgically, the kind of Southern Baptist I am has been excised from policy making posts. This is painful, since all the while we thought we were friends of the denomination. We have viewed ourselves as your defenders and supporters both in word and in coin. A denomination that has no place for us is emerging.[29]

With agency heads mute and moderates deciding that the popular and amicable Draper, with his church's record in evangelism and Cooperative Program giving, could not be defeated, Pittsburgh became the most peaceful convention in years.

Draper did not mention "inerrancy" in his presidential address, "Southern Baptists: People of Deep Belief," yet he said,

> The basis of these beliefs is the Word of God. From every section of our Southern Baptist Convention this year we have heard affirmations . . . of our commitment to the Bible as the final authority for Southern Baptists. To this

conviction . . . we must stand united. Our only hope for
strength and vitality in our denomination is our renewed
and continued commitment to this divinely inspired,
uniquely transmitted, carefully preserved, and totally reliable book. These great beliefs that have so characterized
Southern Baptists are cherished Biblical truths.[30]

Building further on this speech, Draper later called for certain
"minimum parameters" of doctrine as "the irreducible minimum
theology that a person must subscribe to in order to be acceptable as
a professor . . . or as a worker, writer, or policymaker in one of our
agencies; The "undiminished Deity and the genuine humanity"
Jesus Christ; the "substitutionary atonement", the "literal, bodily"
resurrection of Jesus Christ from the grave, a "literal" bodily ascension
into heaven, a "literal", bodily return of Jesus Christ to earth, and
"justification by God's grace through faith." [31]

At Pittsburgh, Draper didn't see recent conventions as marking a
dramatic turn to the right.

The SBC is kind of cumbersome, like trying to take a
sharp right turn in an aircraft carrier. You can't do that
very easily. I see it as a midcourse correction with our
leadership being responsive to the constitutency. A turning
back to where we were.[32]

Paul Pressler called this shift "unprecedented" except for Missouri
Synod Lutheran conservatives who had, nine years before, recap-
tured Concordia Seminary from "the [neo-orthodox] liberals." In an
interview, Pressler explained why he felt his group had been successful
to this point:

We saw the handwriting on the wall and started early. We
sought to work within the system instead of tearing down.
We followed a definite plan that would get conservative
trustees nominated and elected who would change the
system. We did not make frontal attacks on the integrity
of those we felt were liberals. We merely read what they
had written and published and asked our constituency
whether that was what they wanted taught in their
schools.

The interview was conducted over lunch in the lobby restaurant of
the Hyatt-Regency Hotel where hundreds of messengers to the
Pittsburgh convention were staying. As we talked, pastors and
denominational workers kept stopping by our table to offer Pressler
jovial greetings. During a break, the judge smiled and said, "This
wasn't happening just two years ago."

At breakfast the next morning, I asked a gloomy Cecil Sherman why conservatives had been winning. "Because they tagged into our greatest fears and dreams," he said. "Dreams of quantifying in terms of large sanctuaries and many baptisms: fears that liberalism works against quantifying." Adrian Rogers, Bailey Smith, and Jimmy Draper had been elected "because they embody the dreams of so many pastors." Sherman insisted he was not anti-growth, but that to say growth is the result of correct doctrine is a "mistake". "Moonies, Muslims, and Mormons are growing. There are pastors who have correct doctrine who are not in growing churches."

In his usual candor, Sherman admitted conservatives had been right in charging that many of their beliefs were not taught in seminaries.

> If inerrancy for inspiration, creationism as an interpretation
> of Genesis 1-3, and submission of women are to be litmus
> tests for teachers, then they have legitimate complaints. In
> general these things have not been taught in our
> seminaries.[34]

Sherman, who had received prestigious denominational committee appointments at some past conventions, said he had been deeply hurt by being passed by in recent years. Noting that his church [First Baptist, Asheville, N.C.] had given almost 20 percent ($133,000) of its total offering to denominational causes and missions during the past year, and had baptized 47 new converts, he added,

> Suppose you were in a town that had gone from 72,000 to
> 51,000 in population. Suppose you had broken your back
> to keep your church in the hunt while some jerk in your
> state is raising sand and giving two or three percent to the
> denomination. The political spoils system takes him and
> puts him in [as a trustee] running these agencies and all
> he's done is complain. It's difficult for a guy like me to
> have a good spirit about that.[35]

Conservative Charles Stanley, who was perceived to be more hard line than Draper, was elected president of the Pastors' Conference at Pittsburgh. After losing scores of members in the controversy over "standards" for officers and teachers, Stanley had, in 13 years, led First Baptist Church of Atlanta to increase from 600 to 3,200 in average Sunday School attendance. The church had received 282 new members by baptism in 1982 and given four million dollars in offerings, with $120,000 going to the Cooperative Program and $280,000 to other mission endeavors, including the support of some members who served with non-denominational missions. With a TV outreach to every state, Stanley had become, next to Billy Graham, the best known Southern Baptist in America.

Stanley chaired the powerful Committee on Boards at Pittsburgh where moderates failed in attempts to elect substitute nominees. How did he regard his newly acquired prominence in denominational life, when he had been relatively inactive in the Atlanta Baptist Association and the Georgia Baptist Convention?

> What has been true of me has been true of many [conservative] pastors. I was faithful in giving and in every way to the denomination. But for years, I was ignored, shut out, and given no voice. I said nothing, then there came a time when I said, 'I have a right to speak my opinion. I think it's healthy for many others to become involved, rather than just a few.' Now those folks, who have talked so much about diversity, find that it's no longer fair when we give them a little diversity. To me that's a little hypocritical.

Rumors circulated that Stanley would be the conservative nominee for president at the 1984 convention in Kansas City. Would he accept? "Well, I said I would never be elected president of the Pastors' Conference and here I am. We'll just see how the Lord leads." [36]

While moderates made no herculean effort at Pittsburgh, they were clearly looking ahead to Kansas City. At Pittsburgh, an ad hoc committee of moderates organized an evening fellowship at a local hotel, the first such effort since the Mullins Fellowship had disbanded in 1970. There was no program for the 900 attenders at the fellowship in the Steel City. Organizers said there would probably be one next year.

"Women in Ministry" held their first pre-convention meeting in Pittsburgh. They reported 175 ordained "clergywomen" in the denomination, with hundreds more waiting in the wings. With strength at Southern and Southeastern seminaries, they saw themselves as supporters of the moderates' call for more diversity. Women's ordination would lead all other controversies at the upcoming fall state conventions.

Many moderates left Pittsburgh deeply discouraged. The denomination, as they perceived it, was ablaze, and only a disorganized crew of firefighters was trying to put it out. Indeed, most of the hired workers in the buildings—agency people—were going about their business as if nothing had happened, and even saying nice words to the people who had set the structure aflame. How much more must the structure of "unity amidst diversity" burn before the agency heads came to their senses and gained the courage to fight? How much longer could "old mother," as some called the SBC structure, stand?

Of course, conservatives did not see it this way at all. The fire was in the minds of the moderates. The structure had grave weaknesses, thanks to decades of neglect, but it was slowly being brought back to the beliefs of the founding fathers. Two or three more years of informing the people and getting them out to vote and victory would be close. Then in Paul Pressler's words, they could "start cleaning up the mess" left from the theological mudslide.

Neither side doubted that the biggest battles lay ahead.

REFERENCES

1   Walter B. Shurden: "The Erosion of Denominationalism: The Current State of the Southern Baptist Convention." Address given to the South Carolina Baptist Historical Society, November 12, 1984.

2   Many copies of the letter were circulated to individuals and media.

3   Quoted from Powell's comments on back of circulated Harwell letter.

4   "Georgia Committee Affirms Harwell as *Index* Editor, "*Baptist and Reflector*, December, 26, 1979. See also articles and Baptist Press releases in other Baptist state papers during this time.

5   James Lee Young: "McCall Voices Concern Over Stability of SBC," *Baptist and Reflector*, May 7, 1980, p. 3.

6   Toby Druin: "Patterson-Pressler Group Seeks SBC Control, as reported for the *Baptist Standard* and reprinted in the *Baptist and Reflector*, April 30, 1980, pp. 4, 5.

7   Gayle White: "Bible 'Infallible,'" *The Atlanta Constitution*, June 12, 1980, pp. 6A.

8   James C. Hefley: "Conservative Tidal Wave Sweeps SBC," *Moody Monthly*, September, 1980, pp. 122-125.

9   Ibid. See also Convention *Book of Reports* for this year. The resolution was patterned after the "doctrinal integrity" resolution passed by the Missouri Baptist Convention as noted in reference #45 for the previous chapter. In the parliamentary process at Houston the year before, the resolution had been withdrawn by Lewis in order to have another resolution passed supporting Biblical infallibility. The election of Adrian Rogers in 1979 had given conservatives control over the 1980 Resolutions Committee. Previous Resolutions Committees had been prone to take moderates off the "hook" by softening or making ambiguous resolutions on Biblical inerrancy. Adrian Rogers' Resolutions Committee, which included Larry Lewis, served at St. Louis and reported the doctrinal integrity resolution out virtually as presented. Astute members of the "unity" party and moderates saw what was happening, but could do nothing about it. For them, this was one more reason why the election of militant conservatives to the presidency had to be halted.

10   Personal Interview, St. Louis, June, 1980.

11   Personal Interview, Los Angeles, June, 1981.

12   Quotations from a tape recording of the debate.

13   Telephone Interview, March, 1981.

14   Baptist Press, June 22, 1981.

15 James C. Hefley: "That Southern Baptist Battle Over the Bible," *Moody Monthly*, September, 1981, pp. 115-117.

16 Quotation from nomination speech.

17 Bailey Smith: Presidential Press Conference, Los Angeles, June 1981.

18 The indented remarks are as printed in the *Convention Annual* (p. 45) for the 1981 convention. Information on the background of the information came from a personal interview with Larry Lewis in Hannibal, Missouri, February, 1986.

19 Personal Interview, Los Angeles, June, 1981.

20 Baptist Press, September 3, 1981.

21 Dan Martin: "Doctrinal Unity, Program Unity Rise, Fall Together, Rogers Says," Baptist Press, May 14, 1982.

22 "Ex—SBC Presidents Term Statement as Adequate," *Baptist and Reflector*, June 9, 1982.

23 Baptist Press, June 16, 1982.

24 Bailey Smith: Presidential Address, New Orleans, June, 1982.

25 Duke McCall: Impromptu Press Conference, New Orleans, June, 1982.

26 Recalled in Personal Interview with Larry Lewis, Hannibal, Mo., May, 1985.

27 Convention proceedings, New Orleans, June, 1982.

28 Reported by Baptist Press, January, 1983.

29 Quotes from Sherman and Harbuck are from circular letters distributed to moderate leaders and made available to press.

30 James T. Draper, Jr.: Presidential Address, Pittsburgh, 1983.

31 James T. Draper, Jr.: **Authority: The Critical Issue for Southern Baptists,** Fleming H. Revell, Co., Old Tappan, J.J., 1984, pp. 105, 106.

32 James T. Draper, Jr.: Presidential Press Conference, Pittsburgh, 1983.

33 Personal Interview, Pittsburgh, June, 1983.

34 Personal Interview, Pittsburgh, June, 1983.

35 Ibid.

36 Personal Interview, Pittsburgh, June, 1983.

6 THE MODERATES STRIVE FOR A COMEBACK

The score was now Conservatives four. Moderates zero. Four times the moderates had challenged the conservatives and lost. At Pittsburgh, they had decided it was not worth the effort. Draper's reconciling spirit and the tradition of giving an incumbent a second term seemed impossible to beat.

They poured over the percentages of the last elections:

Houston, 1979, Adrian Rogers by 51.36%

St. Louis, 1980, Bailey Smith by 51.67%

Los Angeles, 1981, Bailey Smith by 60.24%

New Orleans, 1982, Jimmy Draper by 56.97%

The conservative victors had defeated able men. Who—what would it take to win?

Jimmy Allen, the last SBC president supportive of the moderate agenda, was now head of the Radio and TV Commission. Tradition and strong feelings ran against active denominational executives running for convention office. Retired agency heads were more acceptable. James Sullivan, a "unity amidst diversity" man, had been elected in 1976. But that was before Pressler and Patterson had started organizing the conservatives. Duke McCall, a denominational statesman if there ever was one, moderates thought, had lost at New Orleans. Working against him had been allegations of liberalism at Southern Seminary, and the Hollyfield thesis suggesting a decline in orthodoxy as students progressed in studies. He had probably received some sympathy vote for the ugly and untrue rumor printed by Bill Powell alleging a drinking problem. But there were not enough votes there for him to win.

The conservatives had won with pastors successful in building large churches and baptizing hundreds of people. Here the moderates were handicapped. Some of their best known men had notoriously poor records in numbers of baptisms. Some also were reduced in popularity by their plain spokenness. Cecil Sherman, for example, was on record in a debate with Paige Patterson saying there were contradictions and errors in scripture. The conservatives would make mincemeat of Sherman, a man held in high honor by moderates and many in the agencies.

One bright light had emerged from Pittsburgh. John Sullivan, a widely-liked and successful Shreveport pastor, had been re-elected first vice-president. Sullivan bore no taint of neo-orthodoxy. He talked as conservatively on the Bible as Adrian Rogers. His church gave 26 percent of its budget to the Cooperative Program. He put his money where his mouth was. He was a good evangelist. Most important, he was believed to be a "company man" all the way, who didn't believe that the moderate interpretation of the *Baptist Faith and Message* phrase, "truth, without any mixture of the error," was grounds for disqualification in denominational service.

Sullivan was well liked among pastors. Some moderates thought he would be their best chance in 1984 in Kansas City, assuming he would be "balanced" in his appointments.

Others thought Grady Cothen the better candidate. Cothen had just retired from the presidency of the Sunday School Board. He had a long career in denominational service and was well known and admired by many. But a court suit won by one of his employees had undoubtedly hurt him?

However, it was months before Kansas City and too much talk of presidential candidates could work against the moderate effort to make a comeback.

The moderates pushed "education." Moderate pastors, such as Cecil and Bill Sherman, spoke on the "fundamentalist threat" wherever they could get an audience. But agency executives were still unwilling to go public against the conservatives, though some worked hard behind the scenes. Baptist Press and state editors, for example, had to be cautious. This meant that when reporting a talk by a leading moderate against the "take-over party of independent fundamentalists," countering quotes had to be printed from the other side, and vice versa.

The conflict was now a full-fledged political contest. Both sides were doing no more than what Democratic and Republican political activists did before an election—calling influentials (pastors), speaking to rallies, copying and distributing letters and newspaper clippings, talking to reporters. It was a battle for the minds and hearts of the numbers of Southern Baptists who had not taken sides, especially those who had not been in the habit of attending national conventions.

The leaders on both sides were devout men who believed that only their respective agendas could "save" the convention. Conservatives kept pushing the Bible issue and the implications they saw for missions and evangelism. Only by proclaiming and teaching Biblical infallibility, conservatives said, could the denomination survive.

Moderates hewed to the line of "unity amidst diversity". All Southern Baptists accepted the Bible as authoritative, they said. Differences in "interpretation" must not be allowed to divide the denomination. Agency trustees, administrators, and programs must represent the wide spectrum of Southern Baptists. Enforced uniformity in Biblical interpretation would destroy the structure, cooperative fellowship, educational institutions, and world-wide mission program which so many had worked so long and hard to develop. The "independent fundamentalist" party must not be allowed to take over the denomination and impose its "far right" theological and social platform on all Southern Baptists. The "Pressler-Patterson" coalition must be turned back.

The moderates had started late. They had blundered in making personal attacks on some conservatives, whose personal lives were above reproach.

In 1980, Chafin called the conservative coalition's cry for biblical inerrancy "a phony issue" used as a front for their "lust for power." *Dallas Morning News* Religion Editor Helen Parmley quoted Chafin's words, in which he said,

> They are sick people with different sets of sick egos with different ego needs—one old one that should retire, one with a secular vocation wanting to be in a religious vocation, and one with a second-rate institution wanting to be in a first-rate institution.

Parmley wrote that Chafin's statement "was an obvious reference to W. A. Criswell, pastor of First Baptist Church of Dallas, Pressler and Patterson, respectively." [1]

They had not been able to generate much enthusiasm in rallies. They could not get much help from kindred minds in agencies, who kept nervously looking over their shoulders. They were having difficulty enlisting many young pastors and lay church leaders who had not been schooled in the SBC way of "doing missions." Some moderates laid this lack to the demise of the Sunday evening church Training Union, which had educated the past generation on denominational agencies, leaders, and programs. Some blamed the aggressive parachurch movement. Many recent and present seminary men had been converted in state colleges through Campus Crusade for Christ and other non-denominational ministries. Lack of approval of parachurch groups from denominational headquarters (SBC and other mainline church structures) had hurt parachurch fund raising and enlistment. It had also made many young people, who had benefited from the parachurch organizations, feel distrust and even resentment toward their denominational establishments. Some were now active in the SBC conservative camp. Others voted the conservative ticket because they did not hold denominational agencies and programs with the reverence of those who had "grown up" in SBC churches.

As for parachurch influence on layman, church historian Bruce Shelley would later write:

> The last 50 years have witnessed a sharp decline in mainline denominational loyalty all over the country . . . Most laymen today simply do not care about the decisions denominational officials make 500 miles away, especially those laymen who find significant expression of the Christian faith in some parachurch ministry.[2]

Moderates recognized these and other handicaps, yet, they believed a greater number of people were "out there" who, if they only knew the immediate danger, would rally to the old order. These, in researcher Nancy Ammerman's words, had

> the denomination in their blood. They even refer to it as their mother, their family . . . [They] grew up with some of the most effective programs of denominational socialization ever devised. The missions education program of Sunbeams, Girl's Auxiliary, and Royal Ambassadors, along with the church training programs offered by the Sunday School Board in the 1930s and 40s and 50s were ingenious at attaching youth not only to their distinctives as Baptists but to the very organizations and personnel of the denomination.[3]

These were the people the moderates felt they had to alert and get to Kansas City for the next presidential election, although they knew many were as conservative on the Bible as Adrian Rogers, Bailey Smith, and Jimmy Draper. They had to get them by appealing to "unity amidst diversity" in building the greatest missionary denomination in the world.

As convention time approached, moderates became confident of winning. They had two good possible candidates in Grady Cothen and John Sullivan, along with several others who were not being mentioned so much. Responses from the field had been good. Some agency people were doing more, in discreet ways, to help. One denominational executive had reportedly permitted moderates to use office telephones in helping to get out the vote. A story spread that Christian Life Commission Director Foy Valentine had bragged that moderates would be busing 8,000 messengers to Kansas City.

Conservatives had also been busy, holding rallies, writing letters, making phone calls, and distributing literature. The conservatives now had another newspaper, classier than the *Southern Baptist Journal* in which Bill Powell was still nailing SBC "liberals" to the wall. It was called the *Southern Baptist Advocate* and edited by Russell Kaemmerling, who happened to be Paige Patterson's brother-in-law.

With Draper ineligible for a third term, conservatives had a number of possible candidates, but the favorite of most was Charles Stanley. Some felt that only Stanley, with his visibility as "America's television pastor," could defeat the moderates who were going all out to win.

The rhetoric began heating up in the pre-convention meetings. Motivational speaker Zig Ziglar, who taught the auditorium Sunday School class in First Baptist Church, Dallas, came out swinging at the conservative-dominated Pastors' Conference against "liberals" in SBC seminaries and colleges, the Baptist Joint Committee on Public Affairs, and the Christian Life Commission. Ziglar sympathized with conservatives who wanted to cut Cooperative Program funds from the Baptist Joint Committee on Public Affairs. Militant Frankie Schaeffer cut a wider swath, challenging the pastors to "take back" their "country" from the liberals. "If someone says to you, 'Do you mean to impose your values on this nation?' I have an answer to that, and it is 'Yes!' " [4] Moderates saw Schaeffer's appearance as one more link in a "New Right" plan to wrest control of the agencies of the Southern Baptist Convention for political purposes.

For the first time, the moderates held their own "pastors' conference," called "The Forum," drawing about 2,000 on Monday afternoon, while the traditional Pastors' Conference was in session with around five times as many. Moderates kept saying, "Wait until the convention opens. Our people will be here." Forum speakers warned about future consequences if the conservative bandwagon were not stopped. Kirby Godsey, president of Georgia's Mercer University, for example, said imposition of conservative theology in the SBC will leave "our children slaves to their ignorance and victims of narrow-minded bigotry."

The moderates were further encouraged by SBC Women in Ministry

(WIM) who were unabashedly pushing women's ordination, a practice anathema to most conservatives. The WIM crowd at Kansas City more than tripled over the 80 in attendance at WIM's kickoff meeting at Pittsburgh.

Suspense grew as time neared for the convention to open with the nominations for president, scheduled for the first business session.

The conservative nominee, as many had expected, was Charles Stanley. As in the case of Adrian Rogers, at Houston, in 1979, he did not agree to run until the last minute. In a prayer meeting late Monday night, before the election on Tuesday, Stanley told his friends, "I can't be nominated. God hasn't told me to do it."

Each person agreed to pray overnight.

Quite early Tuesday morning, Stanley awakened friends to tell them that God had not given him freedom to be nominated. The group reassembled at 7 a.m. and prayed with great fervor until after 9 a.m., when Stanley told them that God had made it clear to him that morning that he should be nominated. "God might be telling me to run so that he can humiliate me, but if that is what God wants to do, so be it." Some moderates openly snickered at the report of his late decision. Besides Stanley, the prayer group included Zig Ziglar, Adrian Rogers, Bailey Smith, Paige and Dorothy Patterson, Paul Pressler, Robert Tenery, Jim DeLoach, Richard Land, D. August Boto, and Russell Kaemmerling.

Jerry Vines, now co-pastor of First Baptist Church, Jacksonville, Florida, nominated Stanley the next day saying the Georgian's church had given $600,000 to various mission causes during the past year and "just may be the greatest missionary giving and sending church in the history of the Southern Baptist Convention." Vines did not mention the low percentage going to the Cooperative Program.

The moderates offered no surprises either. Texas pastor B.O. Baker nominated Grady Cothen, calling him a "bona fide Baptist statesman" whose 40 years of denominational service in varied positions qualified him to lead the convention. Cothen, Baker said, should be called back into service just as England had turned to Winston Churchill in a time of crisis." Baker did not mention Cothen's court suit at the Sunday School Board, nor something else known to many convention messengers which probably did not help Cothen. The *Southern Baptist Advocate* had revealed that Cothen had retired from the Sunday School Board with almost $60,000 in annual pay, plus a $15,000 automobile, and the guarantee of all expenses paid to annual meetings of the Southern Baptist Convention for the rest of his life. The confidential information had been leaked to the *Advocate* by a new conservative Sunday School Board trustee.

James Pleitz of Dallas, who had not been identified with moderate activists, nominated John Sullivan, praising him for leading his church members to give more than a quarter of their budget to the Cooperative Program. Pleitz said Sullivan was a pastor-leader around whom all Southern Baptists could unite.

Few moderates believed either Cothen or Sullivan could win on the first ballot. They hoped that Sullivan would siphon off enough of the conservative vote to force a runoff between Stanley and one of their favored candidates.

Many of the much ballyhooed 8,000 votes which were supposed to be bused in by moderates apparently never arrived. Despite criticism that he was not a committed Southern Baptist, Stanley defeated both Cothen and Sullivan on the first ballot with 52.18 percent of the votes. Apparently the Kansas City messengers did not see Cothen as another Churchill as Los Angeles messengers had not accepted Abner McCall as another Lincoln.

Zig Ziglar then took the first vice presidency with 58.53 percent, probably on the basis of his popularity as a motivational speaker and his speech at the Pastors' Conference. Ziglar's defeated opponent, Kansas City pastor Don Wideman, whom moderates preferred, was then elected second vice president. After the election, it was discovered that Ziglar had never attended an associational meeting, though he taught the largest Sunday School class in the First Baptist Church of Dallas. Moderates made "hay" of that until Russell Kaemmerling pointed out in the *Advocate* that the Sunday School Board had recently hired a vice president for the agency's third highest position who had never attended an associational meeting and who had been a Southern Baptist only three years.

Stanley's post-election press conference reminded some conservatives of Richard Nixon's jousts with the White House Press Corps. Denominational editors quizzed him intensely on his political associations and denominational loyalty. His answers were brief and to the point. No, he had not changed his mind about supporting the Reagan school prayer amendment. Yes, he was a member of The Roundtable, a conservative organization founded by Ed McAteer, a deacon in Adrian Rogers' church, but he was no longer a member of the board of the Moral Majority. And he did personally oppose ordination of women, but said that he respected the autonomy of any local church that chose to do that. He was certainly an inerrantist on the Bible, but thought "you are not going to get all Baptists to agree, and I think we have to accept that . . . I think we have to learn to live together and love each other whether we agree or not." Then as a closing word, the new SBC president gave an "admonition for us all:"

> Let all bitterness, and wrath, and anger, and clamour, and evilspeaking, be put away from you, with all malice: And be ye kind one to another, tenderhearted, forgiving one another, even as God for Christ's sake has forgiven you.[5]

"Tender-hearted," smiling moderates were hard to find at the Kansas City business sessions where conservatives took almost everything except second-vice presidency and the microphones.

Conservatives handily defeated moderate challenges to trustees nominated by the Committee on Boards. The closest vote came on the nomination of Judge Pressler to the Executive Committee, with the conservative strategist winning approximately 54 percent of the votes cast. One of those objecting to Pressler identified himself as Winfred Moore, a pastor from the judge's home state who nominated Dallas pastor Bruce McIver as a substitute nominee. It was Moore's first time to speak on the convention floor, but it would not be his last.

Conservatives almost succeeded in defunding James Dunn's Baptist Joint Committee on Public Affairs from the Cooperative Program budget. The vote was 51.65 to 48.35 percent to keep the money flowing to the Washington-based agency. Some observers felt if this vote had come an hour or two later, after more messengers were present, the defunding would have succeeded.

Conservatives defeated a raft of bylaw amendments attempting to establish minimum Cooperative Program percentages from church budgets of officer and trustee nominees. These amendments were clearly aimed at Charles Stanley and other conservative luminaries whose churches gave low percentages.

Conservatives pushed though resolutions against abortion (except to save the life of the mother), the teaching of secular humanism (including hedonism and relativism) in public schools, and ordination of women. The latter was enacted on the basis that the Apostle Paul "excludes women from pastoral leadership to preserve a submission God requires because the man was first in creation and the woman was first in the Edenic fall."

The resolution opposing women's ordination sent tempers rising among moderates and Women in Ministry members who argued that such passages as 1 Timothy 3:1-13 and Titus 1:6-8 reflected only first century culture and should not be applied literally today. They pointed to Galatians 3:28 as God's ideal: "There is neither Jew nor Greek, there is neither bond nor free, there is neither male nor female; for you are all one in Christ Jesus."

Moderates left Kansas City sobered and fearful. They had bragged about overwhelming the conservatives and had lost again. Most bitter was the election of Charles Stanley, who despite his soft words was viewed by moderates as the most hardline on doctrinal and social issues among leading conservatives. Harold Hime, pastor of First Baptist Church, Anchorage, Alaska called Stanley's win "very distressing, . . . a devastating blow to individual freedom and honesty." [6] Tennessee pastor Dillard Mynatt called his win "the darkest day in the history of our denomination." [7]

For conservatives, "everything" was "up to date in Kansas City." They still had a way to go, but Florida pastor Robert Parker predicted that "within two years we'll see dramatic changes" such as "the firing of seminary professors and presidents" because "we will soon have a majority on trustee boards." [8]

Kansas City did mark one important advance for the moderates. Here, for the first time, a major agency head, Russell Dilday, who was not on the verge of retirement, entered the public arena against the conservative onslaught. And he did it in his convention sermon.

Russell Dilday was no longer in Atlanta, where some had termed him Charles Stanley's cross-town rival in the pastorate. Dilday had received dissenters from Stanley's church into membership and had also pre-empted Stanley's time slot on a local TV station. The station had reportedly canceled Stanley after warning him several times to keep out of "controversy." Dilday was now president of Southwestern Seminary, which was widely regarded as more conservative in theology than some of the other SBC theological schools.

Dilday's main thrust in his sermon, "On Higher Ground", was against conformity to party politics of any kind. Taking a page from the frightening futurist book *1984*, he warned,

> Incredible as it sounds, there is emerging in this denomination, built on the principle of rugged individualism, an incipient Orwellian mentality. It threatens to drag us down from the high ground to the low lands of suspicion, rumor, criticism, innuendos, guilt by association, and the rest of that demonic family of forced uniformity. I shudder when I see a coterie of the orthodox watching to catch a brother in a statement that sounds heretical, carelessly categorizing churches as liberal or fundamentalist, unconcerned about the adverse effect that criticism may have on God's work.[9]

Yet in urging, "Do not dabble in controversies or exhaust your energies arm wrestling for denominational control," Dilday was undeniably positioning himself against the conservatives, for only they were striving to overturn the status quo in agencies which they claimed to be infected with neo-orthodoxy.

Dilday was followed two months later by Roy Honeycutt, Duke McCall's successor to the presidency of Southern Seminary. In a fiery convocation address in the seminary chapel before applauding students and faculty, Honeycutt spoke of "unscrupulous and unethical acts by politicians" heading an "independent fundamentalist party." Party leaders, he said, had enlisted students to tape lectures and speeches by seminary personnel "for the Dallas war room with its reported information banks. I understand there may be files on as many as 400 of us there." One of the Texas leaders of the "inerrantist" political party, he charged, had recently "invaded the privacy of [my] office" by frequently calling "my" student airport driver for information. Honeycutt then called for "holy war" against "the unholy forces" who are "seeking to hijack" the denomination and "take control" of agencies.10

When "holy war" headlines blazed in the media, Honeycutt said he hadn't meant to be "militaristic but ethical." He wasn't fighting anybody's theological views," but a "take-over group who were endangering Baptist principles of priesthood of the believer, pluralism in worship and witness, leadership of the Holy Spirit in decision making, and cooperative world missions.11

In a quick rebuttal, Paige Patterson termed Honeycutt's speech "a demonstration of denominational fascism which is determined to brook no criticism and . . . to squelch and suppress it." (Patterson later wrote Honeycutt that he had not meant to label him a "fascist," the term applied only to the approach he had taken in the denominational quarrel.) Patterson then took a page from church history in replying to Honeycutt's claim that the denomination needed saving from conservatives.

> The burden of proof . . . is upon him, because in the other formerly great denominations, it is the people of his persuasion that kill them—not the conservatives that try to make them vital. As to Honeycutt's claim of hijacking to take control, Patterson said, [This] suggests there is somebody in control now, and I want to know who that is. I thought [the denomination] belonged to the people, not denominational bureaucracy.

The alleged "war room" at the Criswell Center for Biblical Studies, Patterson said, was "nothing more than historical archives." Patterson did admit that some Southern students had met with him at the Kansas

City convention for "breakfast in an open hotel dining room. They asked for the meeting," he noted.

Patterson then challenged Honeycutt "to debate on a public platform and let people ask questions, instead of making unfounded charges and personal attacks" on those who oppose "liberal trends." [12] Honeycutt refused the public debate, but said it might be profitable for "us to write something together." [13]

Randall Lolley at Southeastern followed Honeycutt into the fray, comparing conservatives to the Moonies and cult leader Jim Jones.

Stanley visited Southeastern Seminary and met with professors. He was welcomed politely, but when he asked if they believed the Bible to be "truth, without any mixture of error," none would answer.

Dilday, the most active in speaking against conservatives, was now traveling. Southwestern's faculty, he said, had never allowed "reason to displace faith." None denied miracles and the history of the Old Testament. German higher criticism was an "outdated" theory which "no longer has any serious impact on modern scholarly pursuits." [14]

Patterson also pressed Lolley and Dilday to meet him in public debate. Like Honeycutt, they refused. "They're afraid," Patterson said, "because they'd have to to justify the teaching in their institutions, and that the extent of suppression of evangelical views in their institutions might surface." Patterson said he could present "multifarious examples" of unbiblical teaching in SBC seminaries, but declined to be specific "at this time." [15]

Meanwhile, the colorful Zig Ziglar and Baylor University president Herbert Reynolds were having a mini-battle of words in Texas. Ziglar fired the first salvo by asking why Baylor allowed a Mormon to be on the faculty. Reynolds responded that the Mormon taught only foreign languages and had signed a pledge not to proselyte his students.

The furor over the Mormon teacher apparently encouraged a small group of conservative students at Baylor to present Reynolds a "manifesto" against allowing the teaching of "theistic evolution, R-rated movies, songs with "immoral themes" while "no Christian music" is on the student center juke box, a lecture by a professor on the advantages of being a homosexual, the teaching of evolution, other lectures by speakers they felt "presented viewpoints contrary to the beliefs of Southern Baptists," and other "unchristian" activities on campus. The students also cited three examples where "conservative" speakers had either been denied permission to speak on campus or limited in what they could say. When the story was picked up by

Baptist media and spread by outside conservatives, Reynolds said he was doing all possible to investigate the accusations, but charged the students with using "KGB" tactics, and said "a priestly and self-anointed group [Ziglar, Pressler, Patterson, et. al.] were out to make "clones" by controlling the SBC educational system.16

With some major institutional heads at last speaking up, moderates found it easier to build support bases in several states—"a grassroots response to fundamentalism," said Walter Shurden.17 One of the strongest moderate groups was the Concerned Southern Baptists of Georgia with two statewide and eight regional coordinators and eight state consultants. Their purpose was to "educate" and get more lay church messengers to the upcoming convention in Dallas.

The Georgians sponsored a series of informational meetings. The keynote speaker at the third of the series, held in Savannah's First Baptist Church, was Randall Lolley from Southeastern Seminary. Speaking to about 200 persons, Lolley said Stanley had told him "personally" that "he had no confidence in the six Southern Baptist seminaries when he became [SBC] president and therefore had counseled young people, including his own son and daughter, not to attend one of the Southern Baptist seminaries.18

"That's his business," Lolley continued, "but he ought not to be president of a group that he doesn't love."

Lolley then turned to First Baptist, Atlanta's support of missionaries [local church members who had chosen to go out under another group or had been unable to secure appointment by the SBC Foreign Mission Board] serving under non-Southern Baptist boards. He asked,

> Does it make any person less a Southern Baptist to do missions differently than the way the denomination has determined we'll do it? No. If a Southern Baptist church decides to do missions congregationally, it's their business. But the people who decide that ought not to be elevated to the highest position in this denomination.

Lolley further criticized the appearance on the Christian Broadcasting Network's "700 Club" of three former SBC presidents—Adrian Rogers, Bailey Smith, and James T. Draper, Jr., who, Lolley said, "effectively smeared" all six of the seminaries. The Southeastern president continued,

> Your seminaries are not perfect, but we use the best tools of scholarship in our seminaries and they do not lead us to doubting Scripture; they lead us to loving Scripture as the Word of the Lord.

Lolley suggested that the conservative trio might have less than loyal motives in criticizing denominational seminaries.

> When the three most recent presidents of the SBC say what they said about the six Southern Baptist seminaries, I think there's at least the possibility they're trying to sell another set of schools.

Lolley then referred to an announcement by Stanley that he would seek a second term at the 1985 convention in Dallas. He was not prepared to endorse the Georgia conservative for the traditional reelection of an incumbent.

> We Baptists elect presidents one year at a time. And to talk in terms of absolute commitment without any questions asked . . . of a president for a second term . . . is not the way we Baptists usually conduct our affairs. It is entirely appropriate for someone else to be nominated. If you go to Dallas, I can guarantee you there are going to be some other nominees. Baptists are just Baptist enough to say that they want a chance every year to review their leadership.[19]

Moderates were now more active in journalism. Walker Knight's professional-looking *SBC Today* was reinforced by Gregory Hancock's *The Call*. Hancock, a militant Kentucky moderate pastor, took the line in one editorial that conservatives did not deserve leadership because they lacked experience in denominational affairs.

> [This] is akin to setting persons up as physicians without the proper credentials. The propaganda of the fundamentalists is aimed at convincing us that certain people are worthy of authority even though they have paid no dues in terms of study or services to the denomination . . . You and I must make known by our presence and our respective votes at the upcoming convention that we will not tolerate the abuse of the will and direction of God . . . Let's elect leaders who have *paid their dues.*[20]

Moderates cited conservative connections to the Luther Rice and Mid-America seminaries and the Criswell Center for Biblical Studies as further evidence that they were independents in denominationalist disguise. It was not hard to link conservatives with the triad of "alternative" schools. Criswell Center for Biblical Studies was controlled by First Baptist Church, Dallas, Mid-America Seminary, with former SBC seminary professors as faculty, received help from Adrian Rogers' Bellevue Baptist Church. Luther Rice had close ties with First Baptist Church, Jacksonville,

Florida, where Jerry Vines was now co-pastor with Homer Lindsay, Jr. Many well-known conservatives, including Charles Stanley (who also graduated from Southwestern Seminary) held doctorates from Luther Rice. The Florida school had chosen Stanley as its "alumnus of the year for 1984," happily coinciding with his election to the SBC presidency.

Furthermore, Mid-America Seminary established a precedent by contributing to the Cooperative Program and special SBC mission offerings. No official SBC seminary could make such a claim.

Moderates studiously avoided talking about the successes of graduates of the three independent schools. In 1983, half of the pastors with churches in the top ten of baptisms in the Georgia and Florida state conventions were graduates of Luther Rice.

Moderates also failed to note that all three schools encouraged their students to promote the Cooperative Program, even though the institutions received no Cooperative Program money, as did seminaries inside the convention structure; offerings for the Cooperative Program and SBC mission endeavors are sent annually from Mid-America Seminary; and that it was against policy at Mid-America and Luther Rice for faculty members and visiting speakers to criticize SBC agencies. Mid-America president Gray Allison had once interrupted a chapel speaker to rebuke him for a critical remark against a denominational institution.

Moderates also did not direct attention to the denominational background of the three presidents of the independent schools. All three—Paige Patterson of the Criswell Center for Biblical Studies, Gray Allison of Mid-America, and Gene Williams of Luther Rice—held doctorates from New Orleans Seminary and had served as pastors of cooperating SBC churches.

Conservatives, and probably many other Southern Baptists as well, were becoming resentful that the presidents of Southern, Southwestern, and Southeastern seminaries were taking time off from their regular duties to speak against some of their supporters and also using alumni periodicals for the same purpose. Retorted W.A. Criswell, "It isn't right for them to take our [Cooperative Program] money and damn us." [21] Criswell called for the seminary presidents to stick to institutional business or quit. Seven Southwestern trustees demanded that Dilday get out of denominational politics. Dilday refused and rode out the rebellion on his board.

Moderates defended the right of agency heads to speak in the controversy. Said Walter Shurden:

> Moderates would have been delighted if a "middle" had
> emerged [at Kansas City] and restored balance to the

Convention . . . The fact that it did not happen is exactly why SBC agency heads such as Dilday, Honeycutt, and Lolley came to the front of the conflict. They waited five years. They finally realized that they could wait no longer. So they have now risked their positions of leadership to try to halt the blitz of Fundamentalist leaders on the Southern Baptist Convention.[22]

Draper, for one, did not accept such reasoning. He warned that if the agency heads didn't cease their attacks on the conservative movement, his church might start putting Cooperative Program money in escrow. Draper thought thousands of other churches might follow suit.

Other moderates, had warned previously that churches on their side might do the same if conservatives took control of institutions. Cecil Sherman had said, "If the swell of support for moderates wanes and fundamentalists prevail in their announced intention to rule the denomination, the moderate churches in North Carolina and Virginia will quietly step to the edge of the denomination," divert their annual contributions from denominational agencies to other mission programs and purchase Sunday School materials from non-Southern Baptist groups. [23] This threat was ignored in speeches and letters to editors by moderates crying blackmail and intimidation.

Charles Stanley, who had said little about the struggle since Kansas City, except to state his willingness to serve a second term, thought Draper was only "trying to get people's attention . . . to get them to admit we have problems and be willing to sit down and talk about them." [24]

Bailey Smith said his church had already cut Cooperative Program giving from $175,000 in 1984 to $125,000 in 1985 as a protest against a seminary president [Dilday] who is going around the country on Cooperative Program money trying to defeat Charles Stanley. My deacons said they weren't going to pay for that. I had to work to keep them from cutting it more.[25]

Conservative Jim Henry, whose FBC, Orlando, Florida, ranked third in the SBC in dollar Cooperative Program giving, said his church would continue supporting the Cooperative Program, but "if we see a deterioriation, we would have to consider changes." [26]

Roy Honeycutt and Russell Dilday did not retreat in calling for defeat of the conservative movement, though Dilday said friends were now paying his travel expenses. Lolley stopped speaking against Stanley altogether. Other agency heads restricted themselves to pleading for the fighting to stop. Said the Home Mission Board's

William Tanner, who affirmed both a "Bible-centered conservative theology" and "unity within diversity":

> We must stop assulting each other with counterfeit labels
> and start assaulting the gates of hell . . . No issue should
> overshadow the fact that there are infinitely more things
> and deeper things that unite us than divide us.[27]

Foreign Mission Board President Keith Parks said the conflict was hurting missions. Then, a few months before Dallas, Parks announced that he could not support Stanley for a second term. In a statement released to the press and sent to all SBC foreign missionaries entitled, "Will Missionaries Become Hostages to Convention Conflict?" Parks deplored alleged threats by some churches to withhold funds from the Cooperative Program. He bewailed attacks on the Cooperative Program, "liberalism" in seminaries (he denied any "drift"), and "actions of the Baptist Joint Committee," by those who would "dismantle the denomination" and destroy the foreign mission enterprise. He urged missionaries who would be messengers to the convention to "choose officers of the convention and trustees of agencies who are unquestionably committed **both** to the Bible **and** to our convention approach to missions." [28] After Paige Patterson said he had been "deeply hurt" by an agency head whom conservatives greatly respected and supported, Parks made no further public comments about the convention.

As Dallas approached, recruiting activity and passions on both sides intensified. Moderates kept claiming that a group of independents were using power politics to "take over" the institutions and creedalize the denomination. Conservatives kept saying that no one could creedalize autonomous churches and their members. The problem was, Paige Patterson kept insisting, that the denomination had been "taken over" years before by those who would accomodate more theological diversity than the founders had intended.

> For the last 25 years, people at the Louisville seminary, for
> example, have imposed their beliefs on all Southern
> Baptists, including conservatives, who have paid the bill.
> They, and others, were in control of the convention pro-
> cesses, as they so now accuse conservatives. Dr.
> Honeycutt and others are sore about it because the
> Convention is not working their way at this time. They are
> learning how some of us have felt for 25 years.[29]

Then, the moderate argument that there had been no control politics before the conservative challenge was pricked by retired Editor C.R. Daley's class lecture at Southern Seminary. Daley admitted that there was "some truth" to the claims of the "inerrantists" about politics. He recalled once being asked if he would agree to being nominated for recording secretary of the SBC, an important position because it carried membership on the influential Executive Committee. When Daley declined the offer, the inquirer asked that Daley nominate him as the group's second choice, something Daley told the class, "I was more than willing to do."

> I learned at that time there were mixed motives . . . It turned out that at the convention there were two nominees, the one I nominated and the enemy of the friend who led me to make the nomination. If my nominee had lost, I probably would never tell this story, but he won and has made a magnificient contribution in the office. Now you judge. I'm judging myself. I think there is no way but to admit that there was something unethical about that, particularly, I was willingly manipulated to nominate a person, not only because he [could do the job], but to head off someone else whom I did not care much for and whom my friend [did not want elected]. So that is the way the system works and I am speaking to you as a very small fish in a big pond. Someone, like Dr. Wayne Dehoney [a past SBC president] or others who have been in the inner circles, could make your hair stand on end by stories similar to the ones I'm telling you.[30]

Moderates ignored Daley's admission, except to decry the "unethical" use of the tape, and continued their campaign to get church messengers to Dallas who would defeat Stanley and halt the conservative juggernaut. The charge of "unethical" use of the tape was somewhat humorous since a videotape was made by the seminary and placed in the library for circulation.

At Southern and Southeastern seminaries, course credit was offered students who would attend and learn the processes of the convention. Seminary students were further urged to get themselves accredited as church messengers. Kenneth Chafin, back on the Southern faculty after a stint in the pastorate, urged a chapel audience, "Start saving your nickels and dimes. Get on as a messenger from some church. Get to Dallas and . . . vote." [31]

Moderates worked hardest in states in the Old South which had more denominational history. Two thousand Georgians signed a full-page ad in the *Atlanta Constitution*, stating their opposition to the reelection of the pastor of First Baptist Church, Atlanta. Charles Stanley made no public comment on the ad.

W. A. Criswell was talking to everybody who would listen.

I had a seminary professor here in my church to teach a Bible study. After he made some statements that parts of Genesis were not historical, I took him aside and said, 'I'm going to ask you a question and I want you to take a couple of days to think about the answer. The question is this: Do any more of you fellows at the seminary believe like this?' When the time came I said, 'Have you thought about the answer?' He had and said, 'Just about all of us think this way.'

Gathering steam, the veteran warhorse pastor of the denomination's biggest church, asserted,

We've got a hierarchy more dominating than the Episcopal Church. They say we [conservatives] are against missions. That's a coverup. Our dispute is not over the Convention way of doing missions but over liberalism and denial of the integrity of the Word of God. There'll be a terrible reaction from churches after the convention in Dallas if Stanley is not re-elected. They'll be taking a long, hard look at their giving to the Cooperative Program.[32]

Then to insure that this would not happen, Criswell sent letters to 36,000 pastors urging them to bring every church messenger they could to Dallas and help elect Charles Stanley.

With charges and countercharges flying and both sides working zealously to get out their vote, fears rose that the Convention might split at Dallas, with the losing side staging a mass walkout. Worried state convention presidents had already been meeting to discuss formation of a Peace Committee. Former SBC president H. Franklin Paschall, who had also been pushing this idea for several months, offered help in getting such a committee ready to present at Dallas. Some said it was the only hope of averting disaster.

So the stage was set for the largest parliamentary church meeting in U.S. history.

REFERENCES

1   Helen Parmley: "Baptists Plan 'Rescue' From Conservatives," *Dallas Morning News*, October 4, 1980, p. 33A.

2   Bruce Shelley: "The Parachurch Vision," **Christianity Today**, November 8, 1955, pp. 41-43.

3   Nancy T. Ammerman: "Organizational Conflict in a Divided Denomination: Southern Baptists and Abortion," Candler School of Theology, Emory University, A paper presented to the meetings of the Society for the Scientific Study of Religion,

Savannah, Georgia, and the conference on Religion and the Political Order, Hilton Head Island, South Carolina, October, 1985, pp. 25, 26.

4   Steven L. Higdon: "Pastors Urged to Battle Pornography, Abortion," *Baptist and Reflector*, June 20, 1984, p. 6.

5   Ephesians 4:31, 32, *King James Version* of the Bible.

6   Helen T. Gray and Sean Hillen: "Southern Baptists Elect Conservative," *Kansas City Times*, June 13, 1984, p. 1.

7   Baptist Press. Reports for press at the Kansas City Convention, June 1984.

8   Ibid.

9   Russell H. Dilday, Jr.: "On Higher Ground," Convention Address as printed in *Baptist and Reflector*, June 13, 1984, p. 9.

10   From printed copy of speech supplied by the seminary news department.

11   Telephone Interview, October, 1984.

12   Mark Kelly: "Concerned" Arkansas Pastors Condemn 'Liberal Drift,' " *Arkansas Baptist Newsmagazine*, March 14, 1985, pp. 10, 11.

13   Telephone Interview, October, 1984.

14   James C. Hefley: "Southern Baptist 'Moderates' Regroup for a 1985 Battle Against Inerrantists," *Christianity Today*, November 9, 1984, p. 44 (see also Baptist Press reports).

15   Telephone Interview, October, 1984.

16   Baptist Press and report in Baptist state papers, October, November, 1984. See, for example, Craig Bird: "Baylor Students Deliver 'Manifesto' to Reynolds," *Baptist and Reflector*, December 26, 1984, pp. 1, 3. This same issue (p. 3) also carried a Baptist Press report of the organization of other students at Baylor and other Baptist colleges in an "information movement" which they hoped would reverse the trend of high school and college-age Southern Baptists ignorant of SBC history and heritage, current denominational issues, and future SBC goals. This group claimed to be neutral in the wider SBC conflict, but their goals were welcomed by moderates. Baylor received more unwelcome publicity during this period, when President Herbert Reynolds also called conservative SBC leaders a "little Baptist 'college of cardinals.' " See the BP dispatch, "Baylor President Denounces SBC 'College of Cardinals,'" in *Baptist and Refector*, October 17, 1984, pp. 1, 2.

17   Walter B. Shurden: "In Defense of the SBC: The Moderate Response to Fundamentalism," "The Controversy in the Southern Baptist Convention," Special issue of *The Theological Educator*, published by the faculty of New Orleans Baptist Theological Seminary, 1985, pp. 11-14.

18   Robert Dilday: "Randall Lolley Speaks to Group in Georgia," *Baptist and Reflector*, April 17, 1985, p. 8.

19 Ibid.

20 Gregory L. Hancock: "Ruse or Reason," *The Call*, March, 1985, p. 2.

21 Personal Interview, Hannibal, Mo., May, 1985.

22 Shurden, op. cit.

23 Ed Briggs: *Richmond (Va.) Times-Dispatch*, December 11, 1982.

24 Dan Martin: "Key Leaders in SBC Comment on Threat to Withhold Funds," *Baptist and Reflector*, April 10, 1985, pp. 1, 3.

25 Ibid.

26 Ibid.

27 Baptist Press reports, Fall, 1984.

28 The statement released April 19, 1985 was sent to missionaries on May 2 under a cover letter by Charles W. Bryan, Senior Vice President for Overseas Operations. Bryan asked only for prayer for the Board and the convention and noted that "persons with widely differing viewpoints are seeking God's leadership."

29 Frequently stated by Patterson in countering charges by Honeycutt and other moderates.

30 Excerpted from tape as cited in Chapter 3.

31 Reported by LaVern Butler who was present on the occasion.

32 Personal Interview, Hannibal, Mo., May, 1985.

7 DALLAS: DIVISION AND HOPE

Both sides worked furiously to get church messengers to Dallas. Both sides expected a record turnout, perhaps 30,000 to 35,000. Above that, some moderates admitted, they could be in trouble.

The numbers kept swelling until, by the time the convention opened on Tuesday morning, June 11, 1985, 45,404 church messengers—more than twice the previous record—had registered for the 128th session in the 140th year of the Southern Baptist Convention. They came for what most believed would be the most important meeting in the history of the country's largest non-Catholic denomination.

Excitement built during the weekend as early comers poured into local churches to hear convention luminaries. Thousands of conservatives converged on First Baptist Church, Dallas. Many said they had come after receiving Criswell's letter and that they agreed with him that agency heads should not involve themselves in convention politics. They packed the auditorium (many church members stayed home to give visitors their seats) for two sermons by Criswell and the auditorium Bible class by deacon Zig Ziglar sandwiched between.

They heard the 75-year-old firebrand pastor shout, "All Scripture is inspired of God. All of it. Not parts of it. If this Bible, which is supposed to be written by the Holy Spirit of God contains errors; it is a work of men; it is not a work of God. It is that plain." Special guest Charles Stanley, seated on the platform, joined the roar of amens.

A much smaller number heard Cecil Sherman at Wilshire Baptist Church rawhide his conservative opponents for financing "independent" missionary programs (he apparently had Stanley in mind), using non-Southern Baptist Sunday School literature, giving small percentages of the church budget to the Cooperative Program, and other low activity in denominational life. "Anyone who does not choose to be inside the Southern Baptist system [is] free to drop out and do independent missions," he invited. "Coerced cooperation is not cooperation at all."

Repeating what he had said many times before, Sherman charged, "It's the spirit of fundamentalism that has made our division; they're good and we're bad; they're orthodox and we're unorthodox, they believe the Bible and we don't."

Sherman said the denomination was not split between theological moderates and fundamentalists but between those who like the SBC as it is and those who want to change it. "We've always had" conservatives and moderates. "There has always been a spirit of live and let live and now [the militant fundamentalists] are putting us out of policy-making posts as they exercise their political rhetoric."

If "they do not love [the SBC]," he asked, "Why do they want to rule it?" [1]

"Women in Ministry" held their own worship service in a downtown hotel meeting room. Five hundred heard Molly Marshall-Green, a new theology professor at Southern Seminary and interim pastor of Louisville's Deer Park Baptist Church, urge them to keep moving forward. "Our gaze and our yearning efforts," she said, "should be toward the horizon God places before us rather than a stultifying preoccupation with days gone by." [2]

Reba Sloan Cobb, editor of Women in Ministry's publication, *Folio*, said they planned to introduce no motions at the Dallas convention. The resolution against women's ordination, adopted at Kansas City, she said, "has helped us more than it has hurt. There are now at least 350 ordained Southern Baptist women." When convention bulletins, giving the order of business, later came out, an ordained woman was listed to give a prayer from the podium—"a first, so far as we know," she said.[3]

The largest Pastors' Conference on record opened on Sunday evening. Moderates groaned when they heard a crowd estimate of 20,000. By Monday night the attendance had mounted to around 25,000. Most, moderates feared, would be voting for Charles Stanley.

Stanley and Criswell appeared together at the final session of the Pastors' Conference. The SBC president said that the convention, which would begin the next morning, would send "a very certain signal to the world that we still are bound to the Word of God as the revelation of God." Stanley hoped a second signal would go out; that Southern Baptists "still know how to be forgiving and loving toward one another." The mass of preachers stood and gave sustained applause.[4]

If Stanley was the man of the hour for the conservatives, Criswell was the timely orator in giving a sermon for which he said he'd spent more time preparing than for any other message he ever preached. Slowly, methodically, then building steam, the veteran pulpiteer, who holds a Ph.D. from Southern Seminary, traced a pattern of decline among British Baptists that he said had been caused by neo-orthodoxy and German higher criticism. Then raising his voice like a prophet shouting across a desert, he thundered, "There's a lesson here for Southern Baptists. Whether we continue to live or ultimately die lies in our dedication to the infallible Word of God." If higher criticism, he warned, "continues to grow like a parasite in our seminaries, there will be no missionaries to hurt—they will cease to exist."[5] The walls resounded with amens.

The moderates' Forum drew a record, but disappointing, 5,000 people Monday afternoon. Many bore "TEN PLUS" lapel stickers, proclaiming their belief that every SBC church should give more than 10 percent of its budget to SBC agencies through the Cooperative Program. Undismayed by the big gap between their crowd and the number at the Pastors' Conference, leading moderates said many of their people had been counted in the Pastors' Conference sessions. Others were just a little late in arriving. They would be in the convention center "when the voting starts." That had been heard at Kansas City.

And, as at Kansas City, Forum speakers filled the air with dire predictions of what could happen if the "takeover" faction were not stopped. Atlanta's William Self alleged that Southern Baptists were being manipulated by such right-wing political leaders as Moral Majority head Jerry Falwell, Senator Jesse Helms, and broadcaster Ted Turner, who were trying to break down barriers between church and state. Self warned that the Annuity Board with almost $1.5 billion in assets might lose its religious status if the "political" takeover was not averted. "We may not have retirement funds if we do not continue as we have historically. When church and state go to bed together, they do not make love, and they do not produce offspring. One always rapes the other."

Thundered Self, "We're not dealing at this convention with who's going to be our next presiding officer," but with "some kind" of political and religious" coalition who wants "access to the resources of our convention."[6]

As the crowds increased Monday, small children were seen in the long lines leading to the registration counters. The children—some as young as four—brought standard church messenger cards, signed by the proper church officer, and asked to be registered. Accreditation procedures had been tightened in recent years. Without the proper card, duly certified by the church clerk, no one could register. But convention bylaws specified no minimum age and at least 100 children, age six and under, were given ballots for voting.

Meanwhile, the group of state convention presidents and former SBC president Franklin Paschall had continued working on a proposed Peace Committee. They brought together key leaders from both factions in a midnight prayer meeting in a room at the Dallas Hilton. Several reporters happened to wander in and saw the key players in the conflict joining hands in small subgroups and praying. In one group Jimmy Draper was heard to pray, "We are not enemies, but brothers and sisters with differences. Forgive us when we have handled our differences wrongly."

In another was Charles Stanley and Winfred Moore, Stanley's expected challenger for the presidency. When the prayers ended, Stanley and Moore embraced, and Stanley was hear to say, "I love you." [7]

The 1985 SBC convention and related activities would be the biggest media event in Dallas since the Republican National Convention met in the same convention center the previous fall. Over 625 writers and broadcasters—well over twice the registered messengers for the first meeting of the Southern Baptist Convention—received accreditation in the press room, including crews from the major TV networks, Cable News, PBS, and many independent TV stations, along with reporters and editors from the national newsmagazines, most major American newspapers, the leading non-SBC religious journals of the country, and the usual spread of denominational periodicals.

Thousands of copies of papers, tabloids, and magazines were distributed in the corridors and the press room. Moderates now had three supportive newspapers, with the *Laity Journal* joining *The Call* and *SBC Today*. The publisher of the *Laity Journal* was listed as Owen Cooper, a former SBC lay president, widely respected across the denomination.

Bill Powell's *Southern Baptist Journal* was still naming and quoting "liberals" in denominational employment. A report on a speech by Zig Ziglar, for example, accused six state Baptist colleges—Wake Forest, the University of Richmond, Stetson, Furman, Baylor, and William Jewell—of departing from the purpose for which they were founded.

Russell Kaemmerling's *Southern Baptist Advocate* had matured into a 40-page magazine. Far less strident than the *Journal*, it was fast becoming the "establishment" periodical of the conservatives. Yet Kaemmerling minced no words in his convention editorial:

> Two messages need to be sent in Dallas. One is a reaffirmation of our absolute commitment to the Bible as the inerrant and infallible Word of God. Secondly, a message needs to be sent to the bureaucracy, whose salaries we pay, whose budgets are supported by us. A message needs to be sent that says, we, the people of the Southern Baptist Convention, committed to the Word of God and to our world missions program, will determine the course and the direction our Convention will take.[8]

The independent moderate and conservative papers were decidely partisan for their respective causes. The state denominational papers defended unity amidst diversity, taking the line that the denomination was solid on the Bible and did not need changing. Presnall Wood, editor of the Texas *Baptist Standard*, which published a daily edition for convention messengers (another first) declared,

> There are definite doctrines Baptists believe and a consensus of such is found in the *Baptist Faith and Message*. Baptists must be sure to believe the Bible and not just a belief about the Bible. Southern Baptists are biblical conservatives in spite of the efforts of some to wear the label to the exclusion of others.[9]

Only the California and Indiana editors had openly backed Charles Stanley with the former saying Stanley had "given the denomination leadership skills expected of his office" and deserved another term.[10]

Only one handout paper broke the solemnity of the convention. Rumored to have been put together by a group of irreverent seminarians, the short-lived *SBC Enquirer*, published by "Southern Baptists for Integrity in Media" and edited by Dr. U. Ben Took, D.D., Litt.D.," referred "all honest seekers after truth to the following controversy experts: Dr. Jihad [holy war] Honeycutt, Dr. Tenure Reynolds, Dr. Pre-Heresy Dilday, Dr. Brewery Blessing Lolley, Dr. Sacred Cow Rogers, Dr. Jews Can't Pray Smith, and Dr. Escrow Draper." The rag also listed "new Broadman books" available in the Convention book store:

How to be Supportive When Your Pastor Has a Hysterectomy

Honeycutt's Holy War & End Time Prophecy

The Art of Objective Journalism by Presnall Wood

How to Get Paid by Southern Baptists While You Travel the U.S. by Russell Dilday.

Unamused convention managers confiscated every copy of *The Enquirer* they could find, denying most messengers its wisdom.

Grand Hall, the main auditorium in the Dallas Convention Center, where Republicans had nominated Reagan and Bush, could seat only 31,000. It was full long before the Tuesday morning opening of the convention. Other messengers had to settle for large-screen TV in two lesser-sized halls.

In a camp meeting atmosphere, conservative messengers claimed the front rows in Grand Hall, bringing bags of sandwiches and cold drinks in coolers, intending to hold their seats during the noon recess. Moderates were mostly scattered further back, with key spokesman seated near floor microphones where they could be ready for action when the parliamentary proceedings began. Somewhere in the crowd were the seminary classes from Southeastern and Southern, "taking" the convention for classroom credit. One conservative leader passed the word that the Southeastern class had been "heavily infiltrated" by the "inerrantist club at the seminary."

Agency heads and press huddled along rows of tables positioned to the right of the high speaker's platform. Here was affable, grandfatherly, "holy war" Roy Honeycutt smiling as if he were at an alumni reunion. Within speaking distance sat his more somber colleagues, Randall Lolley of Southeastern, Frank Pollard of Golden Gate, Landrum Leavell of New Orleans, Russell Dilday of Southeastern, Milton Ferguson of Midwestern, and executives of other agencies.

On the platform sat various committee members, President Stanley, First Vice-President Zig Ziglar, Second Vice-President Donald Wideman, and a number of other notables. Armed security guards, a first for the SBC, hovered near the president. Stanley's new senior associate pastor stood atop the short flight of stairs from which personalities ascended and descended. Observers would note that the agency heads, who, before the conservatives took elective power had frequented the platform, remained at the floor tables, except when coming to give their reports.

Except for the absence of large state banners and the aisle parades, the SBC Convention in Dallas was much like the Republican Convention of the preceding summer. The conservative wing controlled the platform and key committees. A small band of vociferous moderates, peppered with a few conservatives, occupied the open space between front row seats and the high podium, some standing, others squatting on the floor. Reporters and camera crews roamed among the agency tables, through the crowd, and around the base of the platform, buttonholing newsmakers for spot interviews.

Moderates were putting their hopes and votes on folksy Winfred Moore, 65, pastor of First Baptist Church, Amarillo and President of the Baptist General Convention of Texas (giving him the home state advantage). Moore had endeared himself to moderates at Kansas City by contesting Judge Pressler's nomination to the Executive Committee. After failing three times with retiring institutional heads, they were going with a much loved pastor who had a healthy track record in baptisms and Cooperative Program giving (four times as much as Stanley's church during the past year). In nominating Moore, Milton Cunningham, a pastor from Houston, called him, "a man of God, with absolute integrity and a healer who would be 'good news for missions, good news for evangelism, and good news for the kingdom of God' if elected president of the SBC." 11

That Moore had never attended seminary seemed not to trouble his backers, who were strong supporters of graduate theological education. That he believed "every word" in the Bible was "absolute truth" did not cool their ardor, for it was now plain that only a personal inerrantist could win a majority. What made Moore different from Stanley, besides his greater experience in denominational work, was his stated perception that he saw no "liberal drift" in the seminaries or elsewhere in SBC life. They loved one of Moore's "favorite Scriptures, Second Babylonians 4:12, 'For behold it is not given unto any man to ring every man's bell.'" 12

They cheered his loyalty to agencies, although he had once led his church to withhold Cooperative Program funds from the SBC Christian Life Commission in protest over inviting a defender of the *Playboy* ethic to participate in a Commission-sponsored debate on morality. Moore said he had since repented and, if he had it to do over, would pursue quiet diplomacy with Foy Valentine, Executive Director of the Christian Life Commission.

So it was Moore versus Stanley, who had been promoted by Criswell as "the pastor's ideal and the kind of man we ought to have as head of our convention." Two who held the same view on the Bible; two who had no preacher's reputation for mud-slinging, preferring to talk about love and forgiveness; but two who were poles apart on balancing theological freedom and responsibility in denominational agencies.

Despite the large attendance at the pre-convention Pastors' Conference, moderates thought Moore, because of his personal conservatism, church record, and easy-going ways had an excellent chance for becoming SBC president and stopping the conservative drive. He had been elected president of the "conservative" Baptist General Convention of Texas, why not now the Southern Baptist Convention?

Still, moderates were faced with some worrisome questions, none of which related directly to Moore.

Would there be a sizable boomerang vote against the entry of agency heads into denominational politics? How much resentment had Russell Dilday, Roy Honeycutt, Randall Lolley, and Keith Parks aroused in opposing Stanley's reelection and criticizing the conservative movement?

There was also the question of breaking tradition in failing to reelect an incumbent to a desired second term. Moderates had failed to unseat incumbent Bailey Smith at Los Angeles and they had not even tried to prevent Jimmy Draper from receiving a second term at Pittsburgh. How many would honor the tradition of incumbency by voting for Charles Stanley?

Most disquieting of all was Stanley's television and pulpit image as a reconciler. He had answered none of his critics by name during the past year. He had called for the fighting to stop, and was "playing Reagan," one of his friends said. In his presidential address at Dallas, which preceded the election, he said, "Love, forgiveness and humility aren't feelings we have, but commitments we must make." [13]

Then, on Tuesday morning, the local papers broke a story that Billy Graham, in Europe for evangelistic crusades, had endorsed Charles Stanley. According to the report, the evangelist had called his long-time aide Grady Wilson and said, "Do me a favor: . . . Call Charles Stanley . . . and tell him if I could be there I would vote for him." Wilson then telegraphed the message to Stanley. [14]

A stunned Kenneth Chafin, who had formerly directed Graham's School of Evangelism, could hardly believe it. "I saw him two weeks ago, and he told me he was not going to get involved in our conflict." [15]

A hurried call was made to Graham's office in Minneapolis where spokesperson Donald Bailey confirmed that Graham had asked that the message be sent. Bailey, however, did "not know if Dr. Graham intended for it to be made public." [16]

Further inquiry revealed that the message had been sent several days before the convention. Stanley had not wanted to make it public, but friends had prevailed on him to let them release it to the press on Monday evening. Incensed moderates called the timing, "A Nixon dirty trick." [17]

Graham apologized several days later for any "confusion" he might have caused. He had given the endorsement for two reasons: "Because it is the custom of the convention to give a two-year term," and he "had been told that if [Stanley] were not elected, it might split the convention," But he had not expected the message would be made public.[18]

Buoyed by publicity over the Graham telegram, some conservatives on Tuesday morning forecast a Stanley win by as much as a 65-35 margin. Judge Pressler was much closer with a 55-45 prediction.

When Recording Secretary Martin Bradley announced that Stanley had turned back the challenge with 55.3 percent of over 44,000 votes cast, conservatives leaped to their feet in a long cheering ovation. Bill Powell strode through the crowd, slapping shoulders of friends, and shouting, "Victory! Victory!" "Glorious!" beamed a jubilant Judge Pressler. "With all the power and Cooperative Program money the liberals used against us, Charles Stanley's election is a miracle. I hope the bureaucrats will now quit waging war on their constitutency, so we can turn our convention back to the principles of the founders." [19]

Grim-faced moderates could only take solace in their best showing since the conservative drive for power began. Said Bill Sherman, "We've gone from 39 to 41 to 43 to 45 percent [in presidential elections]. And don't forget, Stanley was running this year as an incumbent." [20]

As nominations for first vice president got under way, reporters spotted Moore a few rows down from the front and hurried back for reaction to his defeat. "Of course, I'm disappointed," he said, "but we have to somehow get together." Had the published report of Graham's endorsement made a difference? "It must have, and I'm bitterly disappointed." [21]

Eyes in the crowd were turning towards Moore. A friend tugged at his arm. "You're wanted on the platform."

Moore hurried up to Stanley's side who reached out an arm and smiled. "Would you accept the nomination for first vice-president?"

"Are you asking me?" the surprised Moore drawled and the crowd roared. Stanley hastened to explain that a messenger from Virginia had nominated him while he had been talking to the press.

Against Zig Ziglar, running for a second term, the amiable Moore won by a solid two-thirds majority. The hall rang with cheers and exultant yells of delight. Many messengers shouted "Praise God" in the joy of the moment, thinking a miracle in reconciliation might be on the way.

Moore pledged later, in a press conference, to work with President Stanley "and do everything I know how to put the convention back in the mainstream of evangelism and missions. . . . Maybe it was the hand of God putting us in relationship to work together." [22]

Conservative leaders told reporters that many of their people had voted for Moore as a gesture of reconciliation. The first vice presidency carried no appointive powers and nothing had changed. Shortly, as if to confirm this opinion, a majority of messengers approved, over moderate challenges, the full slate of trustee nominees from the Committee on Boards.

Tuesday evening, the crowd thinned. Moderates elected layman Henry Huff of Louisville, a strong backer of Southern Seminary, as second vice president. Moaned Russell Kaemmerling, "Our people have a record of voting for the president and going home. Some may have gone to Six Flags [amusement park]." [23]

Earlier that afternoon, Franklin Paschall and the state convention presidents had held a press conference at the Dallas Hilton to announce 18 nominees for the proposed Peace Committee. The group—all men—covered the spectrum of the controversy and included, on the left, Cecil Sherman and William Hull, the former dean of theology at Southern Seminary who had been a Bill Powell target a decade before, along with conservative notables Adrian Rogers and Jerry Vines. Charles Fuller, pastor of First Baptist Church, Richmond, Virginia was designated chairman. President Stanley would be an ex-officio member. Fuller, who later gave the Convention sermon, declared himself "a 'non-union' conservative, who pays dues to no one . . . [and believes] the Bible is truth . . . without mixture of error." [24]

Paschall and Bill Hickem, who chaired the group of state presidents, presented the "Peace Committee" to the Dallas Convention Wednesday morning. Paschall called the Committee's task "urgent . . . We've been pitting power against power and it's a no win situation. Whoever wins, we all lose." The Committee, he said, would deal with "issues, personalities, and spiritual problems." [25]

A brief discussion ensued during which messengers added two women, a conservative and a moderate. Women had not originally been proposed for the committee, Hickem said in an interview, because, "We didn't want to upset some of our strict fundamentalist brethren." [26]

With messengers still glowing in the euphoria of Moore's election as first vice president, the Peace Committee was then accepted with such unrestrained enthusiasm that a Dallas TV newscaster declared, "It looks as if the big shootout has turned into a family reunion."

Hardly. The skies turned black within the hour. The Convention was turned into heated debate after Virginia moderate James Slaton moved for "the sake of peace and unity" to set aside the Committee on Committees' nominees to the Committee on Boards, two from each state convention, and substitute the names of presidents of state Baptist conventions and state Woman's Missionary Union organizations. It was a new version of an old moderate plan designed to transfer nominating power for trustees to states where moderates had more pull in a majority of state convention bureaucracies.

Tempers ran short as messengers lined up at floor microphones to speak for and against the proposal. Stanley ruled that Slaton would have to nominate and the messengers discuss the 52 names one by one, rather than try to substitute as a group. Given the division and heatedness of the occasion, this might take hours, perhaps days. At the very least other important Convention business would be derailed.

Three years before, at New Orleans, when trustee nominees were being challenged, conservative Larry Lewis and moderate Kenneth Chafin had presented a compromise which probably forestalled endless bickering. Lewis, Chairman of the Resolutions Committee for the Dallas convention, and his committee members had come into the hall only minutes before and were waiting to present their report. When he realized what was then happening, Lewis reached for a copy of the official *Book of Reports* lying on one of the agency tables and began checking the constitution and bylaws which were printed in the back of the book. He found five legalities which he felt rendered Slaton's motion out of order.

Making officers of one entity, state conventions, to be officers of another, the national convention, would be stepping into connectionalism, forbidden by denominational polity. Second, the bylaws specifically stated that the Committee on Boards "shall be nominated to the Convention by the Committee on Committees." Nothing was said about nominations from the floor of the convention. Third, prospective nominees for the Committee on Boards had to give permission for their names to be put before the convention. Fourth, committee nominees had to be residents for at least a year in the respective states from which they were chosen. Fifth, only one of the two nominees from each state could be a full-time employee of a church or a denominational agency.

On the last three, Lewis doubted if messenger Slaton had complied with the rules before making his motion. He turned to Carolyn Miller, a member of the Resolutions Committee. She was president of the WMU in Alabama and was included in the group which Slaton had asked to be substituted for the Committee on Committees report on the Committee on Boards. "Has anyone talked to you about this?" he asked. When, by his recollection, she replied, "No," he said, "I thought that was the case." Then he headed up the platform in hopes of getting to speak.[27]

John Sullivan, from Shreveport, was just ahead of him. "What are we going to do? This is awful," Lewis asked the man whom many moderates admired. He understood Sullivan to say something like, " 'I know,' " But in the confusion neither was able to get to the podium.

Cries for "point of order" were reverberating across the hall. Moderates and conservatives gathered around the platform exchanged strong words. "You're trying to run over us with a train," accused one moderate. Retorted Russell Kaemmerling, "Moderates want peace like the Russians. They want us to lay down our guns while they build better ones."

Stanley rapped his gavel sharply for order. A speaker at one of the microphones asked for a vote to appeal the chair's ruling. When a standing vote proved too close to count, ballots were taken and the count showed 12,576 to 11,801 against Stanley's ruling. Long-time observers noted that it was extremely rare for messengers to overturn an SBC president on a parliamentary ruling.

There was no session on Wednesday afternoon. Conservative leaders manned telephones and frequent announcements were made over KCBI-FM, the Criswell Center for Biblical Studies radio station, urging messengers to return.

Charles Stanley spoke to the staunchly conservative Southern Baptist Evangelists' Association during the afternoon and warned that if the procedure for nominating trustees by the Committee on Boards were changed, the conservatives would have failed in their strategy. "Go without your supper," speaker Mike Gilchrest, told his fellow evangelists, "but be there to vote."

That evening Stanley reported that he and his parliamentarians had conferred with a battery of lawyers (about 20) that afternoon and concluded that, according to Bylaw 16, both the motion to substitute the Committee on Boards and the vote overruling the chair had been out of order. Bylaw 16 stated plainly that "the Committee on Boards . . . shall be nominated to the Convention by the Committee on Committees." [28] Messengers could only reject the 52-member slate, thereby requesting the Committee on Committees to bring back a new Committee on Boards which they could approve. With the light at every floor microphone blinking red and objectors shouting across the auditorium, Stanley quickly called for the vote on the

Committee on Boards as presented earlier. It was approved by a margin of 13,123 to 9,581 and conservatives cheered the results. Registration Secretary Lee Porter then reported tellers had seen numerous persons passing out ballots outside in the corridors and the parking garage. "I can't do a thing about it," Porter bemoaned. "The integrity of the balloting system has to depend on the integrity of local churches and individual messengers." [29]

Slaton and the Sherman brothers were already enroute to the press room where reporters quickly gathered about them. Clearly angry at Stanley's decision to cut off debate, Bill Sherman declared, "That business session was not justice. When every voice is not heard, every vote is not heard."

"They'll say we were disturbing the peace," said Slaton. "I say a guarantee of peace is due process and a structure that makes peace possible. Regrettably, we don't have due process . . . They have made the Committee on Boards a recipe for war."

"It is one thing to talk peace," said Cecil Sherman. "It is another thing to set up a structure that makes peace possible."

The trio vowed that their group would not leave the Convention, despite the reported presence at the convention of American Baptist leaders who were courting moderates. "We will continue to stand our ground and plead for fairness," Bill Sherman stated. "Forty-five percent of the messengers voted with us. If the president will show some statesmanship and give a balance to the Committee on Committees, with representation from the 45 percent who voted against him, then Southern Baptists can be united. If not, I can assure you we will continue to have confrontation."

Bill Sherman was not optimistic that this would happen or that the Peace Committee could bridge the chasm. "I met with Adrian Rogers and told him, 'I don't see eye to eye with you theologically, but I can work with you and you interpret Scripture as you wish.' Quick as a flash he snapped his finger and said, 'Bill, that's good enough for you, but I will not work with liberals.'" [30]

Rogers said he was "willing to sit down and talk. I understand the Peace Committee has been given an open door to our seminaries and institutions. They've been defensive before. I certainly hope they will [now] welcome sunshine. If I were falsely accused, I know I would. I love the truth." [31]

Thursday, the last day of the convention, brought fears of a walkout by aggravated moderates. In the morning business session, moderates kept pressing their objections to the parliamentary ruling on the Committee on Boards. After reminding them several times that they were out of order, Stanley shut off their microphones and declared he would hear no more "on this subject." As a rumble from moderates was heard across the hall, John Sullivan, a previous moderate candidate for the presidency, and Winfred Moore, the vice president elect at Dallas, made personal, eloquent pleas from the podium for calm and urged that all messengers support the president as presiding officer. The tension relaxed a bit and the business turned to resolutions.

A record 71 resolutions had been presented to the Resolutions Committee. Five called for unity. Four criticized denominational employees for political involvement. A fifth asked the resignations of seminary presidents Roy Honeycutt, Lolley, Dilday, and Foreign Mission Board President Parks, "in the interest of peace and unity in the Southern Baptist Convention."

Resolutions chairman Larry Lewis remarked that the calm following Sullivan and Moore's appeal "reminds me of the fellow who bought a ticket and went to the arena to see a fight and behold a hockey game broke out." Lewis said that, in the interest of peace, his committee had decided not to report out any "controversial" resolutions. When messengers seemed to be going along, Lewis remarked, "It looks like our fight has turned into a hockey game."

The calm was broken when William Shoulta offered a resolution from the floor condemning "secret tape recordings." When the hubub began anew, Lewis said, "Okay, if you want a fight, we can have a good one. We can beat one another to a pulp if we wish. It's up to you." Shoulta's resolution was decisively rejected and calm prevailed through the closing minutes of the morning session.

Then, in the very last session on Thursday afternoon, after many persons had left, the Denominational Calendar Committee presented its report. Few in the hall were paying close attention, for the Calendar Committee seldom presented anything of great interest. Some would later find it significant that Second Vice President Don Wideman, a friend of many moderates, had finished his "courtesy time" of moderating and President Stanley was now back at the podium.

The Calendar Committee had been nominated by the Committee on Boards and elected by convention messengers the year before, in Kansas City. Shortly afterwards, a messenger moved that the committee investigate the possibility of recommending to churches that a Sanctity of Life Sunday be observed on a Sunday in January, a "day" which was already being observed by many in the Right to Life movement outside the SBC. (January was the anniversary month of the Supreme Court's Roe v. Wade decision which had effectively opened the floodgates to the millions of abortions which had occurred since.) This would later be seen as a shrewd "end run" around the usual convention procedure and the Christian Life Commission which opposed the pro-life coalition's crusade to persuade Congress to enact, and the president to sign a Federal constitutional amendment to outlaw abortion. The resolution, pushed through by SBC conservatives at a previous convention, endorsing the requested amendment, had been virtually ignored by the Christian Life Commission which was supposed to educate SBC churches on abortion and other socio-moral issues.

If the messenger desiring the January observance had not referred his motion to the Calendar Committee, his request would probably have gone to the Christian Life Commission or to the Executive Committee and would likely have died there. Conservative sponsored motions had met that fate many times in the past. But he asked specifically that a convention committee study it.

Stanley's appointed Calendar Committee met the following January to weigh the request. Commission head Foy Valentine presented them with an alternative proposal, urging a "Concern for Life" Sunday in April. The Sunday he favored fell on the day when humanists and others favoring Roe v. Wade recognize sanctity of life. Valentine obviously feared that observance of a day in January would draw more Southern Baptist support for the amendment which the pro-life movement wanted.

The committee rejected Valentine's proposal three to two. Since the motion was not assigned to his agency, his only remaining recourse was to oppose it when the committee presented it to the Dallas convention.

Valentine was expecting the matter to come up when the Calendar Committee gave their report at the closing session in Dallas. He had lined up a number of articulate persons to follow him in speaking against the motion. After Stanley introduced the committee chair, who recommended the third Sunday in January as Sanctity of Life Day, Valentine had the Commission's trustee chairman, moderate Charles Wade of Arlington, Texas, present, from the podium, an amendment that a "Concern for Life" day in April be observed. This would, of course, not coincide with the anniversary of Roe v. Wade.

Other Christian Life Commission supporters were waiting at the foot of the stairs leading up to the platform. But they were not permitted up. Conservatives Larry Lewis and Adrian Rogers were already on the platform, having been tipped off earlier that the proposal would be coming up. Both spoke eloquently from the podium for the main motion, designating the day in January. The rules required that proponents and opponents of a motion alternate in addressing the Convention. Moderator Stanley recognized as spokesmen for the "Concern for Life" day only persons at floor microphones, who could only be heard and not seen and were relatively unprepared. Nancy Ammerman perceptively notes,

> The visual impact of this contrast should not be ignored, since everything was being shown on three huge closed-circuit TV screens. Those on the platform looked "staged", while those on the floor looked "unrehearsed." The result [was] a kind of visual legitimation of platform speakers. These and most of the rest of the communication resources were clearly in the hands of fundamentalists during the Dallas convention. [32]

Staged or not, it was not unlike parliamentary maneuvering of past years when the old establishment had effectively "bottled up" undesirable motions from challengers. Valentine's amendment was defeated. The original motion passed by a substantial majority. By program assignment, the Christian Life Commission would have to provide materials for observance of the day. The designation of the January day as "Sanctity of Life" Sunday would not be binding on churches, although many would be more likely than not to observe an "official" day. It would give the impression to the world that the SBC was solidly linked with the pro-life movement, which was what conservatives wanted and moderates, as represented by Valentine and the Christian Life Commission did not. It was a further indication of growing conservative power through the process of electing supportive presidents.

First Vice President Moore had been trailed by reporters all day. Would he apply pressure to have a part in Stanley's crucial committee appointments? Moore noted that appointive power still rested with the president, but he "hoped" Stanley "will consult with me on these appointments." What if the conservative president refused? he was asked. Moore did not answer.[33]

Georgia Editor Jack Harwell, standing nearby in the press room, declared, "If Moore is not consulted, he can call press conferences and issue statements." [34]

Conservatives thought the resistance of agency heads might have cracked a little at Dallas. One seminary professor, long criticized by conservatives, was reported to be going on sabbatical with instructions from his president to look for a position elsewhere. Southeastern's President Lolley, who didn't know if I have any inerrantists on my faculty," said he was "open" to hiring "convictional inerrantists." [35]

The next stop is Atlanta, and another chapter—perhaps the deciding one—in the struggle for control of the denominational structure and agencies. With presidential appointive powers still intact, the focus will again be on the presidential election. Moore is expected to again be the choice of the moderates. Said Harwell, "He's the best horse they've got, maybe the only horse they can go with and win."

And the conservative candidate? "The word I'm hearing," added Harwell, "is that the fundamentalists have been saving Adrian for the most critical time. Atlanta will be it. The confrontation will be bigger than Dallas." [36]

REFERENCES

1   Stephen Johnson: "Angry Fundamentalists May Pull Out, Baptist Leaders Says," *Houston Chronicle*, June 10, 1985, Section 1, p. 4.

2   Baptist Press Convention Reports, 1985.

3   Personal Interview, Dallas, June, 1985.

4   Baptist Press Convention Reports. Pastors' Conference Wrapup (Revised), 1985.

5   Ibid.

6   Baptist Press Convention Reports, 1985.

7   Louis Moore: "Graham Endorses SBC Chief Stanley," *Houston Chronicle*, June 10, 1985, Section 1, p. 1.

8   Russell Kaemmerling: "In Conclusion," *Southern Baptist Advocate*, June, 1985, p. 39.

9   Presnall Wood: "Editorial," *Bapist Standard*, Convention Edition, June 11, 1985, p. 2.

10   *Southern Baptist Advocate*, June 1985, p. 20.

11   *Baptist Standard*, op. cit., p. 1.

12   Press Conference, Dallas, 1985.

13   Baptist Press Convention Reports, 1985.

14   Ibid.

15   Ibid.

16   Ibid.

17   Talks with reporters.

18   Helen Parmley: "Graham Offers Apology for Public Endorsement," *Baptist and Reflector* July 3, 1985, p. 7.

19 Personal Interview, Dallas, June, 1985.

20 Sherman's figures on moderate votes are understated. Correct approximate percentages are 39-43-48-45 for years he has in mind.

21 Response to my questions.

22 Press Conference, Dallas, 1985. (A vice presidential press conference is a new development at conventions. Moore was probably newsworthy because he had opposed Stanley and because he was the expected moderate candidate for 1986.)

23 Personal Interview, Dallas, June, 1985.

24 Baptist Press Convention Reports.

25 Ibid.

26 Personal Interview, Dallas, June, 1985.

27 I was standing among a group of other reporters directly below the platform during the tumult over the Committee on Boards report and heard the proceedings as stated in these paragraphs. Larry Lewis later recalled to me in an interview his failed effort to have Slaton's resolution ruled out of order.

28 *Book of Reports*, 1985 Southern Baptist Convention.

29 Baptist Press Convention Reports, 1985.

30 Informal Press Conference, June, 1985.

31 Personal Interview, Dallas, June, 1985.

32 Nancy T. Ammerman, as cited in previous chapter, p. 16.

33 Baptist Press Convention Reports, 1985.

34 Personal Interview, Dallas, June, 1985.

35 Personal Interview, Dallas, June, 1985.

36 Personal Interview, Dallas, June, 1985.

8 AGENCY POWER AND CREEPING CENTRALISM

Whether Adrian Rogers or someone else, the next conservative presidential nominee will almost certainly be the pastor of a mega-church with thousands of members and a multi-million dollar annual budget. He will have a reputation for possessing strong convictions on the inerrancy of Scripture, the discernment and commitment to appoint a Committee on Committees that will keep the conservative "reformation" going, and the courage to stand against criticism.

The moderate nominee is also likely to be a pastor, with conservative beliefs on the Bible, like Winfred Moore, but with a commitment to appoint a Committee on Committees that will work to restore a "balance" on boards aimed at returning the convention to "unity amidst diversity", as held before 1979.

Only once since 1947 has a retired agency head—James L. Sullivan in 1977—been elected convention president. Only two laymen have been honored with the denomination's highest office in recent times, Brooks Hays in 1958-59 and Owen Cooper in 1973-74. All others have been pastors, but with a difference. Before 1979, those elected did not announce their intention to challenge the power of agencies. They probably could not have been elected otherwise. Since 1979, all have called for changes in trends and policies in the agencies. They probably could not have been elected otherwise.

The difference before and after 1979 reaches into the committee system of nominating trustees. Before 1979, agency heads had heavy input into the appointment of the Committee on Committees. After 1979, the staff executives were little consulted. The same held true for the first Committee on Boards and the trustee nominees which were presented a year later. Agency heads were virtually ignored in deciding who would serve on their boards.

Before the conservative drive to turn the denomination away from perceived liberal drift began producing hard-line trustee nominees, agency heads were often asked who they'd like to have to replace trustees rotating off their boards. And if not asked, it was assumed they would have veto power over any proposed nominees by the Committee on Boards—before the names were presented to the convention for messenger ratification. No one of influence objected to this. No one proposed doing anything about it until Judge Pressler came along and studied the system and told complaining conservatives that they could change agency policies by electing trustees who would, in effect, show the agency heads who was boss. Adrian Rogers, Paige Patterson, Bailey Smith, Jimmy Draper, Charles Stanley, Larry Lewis, Ed Young, Jerry Vines, and other leading conservatives saw the wisdom of this and said, in effect, "Let's get going."

Larry Lewis, among the above, is now a denominational college president who must answer to trustees elected by the Missouri Baptist Convention. "Every staff executive wants trustees who will support his programs." he says. "It has long been the custom in Missouri for a nominating committee to consult with institutional heads about nominees. This system seems to work well in this state, as it probably does in others, and as it did in the national convention for many years. Unfortunately, some of our national agency heads ruined it by failing in their responsibility to the people on the matter of doctrinal integrity. Now I think the system must change with the Committee on Boards nominating board members—whether the agency heads approve of them or not—who will make the agencies become responsible on doctrinal integrity. That's why I've backed every conservative president since Adrian Rogers was elected." [1]

We saw, in chapter two, that SBC conservatives and moderates differ on the nature of Scripture, ecclesiology, ministerial life styles, sociomoral issues, and political alignments. In power affiliations, the broad division is now between elective leadership (conservatives) and agency or staff leadership (supported by moderates). As Nancy Ammerman aptly notes, "There are essentially two groups of leaders in the convention, each 'official' in its own way." [2] Both have extensive power bases.

W. A. Criswell claims that SBC agencies, created to be servants of local churches, have evolved into a hierarchy more powerful than the Episcopal Church. This, he says, is "why our big preachers had to lead out in the fight against liberalism. Their positions are secure. Their churches have influence. The hierarchy in the agencies can't get to them. So the little preachers fall in behind the big preachers, because they don't dare go it alone, or they would be blackballed by the hierarchy. And there have been enough of the little preachers and their church messengers to elect strong conservative presidents in recent years." 3

Paige Patterson says one of the three major concerns which "activated the recent conservative resurgence" was the "gradual development of a powerful ecclesiastical bureaucracy, which, if not in theory, at least in practice, increasingly threatens the autonomy of the local churches." 4

Thus, according to Criswell, Patterson, Lewis and others, conservatives decided that the staff leadership had effectively taken control of the denomination, with one result being an accomodation of doctrinal drift beyond the beliefs of most Southern Baptists. This drift, they felt, had to be reversed and the only way to do it was to reassert elective power over staff power.

Some moderates have been critical of agencies in an earlier day, while becoming mute in recent years, perhaps because they see the conservative challenge as the greater of two evils. Moderates do not necessarily believe that staff leadership should be super imposed over elective leadership.

As for the agency executives, all claim to be servants of the denomination through convention-elected trustees. Their responsibility, they say, is to help the churches do a better job in Christian witness, stewardship, theological education, benevolence, evangelism, and missions. All agency programs are purportedly designed with this purpose in mind.

The six seminaries, the Executive Committee (which operates Baptist Press, among other services), the Seminary External Education Division, the SBC Foundation, the four major boards, the seven commissions, the Baptist Joint Committee on Public Affairs (operated with eight other cooperative Baptist denominations, although the SBC provides 80 percent of the budget), and the auxiliary Woman's Missionary Union employ thousands of people. Over 1,500 work for the Sunday School Board alone.

Agencies are well financed. The basic Cooperative Program allotment for all agencies is set at $120,600,00 for 1985-86. This does not include a separate capital needs budget of $7,450,000, the two big mission offerings projected $96,500,000, and sales revenue for the Sunday School Board which could reach $150,000,000 during the next fiscal year. The Sunday School Board operates on a profit basis and **gives** money to the Cooperative Program. With other amounts added, operating resources of all agencies will easily reach $400,000,000 for the upcoming year—no small sum indeed. And this does not include the budgets of the state conventions and local associations, nor the pension assets of the Annuity Board, now approaching one and a half billion dollars and held in trust for future retirees.

The SBC is the envy of all other U.S. denominations, including the Catholic Church. Says Fr. Robert Dalton, the official "observer" of Southern Baptists for the U.S. Catholic Conference: "Your structure, with its interlinkages among agencies and churches, is a marvel to me. We have nothing like it in the Catholic Church, nothing to compare with your Cooperative Program and Sunday School Board." [5]

To an outsider, such as Fr. Dalton, the interlinkages are impressive.

"Junior" models of many SBC agency programs extend to state conventions and are even found in many associations and large churches. SBC agencies cooperate in providing materials and experts for work on all levels. Promotional slogans such as "Bold Mission Thrust," in which Southern Baptists are called on to witness to every person in the world by the year 2000, are stamped on millions of pieces of literature and incorporated into thousands upon thousands of sermons and Sunday School lessons. No American corporation has such a pervasive informational system.

The agencies, large and small, have grown enormously in recent years, in both funding and personnel. The "small" Christian Life Commission, for example, operated on a budget of only $24,000 in 1959, with $16,900 of this amount allotted to salaries. The Commission's projected budget for 1985-86 is set at $873,850 (more than 36 times larger than in 1959) with $656,000 designated for personnel related expenses.

The agencies can point to phenomenal growth in fund raising through the Cooperative Program during the past two decades. In 1964, national agencies received $20,891,636. In 1984, Cooperative Program allotments to these agencies amounted to $108,822,233, a gain of 420 percent. Endowments of seminaries also increased greatly, while seminary enrollment jumped a healthy 135 percent from 1964 to 1984. During this same period, total annual gifts in local churches jumped 481.3 percent. Church and agency building debt also increased dramatically. Yet Sunday School enrollment, which had gained 127.4 percent from 1944-1964, increased only 2.4 percent during the next 20 years. More money has not meant many more Sunday School members.

The Sunday School has long been proven to be the primary seedbed for evangelism. Lagging Sunday School enrollment helps explain, at least in part, the decline in baptisms. In 1959, 429,063 baptisms were registered among a membership of 9,485,276. A quarter century later, in 1984, 372,028 baptisms were tallied with a membership of 14,349,657. The ratio of baptisms to members was one in 22 in 1959. Twenty-five years later the proportion was one in 38. For 1985, the projection is approximately one to 40. [6]

W. C. Fields, director of Baptist Press, notes that the annual membership growth rate dropped from three to four percent in the 1950s, to two percent in the 1960s, and below two percent in the 1970s. Growth for 1985 is projected at only 0.7 percent. Fields thinks the sharp decrease in recent years is partly due to the conservative-moderate conflict and partly to "the normal inertia of a large organization getting larger and getting older." [7]

A sound research study of comparative growth statistics between "conservative" and "moderate" churches needs to be made. Spot checks, as in Louisville, suggest that the sharpest decrease in Sunday School enrollment, membership, and baptisms may have occurred in churches pastored by moderates. Research studies have been done comparing growth rate by size and location of churches, but none, to my knowledge, have been done to show comparisons between churches led by moderates and those having conservative pastors. The differences might be found to be astounding, confirming conservative claims that the "theology of the left" (to use Draper's term) stifles evangelism.

We know only that growth has slowed dramatically across the denomination as a whole. Baptisms are down while Cooperative Program giving has increased over 400 percent since 1964—a significant jump even when inflation is taken into consideration. Conservatives think this has been largely caused by a liberal trend in seminaries and other agencies, which influences a broad spectrum of the denomination; more emphasis on money and programs than actual evangelism; bureaucratic inefficiency in some agencies; a deadness in churches; and a stifling of initiative in some local churches which are content to be loyal to denominational structures.

The agencies are factored into the controversy in at least five ways.

First, agency executives uniformly support "unity amidst diversity", the cause celebre of moderates. The glue for unity, they say, is the cooperative method of raising funds and doing "missions" through agencies. ("Missions" has become a catch all term among agencies and moderates to include everything the agencies do, from Christian Life Commission seminars which often showcase political liberals, to direct evangelism in foreign countries.) Conservatives, as we have noted before, say the Bible, with its corpus of doctrine as defined in the *Baptist Faith and Message* forms the basis for agency programs and far-flung affiliations.

Second, many agency personnel hold "moderate" theological positions on truth in the Bible, although many others are as much an inerrantist as Paige Patterson. No national agency executives, however, have spoken, to any noticeable extent, against moderate theology. None have suggested that the seminaries are anything but conservative.

Third, some agency heads have personally taken stands against the conservative movement, while those remaining neutral have supported the right of colleagues to speak out.

Fourth, agencies are accused by conservatives of departing from the intentions of the SBC founders, becoming too powerful and centralized, and assuming too much control over local churches.

Fifth, the SBC press system is accused by conservatives of one-sidedness and unfairness in the controversy.

The first three characterizations are patently evident to all who read Baptist media. The fifth is examined in the next chapter. We will consider the fourth, perceived agency power and creeping centralism, in the pages following.

We should understand first how the Southern Baptist Convention system developed. The denomination was born in 1845 of a split from the General Missionary Convention of the Baptist Denomination in the United States of America for Foreign Missions (popularly known as the Triennial Convention because it met in assembly every three years) in a dispute over anti-slavery policies of abolitionist dominated national mission societies.

To demonstrate that some denominational papers were working against their pro-slavery supporters, Robert C. Howell, editor of the Tennessee Baptist paper, published a letter from a missionary in Burma that set southern tempers aflame. Declaring slavery to be "the foulest blot on the American flag," the missionary had "the pleasure" to enclose a ten dollar check for his church treasurer "to assist in the escape of runaway slaves." Editor Howell declared that by helping support the missionary," we indirectly contribute the means by which our own slaves are kidnapped and dragged off. Brethren will you do this? We know you will not." Other Baptist editors in the South echoed his inflammatory editorial. 8

Southerners also feared that slave owning had become a reason for northerners, who were more powerful in the mission societies, denying missionary appointment to some. As a test case, the Georgia Baptist Convention presented an eminently qualified preacher on every count except slave holding as a candidate to the national Home Mission Society. The agency quickly rejected him.

The Alabama convention then asked the Foreign Mission Society if slaveholders could be appointed to serve abroad. The Society answered, "We can never be a party to any arrangement which would imply approbation of slavery." 9

Believing that the die had been cast, the board of managers of the Virginia Baptist Foreign Mission Society called on churches to send representatives to meet in Augusta, Georgia, May 8-12, 1845, to organize a new convention "for the propagation of the Gospel." 10

The preamble to the new Southern Baptist Convention declared that "a painful division has taken place in the missionary operation . . . Fanatical attempts have indeed been made, in some quarters, to exclude us of the South from Christian fellowship." 11

The issue of slavery related to an important difference between northern and southern Baptists on denominational structure. Northerners liked the system in which the mission societies were virtually autonomous agencies. Southerners wanted more central control, the immediate objective being to kill the abolitionist policies and rein in the anti-slavery advocates. When the southerners could not change the policies of the national mission societies on slavery, they organized their own convention. The parallel that exists today finds Biblical conservatives seeking to change agency policies on inerrancy and infallibility of Scripture.

The founders organized the new denomination only "for the purpose of . . . combining and directing the energies of the whole denomination . . . for the propagation of the Gospel" 12 William B. Johnson, the first SBC president, envisioned "separate and distinct Boards for each object of benevolent enterprise, located at different places, and all amenable to the Convention" 13

Walter Shurden, the articulate church historian who has emerged as a leading spokesman for today's SBC moderates, says that the newly organized Convention "turned from the fragmented and decentralized approach of the old society system . . . toward more structured cooperation and a more centralized denominational system."

Distinguished from the old loosely aligned Triennial Convention, the new SBC was, according to Shurden, characterized by "a powerful connectionalism based upon voluntary cooperation" that "found unity in mission and ministry" which "became flesh in institutions".14 Shurden and other moderates correctly note that the method of doing missions was then the unifying point, not theology. There were minor theological differences on which they could agree to disagree. But no differences of consequence existed among them on the inspiration of Scripture. All held substantially to the view of

Scripture which SBC conservatives champion today. It can hardly be denied by moderates that the founders assumed the text of the Bible in the originals to be without error. Moderates are right about the reason for the founding of the SBC. Conservatives are right in saying that the theological climate has changed.

The SBC's first two agencies, the Foreign and Home mission boards, did not immediately become going concerns. The old northern board refused to transfer to the new denomination any funds or mission fields. But the missionaries were left free to choose to work under the new board if they wished, and some did. The first man elected as "secretary" of the Home Mission board (then called the Domestic Board) asked to be excused. The second served only three months and resigned. The third quickly learned the reason why: many of the state conventions and associations preferred to continue with the mission work they had already established. Southern Baptists were sensitive about distant agencies from the start.

Strong feelings continued to exist on the primacy of the local church. The extreme view, Landmarkism, held that only local Baptist congregations, continuous since the first church at Jerusalem and practicing closed communion, could appoint and send missionaries. All other churches, denominations, and so-called church agencies were merely religious societies. Still, the Landmarks remained within the SBC until 1905, when the dissenters departed to organize the General Association of Landmark Baptists, which later became the American Baptist Association.

The present SBC agency system developed from a structure founded on principles intended to protect local church autonomy, insure local church control over agencies, and provide means of efficient cooperation in missionary enterprises. Thus from the beginning, agencies were established only as "means" for local churches to better carry out their mandate from Scripture, and were always intended to be servants of the churches. The board members were elected at the annual convention, to which the churches sent messengers. Each agency was independent of but cooperative with others. Each was answerable through trustees to messengers sent by the churches to the annual convention.

The necessity for trained ministers to serve the churches soon became apparent. In 1859, Southern Seminary was opened in Greenville, South Carolina, with 265 students. Placed under trustees, who were elected by church messengers, the first SBC seminary was later moved to a more central location in Louisville in 1877.

Baptist women, who were then denied participation in convention affairs, began holding prayer meetings for missions while their husbands were taking care of denominational business. Baptist women in Baltimore started a federation of Baptist women's societies, in 1871, called Woman's Mission to Woman. The Foreign Mission Board commended the Baltimore plan and urged that Southern Baptist "sisters" be organized "for the purpose of cultivating missionary spirit and systematic contributions." [15] The Executive Committee of the Woman's Mission Societies was created, outside of the Convention structure, to be an auxiliary to the convention. The name was changed to Woman's Missionary Union in 1890.

The SBC had now almost tripled in membership since its founding. Church literature was a hodgepodge. Some churches were prejudiced against Sunday Schools. Some who did have Sunday Schools used no literature except the Bible. Some ordered materials from the American Baptist Publication Society of Philadelphia, which had branch offices in the south. Some secured printed helps elsewhere.

A convention publishing agency had been proposed and rejected in 1846. Dissenters went ahead and organized their own Southern Baptist Publication Society. It operated until 1863, when the Convention voted to organize a Sunday School Board. Crippled by doctrinal frictions and economic deprivations caused by the Civil War, the Board shut down operations in Memphis and consolidated with the Home Mission board in 1873.

In 1890, Richmond pastor J.B. Frost decided it was time for a Sunday School Board that would stand. "God touched me and I thought it," he later recalled.[16] Opponents, led by J.B. Gambrell, feared this would restrict the freedom of churches in buying Sunday School materials. Both Frost and Gambrell served on the elected publications committee. Gambrell recommended, in the last paragraph of the committee's report, with Frost adding the closing sentence,

> That the fullest freedom of choice be accorded to every one as to what literature he will use or support, and that no brother be disparaged in the slightest degree on account of what he may do in the exercise of his right as Christ's freeman. But we would earnestly urge all brethren to give to this Board a fair consideration, and in no case obstruct it in the great work assigned by this Convention.[17]

The report was accepted and the Board was established the following year. Frost was elected the first employee and given the title "corresponding secretary." Selecting Nashville as the location, he borrowed from his wife's inheritance and set up his desk in a corner of the office of the editor of the Tennessee *Baptist and Reflector*. From that small beginning came the world's largest religious publishing house.

Some institutions evolved from state convention ministries. Southwestern Seminary, for example, first operated under the Baptist General Convention of Texas as the theological department of Baylor University (1901-8), then as Baylor Theological Seminary until 1925 when it became an agency of the Southern Baptist Convention. Some were formed by combining previous agencies. The Christian Life Commission, for instance, grew from the Temperance Commission (1908) and the Social Service Commission (1913). It did not receive its current name until 1953.

Agencies did not develop without problems. There were differences over functions, for one thing, and competition over funding, for another. In 1916, Texas messenger M.H. Wolfe proposed that the SBC Constitution be revised to "create one strong executive board which shall direct all of the work and enterprises fostered and promoted by this Convention." The committee appointed to study the proposal recommended that the boards remain separate and a standing committee be established "to act for the body between its sessions." The Executive Committee was consequently "empowered to act in an advisory way on all questions submitted to it on matters arising between the boards . . . " [18] Again, we see a compromise between those who wanted more centralism and those desiring to preserve the autonomy of Convention entities.

Each agency had been making its own financial appeals, causing churches to grow tired of so many special offerings. Offerings varied widely, depending on the skill of the fund raiser and the emotions he could arouse. The Cooperative Program plan of giving was adopted in 1925, with the Executive Committee, in 1926, authorized to allocate funds to the "various agencies and recommending same to the Southern Baptist Convention for adoption." [19] The plan provided for churches to send Cooperative Program monies to state convention offices which would keep the larger portion for state ministries and forward the remainder to the Executive Committee for distribution to SBC agencies. The Executive Committee later declared the Cooperative Program to be,

> The greatest step forward in Kingdom finance Southern Baptists have ever taken. It arose out of the desires . . . to find a plan whereby all worthy denominational causes might be cared for fully and fairly without conflicting with the necessary progress and work in the churches themselves. It is believed to be sane, scriptural, comprehensive, unifying, equitable, economical and thoroughly workable.[20]

Most Southern Baptists today likely still agree. From 1925 through the 1950s, SBC membership climbed steadily while other mainline denominations declined. The conservative, Bible-based theology and aggressive evangelism of Southern Baptists were certainly major factors, but the growth probably could not have been accomplished without cooperative funding for missions, evangelism, promotion, and other important programs.

Moderates and conservatives alike acknowledge the effectiveness of the convention system of operating agencies under elected boards with the Executive Committee proposing Cooperative Program allotments for agencies, subject to acceptance by messengers at the annual convention. The system of representative democracy and voluntarism presents a middle ground between centralism and individualism, providing controls without coercion and cooperation without wasteful competition.

The system appears to be as perfect as man can devise for a convention of autonomous churches. Yet, recent tumultous history indicates that all is not sanguine in the Southern Baptist kingdom. Conservatives say that the system has evolved into a practical hierarchy where some agencies have violated their most sacred trust by allowing alien beliefs on the Bible to corrupt their ideals. Conservatives further charge that agencies have become too powerful and coercive in enforcing a "group think" through interlinkages and grapevines which compel ministers and other church staffers to cooperate if they desire career advancement.

Researcher Nancy Ammerman, who is presently engaged in a study of the SBC conflict, observes cogently:

> The Southern Baptist Convention has always had a very well-developed career system for its clergy. Those who go to approved schools, make friends with approved people, promote approved programs, and otherwise demonstrate their loyalty to the denomination can expect to be recommended by denominational staff people to good churches, recognized by election to state and national offices and boards, and possibly hired to a denominational staff job. Likewise, those who do not acknowledge their debts to the system are unlikely to be rewarded by it. Nor does the system reward those who "make waves." News about pastors who are "uncooperative" or "troublemakers" travels the grapevine from local associations on up, and those pastors have traditionally been excluded from systems of decision-making and reward.[21]

Ammerman adds,

It is a common complaint among moderates these days that the people being appointed to SBC boards are "unknown" or "known as uncooperative in their local associations." The people who are now getting to lead the convention were previously excluded and are thus "unknown" by the older establishment.[22]

Paige Patterson says "fear of the growing centralization" in the SBC is no "novelty".[23] Creeping centralism, Patterson and other conservatives say, has served to increase agency power and to help build a "we against them" attitude in agencies toward grass root critics. He cites the concern, as far back as 1934, of W.S. Barnes, renowned professor of church history at Southwestern Seminary.

Barnes compared "ecclesiological development" in SBC life with "the development . . . in the first centuries of Christian history . . . that laid the foundation of the medieval Catholic Church . . . "[24] Barnes noted two aspects of growing centralization: First, the crossing of "two distinct species—association and convention bases of representation" toward the "process of evolving, an entirely new species—the ecclesiastical."[25] The second was state convention ownership of Baptist papers.

Associations and conventions are, on paper, separate entities. The SBC national convention is larger than any of the state conventions and associations within the states, but neither of the smaller entities is encompassed within either of the larger. Each is autonomous.

Each is responsible to church elected messengers. Barnes was concerned that the associations were becoming dependent upon the state conventions, which in turn were looking more and more to national convention agencies for guidance and help with programs.

Barnes, in effect, saw a developing hierarchy with national agencies functioning as "headquarters" with "state offices" and "district centers" (associations) on lower levels. A classic corporation model.

As for Baptist newspapers which were once privately owned, Barnes saw,

> objection to private ownership, but the objections to denominational ownership are greater. When an individual owned and controlled the paper the responsibility for the policies was his. Under present public ownership the responsibility is denominational. So long as the denomination retains an editor the denomination is responsible. If the policies are objectionable the editor may be dismissed. But it is not so easy to dismiss the editor of a Baptist paper as it is a French prime minister or a Cuban president. The most objectionable feature

of denominational ownership is that it is but another link
in the chain of centralization. (emphasis mine) [26]

With state ownership, concedes moderate Walter Shurden, "state
Baptist papers became mouthpieces for promoting and reinforcing a
distinct spirit of Southern Baptistness . . . [They] became the informational glue of denominationalism." [27]

Privately owned and edited papers have now come to be regarded
as nuisances and obstructions to kingdom advance by Barnes'
"ecclesiastical species" when the editors criticize agency policies and
practices. So, Roy Honeycutt, in response to Paige Patterson's call for
a public debate on SBC theological problems, demanded that Patterson
and Pressler "and their co-conspirators . . . quit printing their
scandal sheet newspapers and allow Southern Baptists to speak for
themselves without external manipulation." [28] Interestingly, the
independent papers on the moderate side, who support the agencies,
have not been so denounced by Honeycutt and other agency heads
who have rebuked conservatives.

The denominational media's role in the conservative-moderate
conflict will be given detailed scrutiny in the next chapter. Here we
will examine other indications of evolving agency power and
centralization.

In general, the classic characteristics of a bureaucratic structure as
enunciated by Max Weber appear in Southern Baptist agencies: (1)
"Regular activities required for the purposes of the organization are
distributed in a fixed way as official duties." This "clear-cut division
of labor makes it possible to employ only specialized experts in each
particular position." (2) The principle of hierarchy is followed in the
organization of offices. "Each lower office is under the control and
supervision of a higher one." (3) Operations run by a "consistent
system" of rules being applied to "particular cases." (4) "The ideal
official conducts his office . . . [in] a spirit of formalistic imper-
sonality . . . " (5) Employment is based on technical qualifications;
is favored by a system of promotions by seniority or achievement, or
both; and is protected from arbitrary dismissal. (6) The organization
is theoretically capable, from the technical point of view, of "attaining
the highest degree of efficiency." [29]

Other advanced Christian denominations have developed
bureaucracies along the same lines. Many state Baptist convention
offices, as well as large Southern Baptist churches, have moved in
this direction by employing a staff of specialists. We are mainly
concerned here, however, with the evolvement of power in SBC
agency bureaucracies.

Changes in management titles point to increased power of agency executives. "Elder," "Associational Missionary," and "Corresponding Secretary" were commonly applied to denominational "servants" in the 19th century. In time "Secretary" became "Executive Secretary," then "Executive Secretary—Treasurer" in recognition of financial responsibilities. In recent years, "Director," "Executive Director," and "President" (although seminary heads were always "presidents") have become the norm. These titles indicate that the denominational servant is the man on top, the administrator who presides over a corporate structure.

Agency executives argue that corporate nomenclature is needed to bring respect in business relations with the secular world. Agency leaders are entrusted with multi-million dollar programs and can hardly be expected to wear the same titles as low-ranking employees in secular business. Yet the elevation of titles does point to the reality that today's agency leaders have far more temporal power than their predecessors had.

They also make far more money.

National agency heads earn from $60,000 to $90,000 annually, plus good fringe benefits, which usually include a generous travel allowance. Second-level managers receive in the $40,000 to $75,000 range, with salary ceilings depending on responsibilities and the agency employer. Top state convention executives earn from $50,000 to $75,000. The Executive Director of Executive Programs for the Missouri Baptist Convention, for example, received $59,269, in 1984. Missouri's state editor was paid $39,936.[30] Lower ranking professionals earn less, but generally more than average renumeration of pastors and teachers in colleges and seminaries. A woman friend of mine, earning around $20,000 in a Baptist college staff position, recalls being considered for a lower-level staff position in an SBC agency. When someone else got the job, the friend who had recommended her said, "I wouldn't lose any sleep about it. It only paid about $35,000."

These salaries are higher than the average remuneration paid to persons in similar executive positions with leading parachurch organizations, including the Billy Graham Association. A 1984 study, by the Christian Ministries Management Associates showed the average pay of parachurch top executives to be $41,627. [31]

How well SBC executive salaries compare with pay for similar jobs in other denominations is not known. Religious establishments have the penchant, and usually the means, to keep the amount of executive salaries from those who pay the bills. The Reverend Doctor Ralph Bohlman, president of the Lutheran Church— Missouri Snyod, for example, answered a critic who claimed denominational officials had been evasive about executive salaries, "I know of no organization or institution that publishes salaries of even its top management." The critic, Ewald J. Otto, editor of the independent Lutheran publication *Affirm*, replied,

> Even the world believes in full disclosure. The salaries of officials of corporations and civil officials are in the public press. Should not the church be more candid and open that the world? [32]

The highest known annual SBC agency salary ever, $115,000, went to Grady Cothen during his last year as president of the Sunday School Board. Cothen's successor, Lloyd Elder, started at $90,000.

Some state conventions authorize the printing of salaries and/or scales of state executives in their state Baptist paper. The information is thus available to every church. SBC agencies do not release executive salaries to denominational media.

In 1977, a hubbub arose at the Southern Baptist Convention over a motion calling for the publication of salaries of agency heads. The motion was narrowly voted down, with the understanding that any member of a cooperating Southern Baptist Church could learn the pay of any denominational employee by making a written request.

Only one agency head is known to have asked that his pay be cut. Keith Parks, when appointed president of the Foreign Mission Board, was reportedly astounded at the salary offered and requested that trustees reduce the amount substantially. Parks, a former SBC missionary, said he could not in good conscience take such a high salary when Southern Baptists were being asked to sacrifice for missions.

Agency executives, like other professionals, prefer not to discuss their salaries. When pressed, they tend to make two defenses. One, good salaries, equal to those in the corporate world, are necessary to get good people. Two, a few pastors receive salaries higher than any agency executive. Some pastors, mostly in Texas, are reported to be paid in the $100,000 range. The average SBC pastor, of course, earns only a fraction of that amount.

Agency salaries reflect higher budgets and the proliferation of departments and divisions, giving agency heads more status, and requiring more managers with increased bureaucracy and personnel expense. Trustee permission is usually required for national agencies seeking to add divisions and specialized programs. Agency executives must cite needs to justify expansion. Usually this means the promotion of new services to churches.

Many state conventions now have at least one person, directing ministerial relations and/or referrals, to which church professionals are urged to send resumes. Upon request from a proper church personnel committee, this person can quicky provide computerized information on a prospective new church staff member. This can keep a church from getting a "loser," a pastor, for example, who has a record of running up debts, one with sexual problems, one who has flirted with the independent movement, or one who has a record of being "uncooperative" in previous associations and/or states where he served. The advantages to churches are obvious. The motivation for pastors to keep on good terms with agency executives is also obvious.

The denominational man (few women are in denominational leadership, outside of the WMU), of course, feels a responsibility to keep the churches, many of which have been established with denominational funds, bound to their heritage. Conservatives support this in principle, but say that, in recent years, ecclesiastical loyalties have become more important than doctrinal concerns.

The agency executive, like his counterpart in the corporate world, has the people and resources to make himself and his programs look good. Each national agency has a skilled public relations staff with at least one person writing news, on agency time, for Baptist Press. The state convention executive can usually count on the state editors to also provide promotional help, although some editors can be balky at covering up in-house problems. Besides directing a steady flow of "news" stories recounting inspirational activities in the kingdom, the executive can also direct a steady flow of special promotion to the churches.

There is a cyclical dynamic at work here. Agencies use Cooperative Program funding to promote and expand programs, which increase agency budgets for the next fiscal year, which makes more money available for promotion to increase funds for the year following, which brings in more money from the churches. Thus, the agencies have grown as they receive more resources to enlarge and start new programs.

Giving to the Cooperative Program has become the supreme badge of denominational loyalty and commitment to the great Commission of Jesus in Matthew 28:18-20. Since Cooperative Program funds flow to all agencies, as designated by state and national executive committees, the "true" Southern Baptist church must help support all agencies and programs.

Before the conservative movement began, the churches generally heard only positive, glowing reports about the good the agencies were doing. Occasional citations of "liberalism" in schools by publications such as *The Sword of the Lord* could be passed off as coming from independents out to lure churches away from the SBC fold.

Then Bill Powell's *Southern Baptist Journal* came along, followed by Judge Pressler, Paige Patterson, and others alleging problems in agencies. They were called "outsiders" and "independents" and their motives were questioned. But the labeling didn't "stick" after convention votes showed that thousands of Southern Baptists agreed with them. The conservatives, of course, do not make a blanket condemnation of all agencies. They do object to having to support through the Cooperative Program some elements which in Patterson's words, "violate our consciences." [33]

Of course, churches cannot be forced to give all their "mission" dollars to the Cooperative Program and the special official mission offerings. But gifts to "independent" ministries, Baptist or otherwise, are simply not recognized on the loyalty score card. And denominational literature generally publicizes only "approved" ministries. This appears to be standard practice in all major denominations. By reading the missionary magazine of only one denomination, one can easily get the impression that only that church body is pursuing an aggressive mission program in a given area. This builds loyalty for "our" programs and keeps contributors happy. Again, the corporate parallel is evident. Coca-Cola could hardly be expected to do public relations for Pepsi.

State conventions provide lists to Baptist media which print church Cooperative Program giving by budget percentage and dollar amount. These company type financial reports on giving to denominational causes appear every quarter in some Baptist papers.

Churches and pastors are, in effect, graded by the percentage of their budget apportioned for the Cooperative Program. A pastor with a good record of leading churches to give high percentages stands in high favor with executives in state and national agencies. Before 1979, a good Cooperative Program resume was sufficient for nomination to prestigious agency boards on the reasoning that those who put their stewardship where their mouth is should have a say in what happens to their money. Since 1979, in the national convention and in some states, this has not been enough. In many instances, pastors or laity from churches with low Cooperative Program percentages have been selected over those with better records because the nominating committees felt they would have the backbone to make course changes in agencies.

Significant giving to parachurch groups can be used to besmirch an uncooperative preacher, especially one who is a nominee for an important committee or a state or national convention office. Thus, Charles Stanley was branded by moderates and some agency personnel as unworthy for the SBC presidency because his church directed funds to their own nationwide cable TV ministry and supported missionaries, even though they were members of FBC, Atlanta, who felt a call to work with non-SBC missions. Stanley's sin was in failing to put all his missionary "marbles" into the denomination. Thus, conservatives say, moderates speak from both sides of their mouth in calling for soul freedom in theology, while supporting a reward system for uniformity in stewardship, with ostracism for nonconformance.

The same principles are applied to use of Sunday School literature and other materials from Southern Baptist agencies. The pastor who consistently permits or encourages his church to use non-SBC literature, even in a few areas, is soon regarded with suspicion of disloyalty. Moderates have used this deviation to defeat the nomination of certain conservatives for membership on the Sunday School Board. To many Southern Baptists, this seems reasonable. To others, who are perhaps remembering the fears of J.B. Gambrell, it does not. Tying the use of SBC materials to denominational loyalty has certainly helped to make the Sunday School Board the world's largest religious publisher by giving the Board a virtual captive market.

In many respects, the system has worked well. Promotional experts never tire of telling Southern Baptists so. Southern Baptists support the largest number of foreign missionaries of any denomination, they say (3,432 in 1984). It is seldom noted that the non-sectarian Wycliffe Bible Translators,[34] under which many Southern Baptists serve with almost no recognition from the denomination, number over 6,000 members. Or that it takes almost 5,000 Southern Baptists to support one foreign missionary, a ratio fifty times greater than the much smaller Christian & Missionary Alliance which has approximately one foreign missionary for every 100 members. For some Southern Baptists, however, the agency promotion went too far in the program calling for Southern Baptists to witness to every person on earth by the year 2,000. The hype has been toned down. Southern Baptists are now being asked to join other Christians in reaching this goal by the end of the century.

The penalty for disloyalty can be keenly felt by pastors. A reputation for having a "critical spirit" and a low commitment to denominational causes results in a pastor not being appointed to boards and not receiving invitations to speak at denominational conferences. The SBC is not alone here. The "managers" of other denominations follow the same procedure on the rationale that those who pay the freight should receive the honors. Right or wrong, it is a way of keeping the "right" people in office and the "right" programs rolling.

Ministry or machine, no Christian denomination or organization on earth can rank above Southern Baptist Convention agencies in promotional skills. With every passing year, more "experts" (usually persons who have proven their skills in local church situations and in denominational loyalty) are hired, with the corresponding expansion of agency power and influence. Yet, with all this, there has been no correlation in increased church growth. It may be argued, of course, that, without increased agency programs and personnel, church growth might be even more marginal, with yearly statistics even cropping into the loss column. Moderates and most agency executives say the controversy is a major reason, leaving the implication that if Pressler, Patterson, Rogers, Stanley, and their cohorts would shut up and dismantle their "political" machine, then the denomination would start growing again. But the slowdown in growth began long before the conflict became big. Conservatives concede the controversy may be a factor, but shift the larger blame to theological malaise in institutions which they say is counterproductive to effective evangelism.

Agencies, at both national and state levels, have taken on a corporate appearance in structure, with layers of management in large agencies. Funding for "headquarters" programs in some states has greatly outpaced allocations for institutional programs (colleges, children's homes, etc.). In Missouri, for example, the percentage of state Cooperative Program monies for "Executive Board Programs," administered out of the state office, has increased during the past 15 years from approximately 20 to 30 percent while the proportion going to the four Missouri Baptist colleges, the children's home, and the home for the aged has decreased from 23 to 22 percent. At the 1985 Missouri state convention, a proposed restructuring of Executive Board programs along corporate lines was approved by church messengers, however, messengers rejected a "coordinator" for the colleges, who would report to the Executive Director of Executive Board Programs. Objectors saw this as another layer of bureaucracy, increasing the power of the state office. One said, "The state office has been trying to get us to accept this for ten years." Similar struggles probably ensue in other state conventions.

That agency executives are godly and good men should not keep us from looking candidly at their resources for increasing tenure, power, and privilege in their positions. Consider their influence on trustees, especially as it existed before the first change-minded conservative trustees began showing up a few years ago.

Here is Pastor Perry, a new trustee for a major agency, elected
through denominational public relations and the polished skills of
Dr. Harrison, the agency head, in office long enough to be regarded
as a denominational statesman. New trustee Perry comes to the
agency for his first trustee meeting. He and other trustees are put up
at nice hotel and dined (but not wined) at agency expense, given a
tour of the agency, then whisked to their meeting in the handsomely
furnished board room. Dr. Harrison, whom Pastor Perry now
addresses by first name, presents an impressive, documented list of
accomplishments for the past year, then, after discussion, follows
with proposals for new programs and the hiring of key personnel
which require trustee concurrence. With the agency executive,
staffers, including a public relations employee who will "report"
news of the board meeting to Baptist Press for denominational
media, and trustee peers of importance seated at right and left,
Pastor Perry will likely be cooperative. Being human, Pastor Perry
realizes that he needs the good will of his fellow trustees, the executive, and key staffers for career advancement. Almost certainly, he
will not appear rancorous or attempt to create "problems" for
the agency.

Until the rebellious conservative movement began, resulting in
successive waves of trustees who were not so deferential,
denominational executives generally enjoyed smooth relations with
their boards. Occasional problems were discreetly handled in executive
session. Should the agency head or some other executive high in the
organization be found guilty of serious mismanagement or a
misdeed, he would be allowed to quietly tender his resignation and
depart for stated worthy reasons. Or, should he be an extremely
valuable employee, he might be given the choice of changing his
"ways" or departing.

The president of the Sunday School Board, for example, in sworn
testimony relating to the suit (discussed in some detail in the next
chapter) brought against the Board by former employee Donald
Burnett, stated that he gave a sinning executive the opportunity to
keep his job, provided he break off an improper "relationship" with
a woman not his wife. Compassionate, perhaps, but it could also be
argued that the trespassing executive should have been discharged
forthwith for violating a sacred trust. In this case, the trustees—if
they even knew—apparently did not overrule the president's decision.
The executive refused to make the concession and was allowed to
quietly resign.

Some editors in the SBC press system, as will be shown in the next
chapter, refuse to roll over and play dead to please agency public

relations. The truth of a major scandal inevitably comes out. The most sensational incident occurred in 1928, when the respected Clinton Carnes, treasurer of the Home Mission Board, disappeared. Investigators looked in his safe and found he had been keeping a double set of books. The audit showed he had embezzled $909,461 from secret loans made to the Home Mission Board under his name. Further digging revealed that he had used much of the money to finance the career of movie starlets. Carnes' wife fainted when she was told what her husband had done. The Carnes' scandal was reported in great detail. The theft resulted in a financial crisis, with some Home Mission Board funded mission schools having to be closed and personnel discharged. The incident also led to a tightening of financial practices in all institutions.

Because of the checks and balances of the SBC system, an SBC denominational leader could hardly "pull off" such a theft today. This, of course, is not to infer that any executive would even if it were possible.

SBC agency heads have less power than their counterparts in connectional and episcopal structures of some other denominations. The bureaucracy of the United Methodist Church (which once surpassed the SBC in size), for example, can more quickly apply direct pressure on clergy than SBC influentials. United Methodist ministers are appointed. Church properties are owned by the denomination, not the local congregations, as is the case among Southern Baptists.

The United Methodist stucture allows its bureaucracies more freedom to expend church funds on activities which many constituents may not approve. This helps to explain why, in a recent year, the UM Board of Global Ministries could send only $10,047,497 to overseas missionaries from an allotment of $59,326,497.[35] The unofficial Good News, United Methodist organization, claims that the denominational Board of Global Ministries uses a substantial portion of appropriations from churches to support leftist and other revolutionary causes abroad. Influential members of the conservative and independent Good News coalition have established an independent mission board to send missionaries whom the denominational board will not appoint. The UM hierarchy has retaliated by persuading UM bishops abroad not to "recognize" the unofficial missionaries.

Hierarchs of the Seventh-Day Adventist Church (SDA) possess even more power than United Methodist bishops. SDA agencies lost over $30 million and individual members around $40 million during a recent collapse of an investment empire, headed by a prominent SDA layman. The investor was alleged to have given substantial financial inducements to top SDA executives for their willingness to assign church trust funds to his company. Some pastors reportedly lost their jobs for demanding that the officials in question be punished. None of the denominational executives who admitted receiving favors from the investor have served a day in jail. Most are still in sacred office.

The representative democracy of the SBC system would seem to insure that executives cannot long hide deviations from the constituency. However, the structure, as presently bureaucratized, does help to protect paid leadership from constituent pressures on the Bible truth issue. Roy Honeycutt, Russell Dilday, and Randall Lolley, all targets of conservative censure, remain at this writing solidly in office. Dilday told *Time*, "The only way I'll leave is if they drag me out the front door" [36]

One final factor in agency power should be noted: agency employees command from five to eight percent (more if state convention and associational employees are included) of the vote at annual conventions by coming as elected messengers from their local churches. Moreover, their expenses are paid from Cooperative Program monies. This does not include seminary students, whose tuition is paid by Cooperative Program funds and who have been urged by administrators and professors at some seminaries to get accredited as messengers from their churches and go to the convention and vote. Proponents say it would be unconstitutional to deny voting rights to any messenger sent by any church, whether an agency employee or a seminary student receiving benefits from the Cooperative Program. Opponents—principally in the conservative movement—tend to agree, but say the Constitution should be amended to prevent employees from voting on appropriations and other matters in which they have a vested interest. If the hand voting of agency heads at their designated tables before the podium at recent conventions is any indication, agency employees almost always vote against conservative candidates, which, in recent years, has often meant voting against the majority of church elected messengers.

The second major concern with SBC agencies is a growing geographic centralization in Nashville. W.B. Johnson, the chief architect of the SBC Constitution, called for agencies to be "located at different places . . . " [37] So, the Foreign Mission Board was established in Richmond, the Home Mission board in Alabama, the first seminary in Greenville, South Carolina, and the Sunday School Board in Nashville.

The trend toward centralization in Nashville began when the Executive Committee voted in 1927 to establish offices in that city. The Executive Committee and five small agencies eventually came to occupy a building on James Robertson Parkway on the northeastern side of the business district, about two miles from the complex of buildings that accomodated the Sunday School Board. In 1983, the Executive Committee asked the Pittsburgh convention to appropriate six million dollars for a new and larger structure adjacent to Sunday School Board properties which also housed a sixth agency, the Historical Commission.

The funding was opposed by some messengers on the basis that the expenditure was inappropriate in a time when Southern Baptists were being called upon to sacrifice for Bold Mission Thrust. It is safe to say that most of those who favored or disfavored the expenditure did not know that they had been the targets of a skillful public relations plan prepared by the Executive Committee's public relations director, W.C. Fields and presented to the state papers to sell the constituency on the advantages of the new building. Fields' stratagem called for placement of "helpful" stories in state papers at appropriate times. He suggested that the Executive Committee building and the adjacent Sunday School Board buildings might come to be known as The Baptist Center." [38]

The plan succeeded. The funding was voted. The agencies relocated next to the Sunday School Board.

Fields performed admirably by corporate standards. He marshaled the resources of Baptist Press and the state papers to convince the constitutency that the new building was needed. The opposition, which was never strong, had no such resources available.

Because these many agencies are in Nashville, hundreds of leaders from other agencies and from the 37 state conventions (including the state Executive Directors) come to the Music City regularly for meetings. The socialization in these meetings and the daily interactions of the hundeds of employees in resident agencies provide a climate in which an attitudinal consensus can develop against dissidents. Information on the activities of such "troublemakers" as Paul Pressler and Paige Paterson speeds along the grapevine. Ideas develop on how to counter the strategies of the miscreants. Those who cannot conscientiously support the establishment line tend to remain quiet. Objectors do not help their careers. Anyone who doubts this has never worked in a bureaucracy, be it government, commercial, or religious. Insiders and their allies naturally seek to protect their own interests and reputations from outside challengers.

Naturally, agency personnel have become increasingly cautious and defensive as conservatives have increased their elective power base year after year. They naturally feel "under attack" from those questioning their ethics, integrity, and beliefs. Subconsciously or consciously, they identify themselves as the defenders of the denominational heritage. Their opponents are those who would change present policies, expecially on "unity amidst diversity". Their friends are those who support the status quo and seek to turn the fundamentalist barbarians back. Long forgotten are past criticisms by moderate allies of bureaucratic practices and attitudes, criticisms which stand astonishingly similar to some being made by conservatives today.

Some of the sharpest blasts were made at a 1975 Christian Life Commission Seminar in Louisville. C.R. Daley, then editor of Kentucky's *Western Recorder*, declared:

> There is something about becoming a part of the establishment that blunts personal ideals, that tempts us to compromise personal integrity for what is regarded as the welfare of the organization, and that silences our prophetic utterances. We, who were once perceptive observers, become parrots of the party line and once we become defenders of the establishment, it is extremely difficult to be a critic, even a constructive critic.

Daley said it was not known for Baptist leaders "who once cherished editorial freedom" to support a free press when they moved into denominational positions where they are "the observed instead of being the observer.

"One of the saddest spectacles of Baptist life in our times," Daley continued, "is to see denominational offices swallow a man and let him sell his soul for a mess of statistical success and approval by his peers." Such a leader, Daley said, becomes "very self protective and defensive," when "denominational programs and policies are questioned."

Cecil Sherman was "just small enough to say out loud that I question the salaries of some denominational employees. If you quote the words of Jesus, you ought not use the salary schedule of the Sadducees." [39]

Closer to the present conflict, retired SBC Executive-Secretary Treasurer Porter Routh, admits there is "probably some validity" in the "feeling" that as SBC institutions have grown larger "they have become less responsive to the people in general." [40]

Alvin Shackleford, the Tennessee state editor, is more expansive than Routh:

> In the current SBC controversy, there is a feeling by some that the agencies and institutions have abused this freedom [allowed by trustees] and are not as responsive as they should be to the constituency. [41]

Agencies—some more than others—are beginning to feel the "heat" from new conservative trustees asserting muscle not known on previous boards. For one thing, new trustees are reportedly demanding that agency heads exercise more discipline on problem employees. In one situation, the president of an agency reportedly refused to correct a vice president who had allegedly used his "company" credit card for unauthorized expenditures. The trustees asked the president to take action. When the infraction continued, the chairman of the board demanded that the vice president be fired. "And if you won't fire him," he reportedly told the president, "then we'll fire you and get an administrator who will act." [42]

For another, they are refusing to rubber stamp every personnel decision of agency administrators, particularly in hiring new seminary professors. Traditionally, seminary presidents have mailed trustees a short biography of a proposed new teacher and asked them to check yes or no on his employment. Few trustees have ventured to exercise veto power, or even dared to question a prospective professor, believing that the administrator was best qualified to judge the qualifications of the applicant.

Things are changing. In a recent case, a new conservative trustee called and asked a professor being considered for employment to provide "more details on yourself so I can make a more informed decision?" The prospective teacher had apparently been expecting the grilling. "I'll answer your questions," he told the new trustee, "but before you begin, I want you to know that I already have enough votes to get the position." [43]

Should the conservative advance continue, agency heads can expect more trustee "intrusion" in hiring practices, especially in seminaries. Jimmy Draper, for example, claims that parity between inerrantists and those who believe the Biblical text has errors does not exist on some seminary faculties. Draper asks,

> Why is academic freedom only for non-conservatives? Why is it that genuine evangelicals who believe in the total inerrancy of Scripture are not given even token consideration for faculty openings in many of our Southern Baptist seminaries and colleges? It surely isn't because of their lack of academic credentials, because many of them have advanced degrees at least as prestigious as those who are appointed. The fact is that their theological conservatism simply is not welcome on many of our campuses. Where then is academic freedom in these cases? If the concept is valid, it must be applied to all of us and not just to those of us of a more liberal orientation. [44]

Should conservatives keep winning the presidency and should agency heads refuse to comply to such requests from challengers like Draper, who is one of the more "moderate" conservative leaders, the sharpest conflict may be yet to come.

Changes in theological policies aside, conservatives suggest that agency trustees, with cooperation by agency executives, might take some operational steps now to help restore trust and increase church cooperation in their agencies by,

—Ceasing to use agency newsletters and periodicals to harshly criticize any substantial faction of the denomination (in this case, conservatives) demanding the right to have their Cooperative Program monies withheld for programs and teachings which violate their consciences.

—Recognizing that churches can remain "loyal" to the denomination when they decide not to support agencies and programs which they disapprove.

—Working for parity between moderates and conservatives in denominational employment, particularly in seminaries, where imbalances may exist, as Jimmy Draper has urged.

—Urging full-time agency employees, whose expenses are paid from Cooperative Program funds, not to seek church messenger status for the annual convention.

—Cutting back on expensive promotion of some agency programs.

—Lowering of travel allowances of some employees and eliminating nonessential meetings in expensive hotels.

—Reducing excessive salaries of agency executives and setting lower "scales" for positions which pay more than twice what the average SBC pastor receives.

—Being more responsive, and less defensive, to questions about agency policies and operations from pastors and laity.

—Dividing the giant Baptist Sunday School Board—which recently voted to add a music publishing division— into two or more agencies, each with its own board of trustees.

—Moving some agencies from Nashville to other cities.

Some of these proposed actions carry greater priority than others in the conservative camp. Many conservatives have no quarrel with the use of agency influence in theory, but object only to the way the "monopoly" power has been used against them. Some would undoubtedly like to have this power for themselves. Should they succeed, the Convention agencies and their bureaucracies will still stand in violation of the intentions of the founders. Only a new "hierarchy" will be in place to administer its own pressures for corporate uniformity.

Moderates, and many Southern Baptists who have not openly taken positions in the controversy, say such requests amount to coercion, even blackmail. Such, they say, has no place among Christians. Harsh judgments should be put aside with prayer and loving reasoning prevailing over harsh judgments. Let trust be restored.

Sadly, the controversy has gone beyond the point where such requests can be heard and patience given to replies. The murmur in the denomination has swollen to a roar. The challengers of perceived liberal theological drift and bureaucratic trends in denominational agencies and institutions have won seven presidential battles in a row. Moderates have been unable to strip the presidency of appointive power leading to nomination of trustees. Should conservatives keep winning and attain an absolute majority on boards, drastic changes may be expected. Agency power may remain. Centralism may actually increase. But there will be different people in charge, bringing gladness to some and sadness to others. The more "moderate" conservatives believe such great upheavals could be averted by agency responsiveness and recognition by "second-mile" actions that agencies are servants of and not rulers over the churches.

Encouragement comes from one of the newer agency heads, Lloyd Elder, formerly Executive Vice President of Southwestern Seminary and now President of the Sunday School Board. Speaking to a conference of pastors at Baylor University, Elder said,

> We need to focus our attention back on the local church. If we do that effectively, the denomination will be dynamic and flourish. Our institutions and agencies may whimper, but it we do what we're supposed to do, they'll be service organizations for local churches.[45]

REFERENCES

1   Personal Interview, Hannibal, Mo., January, 1986.

2   Nancy T. Ammerman: "Organizational Conflict in a Divided Denomination: Southern Baptists and Abortion, Candler School of Theology, Emory University, Presented to the Meetings of the Society for the Scientific Study of Religion, Savannah, Georgia, and the Conference on Religion and the Political Order, Hilton Head Island, South Carolina, October, 1984, p. 24.

3   Personal Interview, Hannibal, Mo., May, 1985.

4   Paige Patterson: "Stalemate," "The Controversy in the Southern Baptist Convention," A Special Issue of *The Theological Educator*, Published by the Faculty of New Orleans Baptist Theological Seminary, 1985, p. 8.

5   Personal Interview, Pittsburgh, June, 1983.

6   Sources of these figures are from the *Convention Annual* for the years cited and Abert McClellan: "The Southern Baptist Convention, 1965—1985," *Baptist History and Heritage*, 1985, pp. 7-24. McClellan, a long-time staff member of the Executive Committee, provides an excellent statistical study of important demographics in the SBC during the past 20 years.

7   *The Chattanooga Times*, Associated Press, December 23, 1985, p. C-8.

8   James and Marti Hefley: *The Church That Produced a President*, Wyden Books, New York, 1977, p. 99.

9   Ibid., p. 100.

10   Ibid., p. 10.

11   J.W. Storer: "Southern Baptist Convention," *Encyclopedia of Southern Baptists*, Vol. 2, Broadman Press, Nashville, 1958, pp. 1244-1262 (cf. p. 1246).

12   Ibid. (cf. p. 1245)

13   W.W. Barnes: *The Southern Baptist Convention 1845-1953*, Broadman Press, 1954, p. 27.

14   Walter B. Shurden: "The Erosion of Denominationalism: The Current State of the Southern Baptist Convention," Address Presented to the Annual Meeting of the Southern Carolina Baptist Historical Society, Myrtle Beach, S.C., November 12, 1984.

15   Juliette Mather: "Woman's Missionary Union," in *Encyclopedia of Southern Baptists*, as cited above, pp. 1506-1527 (cf. p. 1508).

16   Clifton J. Allen, "The Sunday School Board," in *Encyclopedia of Southern Baptists*, as cited above, pp. 1317-39 (cf. p. 1318).

17   Barnes, op. cit., pp. 92, 93.

18   Porter Routh: "Executive Committee of the Southern Baptist Convention, in *Encyclopedia of Southern Baptists*, Vol. 1, as cited above, pp. 428-433 (cf. p. 429).

19   Ibid., p. 429.

20   Barnes, op. cit., p. 230.

21   Ammerman, op. cit., p. 21.

22   Ibid., p. 22.

23   Patterson, op. cit., p. 7.

24   W. W. Barnes: *A Study in the Development of Ecclesiology*, Published by the Author, Seminary Hall, Texas, 1934, p. 1.

25   Ibid., p. 34.

26   Ibid., p. 60.

27   Shurden, op. cit.

28   Baptist Press, October, 1984.

29   Max Weber: *The Theory of Social and Economic Organization*, Oxford University Press, New York, 1947, pp. 330-340 (Cited by Peter M. Balu: **Bureaucracy in Modern Society**, Random House, New York, 1956, pp. 28-31.)

30   "Missouri Baptist Convention Report," 1984. The Missouri Baptist Convention is one of several state conventions that publishes salaries.

31   Lloyd Billingsley: "To Him That Worketh," *Eternity*, January, 1985, p. 13.

32   "Synod's Leader Assailed," *St. Louis Post Dispatch*, January 11, 1986, p. 4D.

33   Paige Patterson mentioned this to me in several interviews. He has also been quoted frequently on this complaint.

34   The American Bible Society holds the status of "Associated Organization" with the SBC. An unsuccessful effort was made several years ago to obtain this status for Wycliffe Bible Translators, since WBT carries on a distinct Bible translation ministry world-wide. Proponents for such "accreditation" of Wycliffe noted that the Bible Society listed in its annual report translations by Wycliffe, without giving proper credit to the translation group. An informal survey indicated that most Southern Baptists believed the ABS to be the major Bible publishing, distributing, and translat ing agency, while Wycliffe was regarded as a "faith mission." The reason for the SBC "establishment's" keeping Wycliffe at arm's length and continuing to allow the Bible Society a monopoly in SBC promotion may be the larger ecumenicity of the ABS. Wycliffe's statement of faith is conservative. It is probably not coincidental that a number of large conservative Southern Baptist churches give support to Wycliffe.

35   Edmund W. Robb, Jr., "American Methodism at 200: A Case for Hope," *Christianity Today*, November 9, 1984, pp. 21-23.

36   "Battling Over the Bible," *Time*, June 24, 1985.

37   Barnes, op. cit., p. 27.

38   "Public Relations Plans: Southern Baptist Convention Building Project." Distributed to official SBC media.

39   Dan Martin: "SBC Integrity Examined in Christian Life Seminar," *Baptist and Reflector*, March 26, 1975, p. 8.

40   Porter Routh: "An Interview With Dr. Porter Routh," "The Controversy in the Southern Baptist Convention," op. cit., pp. 25-27.

41   Alvin Shackelford: "The Issues in the SBC Controversy," *Baptist and Reflector*, May 8, 1985, p. 4.

42 This incident was related to me personally by the chairman of the trustees of the institution involved. It is my decision not to name the agency and president.

43. This was told to me by the trustee. It is my decision not to name the school.

44 James T. Draper, Jr.: *Authority: The Critical Issue for Southern Baptists*, Fleming H. Revell, Old Tappan, N.J., 1984, pp. 104, 105.

45 "Elder Views SBC Issues as Adulthood Struggles," *Baptist and Reflector*, June 13, 1984, p. 3.

9 WHERE DOES THE DENOMINATIONAL MEDIA STAND?

SBC conservatives see red when asked if the denominational press is fair. "The liberal/moderate element has totally captured the denominational press with a minority view," declares Kerry Powell, pastor of First Baptist Church, Forrest City, Arkansas. Powell says SBC media take "the real theological issue and put the focus instead on a fundamentalist political organization." Denominational media "have discredited and attempted to shut out conservative voices," he says. The official press is responsible for "a large part of the unrest in our convention." [1]

Many conservatives use even stronger words to describe the alleged bias of denominational media toward their challenge.

Disagreeing denominational editors tend to echo Kentucky's Jack Sanford who says, "We are right in the middle, constantly besieged by both sides in the controversy to tell their story in a way that is acceptable to them . . . " [2]

There is little dispute about the power and pervasiveness of denominational media. Will Rogers' declaration, "All that I know is what I read in the papers," is not far short of the mark if applied to Southern Baptists and their denominational papers and periodicals, although they've been reading more lately about the controversy in the secular press. One need only peek in the church literature closet and sample the pastor's mail for a week to perceive the variety and quantity of denominational media available.

Numbers? Peruse the Sunday School Board report in the Convention *Book of Reports*. A circulation of 13,366,161 periodicals for 1984 is impressive. Most are quarterlies, so this figure can be multiplied almost four times over. And there is more, much more, in books, guides, bulletin services, and other special publications coming from the world's largest religious publisher. Add to this, publications from other agencies, including seminary journals and alumni newsletters, plus the nation's largest system of denominational newspapers, the 34 state convention (mostly weekly) papers which range in circulation from 3,100 (Alaska) to 354,703 (Texas).[3] In the midst of this aggregate stands Baptist Press which supplies news copy to the various SBC publications, state papers, other religious publishers, major metropolitan newspapers and broadcasters, and national wire services.

In answering the question of this chapter, we will consider, in order, church curriculum, seminary journals, agency periodicals and newsletters, Baptist Press, and finally the state papers, from which Southern Baptists get almost all of their denominational news.

The Sunday School Board provides curriculum materials and service programs to support SBC churches in their tasks of evangelism and spiritual growth. The doctrinal guideline for editors and lesson writers is the *Baptist Faith and Message*. Board publications consistently steer clear of troubled waters where Baptists disagree, striving not to offend. Specificities on the how of Biblical inspiration and the what of Biblical truth are left for readers to fill in. Writers are supposedly chosen to reflect the diversity of theological thought in the denomination. Mississippi Editor Joe Odle complained at the 1970 "Affirming the Bible Conference", which preceded the acrimonious Denver convention, of a "tendency to allow questions of Biblical criticism to creep into curriculum material." [4]

Some conservatives claim that moderates have been given preference over conservatives as writers for adult curriculum, where doctrine is given more emphasis. If true, this may be because more moderates than conservatives are interested in writing and apply to do sample lessons in the prospect of receiving definite assignments. Or, it could be that more moderates hold seminary doctorates and are therefore judged by editors as better qualified writers. Or, perhaps some editors are more comfortable with moderates, who tend to be less dogmatic than conservatives.

Grady Cothen, who retired from the Sunday School Board in 1983, did not approve of the alleged takeover tactics of conservatives. His successor, Lloyd Elder, who came from Southwestern Seminary, raised conservative hopes when he declared his belief in the infallibility of Scripture. He has not personally involved himself in the conflict, as have some other agency heads.

The personable Elder has taken lumps from both sides on two different incidents, which indicate that the Sunday School Board continues to undergo careful scrutiny by moderates and conservatives alike.

In the first instance, Elder and other Board executives are not likely to forget the mini-tornado which occurred over the July 7 lesson on Job for the summer, 1985 *Adult Bible Study* in the Sunday School Life and Work Series. The lesson commentary stated that the "satan" of Job, chapters one and two, was not "the devil of the New Testament, evil personified," but one of several "heavenly messengers . . . , a kind of heavenly inspector" for sin who "was God's servant, not his enemy. There is, in the Old Testament, no concept of an empire of evil opposed to God," the text asserted.

Many readers disagreed—a record 155 calls and letters of protest rained on the Board. Max Caldwell, manager of the youth-adult Sunday School division, said the commentary did "not reflect the position of the Sunday School Board. We simply failed to catch the errors in this periodical."

Caldwell absolved the lesson writer, Southeastern Seminary Hebrew and Old Testament Professor John I. Durham from blame. The "errors", Caldwell claimed, were inserted by a temporary editor helping out during a staff vacancy.[5]

Critics charged that the unnamed temporary editor was being made a scapegoat and demanded to see the writer's manuscript. President Elder then added to the confusion by stating in a news release about trustee action that the story quoting Caldwell was "accurate" regarding "initial concerns" raised about the lesson. "However, a more complete review of the entire lesson showed the manuscript by Durham is **not unlike** (emphasis mine) what appears in print." Still, Elder said, "the Sunday School Board is accountable and responsible for final editing of all manuscripts."[6]

The trustees expressed "regret" and adopted a motion calling for Board administrators to "exercise special care in determining the doctrinal and biblical commitment of writers by carefully reviewing their published works, their public statements and their personal testimony." This overruled (by a trustee vote of 41-27) a much stronger substitute motion which called for closer scrutiny of future lesson writers.

Following up this trustee action, Board President Lloyd Elder directed a consultation on "Biblical authority" with Board employees. Elder noted that questions to the Board most often related to the article on Scripture in the *Baptist Faith and Message.* "The Sunday School Board is a Bible board," he told them. He did not think that "expectation . . . will ever go away."[7]

The Board, Elder said, was asking prospective writers to provide information about their beliefs and writings.

Editorial and curriculum specialist Bob Dean said editors and writers were being asked to "avoid anything that could appear to cast doubt on Scripture." Editors would scrutinize manuscripts for any unclear writing that could be misunderstood. Unusual interpretations of Scripture would be presented in the context of traditional beliefs.

Trustees of the Sunday School Board also apparently applied pressure on administrators to deal with Howard Bramblette, who had published one article in a magazine for Baptist students perceived as supporting woman's ordination and another opposing political activities of conservatives. Moderates and some state editors, were upset at Bramblette's resignation. Declared Jack Sanford in Kentucky's *Western Recorder*:

> What bothers me is that pressure from persons who disagree puts into jeopardy the professional lives of competent, dedicated Christians. Should our agencies and institutions run scared? How can any progress in spreading the gospel be made if every action must be universally accepted by such a diverse body as the SBC? [8]

Trustee and administrative response to both incidents suggest that the Sunday School Board is becoming more attuned to the concerns of conservatives. Ambiguity and neutrality will not be tolerated on some beliefs which conservatives hold dear. The diversities will not be as wide as in the past.

Researcher Nancy Ammerman thinks the Sunday School Board is now more sensitive to "the direct wishes of people like the [conservative majority] in Dallas," because it is a profit-generating institution which contributes to state conventions and the SBC (over $2.5 million in 1984). If it were to take an oppositional stance, the publisher "would immediately lose revenue—a much more powerful sanction than any censure from convention messengers." [9] The SBC's publishing agency already has an independent conservative competitor in the Baptist Literature Board, which adapts material from non-denominational Scripture Press. With the stance the Sunday School Board now seems to be taking, the unofficial Baptist Literature Board may come in for hard times.

A second category of SBC media, seminary scholarly journals, has received little attention in the controversy, perhaps because circulations are small, or because many conservatives do not read such journals, or because articles by both conservatives and moderates have been published in the journals on the critical Bible issue.

Southern Seminary's *Review and Expositor* has given several quarterly editions to questions raised in the controversy. The Spring, 1974 edition was devoted to "Biblical Inspiration and Interpretation" and included articles by conservatives Harold Lindsell and Carl F. H. Henry and moderates Eric Rust and Morris Aschaft. The edition on Biblical inspiration is must reading for anyone wishing to understand the differences between conservatives and moderates on the inspiration of Scripture. The Spring, 1978 edition centered on "The Problem of Authority of Church and Society," in which writers from several denominations participated. The Winter, 1979 edition on "Baptist Confessions of Faith" included contributions by moderate Walter B. Shurden and conservative Joe T. Odle. The discussions have been brisk, but the tone irenic, on matters which have been fiercely debated in past conventions.

The Theological Educator, edited by New Orleans Seminary faculty, published, in 1985, was a special issue dealing with the controversy itself. Three conservatives (Jimmy Draper, Paige Patterson, and Paul Pressler) and three influential moderates or agency types (Russell Dilday, Porter Routh, and Walter Shurden) were interviewed and allowed to speak for themselves, without censorship by the editors. A concluding summary of the history of the controversy is given by Claude Howe, Professor of Church History at New Orleans Seminary. Howe, however, dips into polemics to indicate that his sympathies are with moderates, "If liberalism is widespread among Southern Baptists," he says, "it must be defined very narrowly . . . The cash value of the words as explained and qualified [about the Bible] is not substantially different." [9] Howe takes the moderate tack in defending Biblical criticism:

> Conservative-fundamentalists desire that students be informed about destructive historical critical methodology only to defend the Bible against it. With few exceptions, they interpret the Bible very literally. Moderates and denominational loyalists believe that the Bible should be studied critically as well as devotionally in order to so understand and apply it rather than simply defend it. Whereas an occasional student may be disturbed by this approach, many thousands learn from it and are enabled better to preach and teach the Bible in churches and schools around the world. [10]

The seminary journals have not mounted heavy attacks against conservatives, although their editors are part of the agency system which feels itself under attack. Professors, who may be sympathetic with some or all of the conservative goals, are not likely to take bold stands in their institutions, unless and until the agencies, as a whole, show more evidence of yielding to the conservative challenge.

Conservative ire against seminary publications has mostly been directed against the institutional news and public relation organs of three SBC schools, Southern, Southwestern, and Southeastern.

The printing, distribution, and promotion of Southern Seminary President Roy Honeycutt's "holy war" chapel speech greatly upset the conservative wing. Seminary funds, from the Cooperative Program, paid for printing the speech in a booklet for mass distribution. Also published was a two-page article, "SBC Takeover Must be Averted," by Honeycutt, in *The Tie*, mailed to alumni and other seminary friends after Charles Stanley's election in Kansas City in 1984. A sampling of quotes indicates the militancy of the Southern Seminary administration against SBC conservatives:

> Undetected by vast numbers of Southern Baptists, a rising tide of Independent Fundamentalism is relentlessly washing away the foundations of the Southern Baptist Convention . . .

> To what extent are the independent fundamentalists succeeding? Look at Kansas City! The annual meeting of the Southern Baptist Convention in that city was interpreted by many, including myself, as the most blatantly politicized demonstration of the Independent party's strategy during the five year political campaign . . .

> To us falls the responsibility of determining that this fate [takeover by Independent Fundamentalism] does not eclipse a denomination so rich in heritage and so challenged by unprecedented opportunities for mission advance . . .

> Every person identified with the Southern Baptist Theological Seminary should rally to this emergency. Plan now to be in Dallas next year; deliver the convention from the bondage of its political exile; recover an open convention process and the priority of our historic commitment to cooperative missions, evangelism, and education.[11]

The seminary news department disseminated this and other articles antithetical to the conservative movement to Baptist Press and secular media. An article by Southern professor Larry L. McSwain attempted to justify the actions by Honecutt and other agency heads in opposing conservatives. Said McSwain:

> [Convention] bylaws and safeguards were never written which would defend the convention against a conspiracy to manipulate the decision-making process. What became apparent in . . . Kansas City is that the

process is indeed corrupted and is likely to remain that way. Honeycutt and others like Keith Parks and Russell Dilday are now trying to alert Southern Baptists to actions they must take to regain the lost democracy they once took for granted.[12]

After the Peace Committee appointed at Dallas asked for restraint from both sides, the acrimony in seminary periodicals cooled. President Honeycutt stated in *The Tie*:

It shall be my intention to offer the [Peace Committee] my complete cooperation and especially to heed its closing exhortation: "All Southern Baptists are urged to exercise restraint, to refrain from divisive actions and comments, and to reflect Christian love, while this Committee is doing its work.[13]

Two issues later, Honeycutt indicated that he had not changed his opinion of the conservative movement:

. . . We will never know the losses to the Kingdom of God because a faction has abandoned our Baptist heritage. No human being can accurately assess where this process will end . . . Who among us can cite a calendar date marking the return to our Baptist heritage? Only in retrospect will we know when Southern Baptists have rejected the spurious rewriting of Southern Baptist polity and the distortion of the convention's self-understanding.[14]

Southern Seminary has been practically silent on the controversy since these remarks by Honeycutt. Southwestern and Southeastern appear to be honoring the plea of the Peace Committee. The other three seminaries have not taken any stand in their alumni and news publications, although Presidents Landrum Leavell of New Orleans and Franklin Pollard, who recently resigned from Golden Gate, have declared themselves believers in inerrancy.

The Foreign and Home Mission Boards, Annunity Board, the seven "Commissions," and the Baptist Joint Committee on Public Affairs (BJCPA) all have publications, as does the auxiliary Woman's Missionary Union. Publications of all but two of these agencies have generally kept clear of controversial theology and topics. Publications of the Christian Life Commission (CLC) and the Baptist Joint Committee on Public Affairs (BJCPA) have not.

The CLC and BJCPA say SBC conservatives are in league with Jerry Falwell, Pat Robertson, Ed McAteer, Tim LaHaye, and other pillars of the so-called Religious Right. The two agencies, and moderate allies in pastorates, have noted in publications that many

SBC leaders serve on the same "ultra-conservative" boards as these independents. Conservatives say the CLC and BJCPA do not publicize the affiliations and associations of moderates with political and religious liberals outside the SBC.

Conservatives have no quarrel—indeed they cheer—crusades by the CLC on world hunger, legalized gambling, pornography, alcohol, and human rights. They stand with the Baptist Joint Committee on Public Affairs on opposing American diplomatic representation at the Vatican and on many other church-state matters. What rankles conservatives most is the refusal of the two agencies to carry out the spirit of certain resolutions at the SBC, notably on abortion and voluntary school prayer in classrooms.

Foy Valentine, head of the CLC, refuses to get behind a proposed constitutional amendment to outlaw abortion on demand. Valentine maintains that he is personally opposed to abortion in all but the most extreme circumstances, although he signed the "Call to Conern," produced by the Religious Coalition for Abortion Rights, which supported the Roe v. Wade Supreme Court decision. As to why the CLC has provided so little educational help to churches in fighting abortion, the veteran social ethicist says his agency is too small and too poorly funded to do everything needed to help Southern Baptists apply Christian principles in society. Because of the convention accepting the Calendar Committee's recommendation that the third Sunday in January be designated "Sanctity of Life Day," the CLC is now obligated to provide help and has done so. Still, the CLC refuses to promote a constitutional amendment to overturn the Roe v. Wade Supreme Court Decision of 1973. Valentine continues to oppose "the effort of the Catholic Bishops to write their dogma [on abortion] into the organic law of the United States of America . . . " [15]

Valentine and his staff have found space in the CLC's monthly *Light* to report on political and social unrest in Latin America, economics, international peacemaking, and nuclear disarmament. CLC articles on these subjects tend to coincide with positions by Congressional liberals. A recent *Light* featured a cover interview with Democratic Senator Albert Gore, Jr. on "Arms Control and Peace." Besides CLC staff, *Light* authors include leading SBC moderates. *Light* has avoided criticizing leading SBC conservatives by name, but has not spared many of the positions they hold on socio-moral issues.

James Dunn, BJCPA executive director, stedfastly refuses to support the convention-backed resolution calling for support of President Reagan's proposed prayer-in-schools amendment. He eloquently proclaims his strict church-state separationist view in BJCPA's periodical *Report from the Capital*. Dunn criticizes some Supreme Court justices, Attorney General Meese, and Education Secretary Bennett for their stances on church-state matters, which happen to coincide with beliefs held by the leading SBC conservatives. Dunn quotes Justice Rehnquist as saying, "The evil aimed at [by the First Amendment] was the establishment of a national church, and perhaps the preference of one religious sect over another." This opinion is held by the SBC conservatives. Dunn continues,

> Attorney General Meese laments the Supreme Court's "hostility" to religion. Education Secretary Bennett would establish a yet unspelled-out Judeo-Christian value system for public schools. He does not bother to reconcile the sometimes conflicting axioms of his hyphenated lowest-common-denominator religion. True believers all, they often labor brilliantly to rewrite history.

> Their revised standard version of the First Amendment holds that it simply rules out favoritism among religious groups and prohibits an official State Church, but endorses God-in-general and allows impartial government aid for churches . . .

> The revisionist view that would turn away from separation of church and state is downright silly.[16]

Report from the Capital, which receives 80 percent of its funding from the Cooperative Program, constantly pushes Dunn's position on church-state separation in editorial matter. The publication schedules articles by authors who oppose the "New Right." For example, the lead article for the November/December, 1985 issue was titled, "The Christian Right Threat to Evangelical Christianity," in which author Richard V. Pierard characterizes the Religious Right, which includes many SBC conservative leaders, in the following terms:

1. "They seek to gain large fellowship and in effect develop personality cults."
2. "They see most issues in conspiratorial terms."
3. They "feature . . . an excessive emphasis on 'absolutes.'"
4. "Many" have "a weak sense of loyalty to their church or denomination." [17]

Many articles and editorials in the CLC's *Light* and the BJCPA's *Report from the Capital* tend to go against the "grain" of the convictions of SBC conservatives who rightly complain that they do not receive equal time in the two agencies and their periodicals. Many conservatives have given up trying to change Valentine and Dunn and believe their only recourse is to get trustees on their boards who will take "corrective" action. With a conservative takeover, this could ultimately mean a drastic change in program and editorial position in the CLC and BJCPA. Short of that, the conservatives would like the CLC and BJCPA removed from the Cooperative Program, or have the Cooperative Program amended to allow "negative designations" from churches.

Periodicals of other agencies have generally steered a neutral course. This is easier for them because their programs relate less specifically to issues in the contoversy.

We move now to a critique of the SBC "news" system in which the "hub"—Baptist Press (BP)—is at the center of a news network conveying and receiving news from SBC agencies and the state papers. Baptist Press receives stories from "representatives" in agencies and state papers, from which Baptist Press editors select and, after editing, transmit to all the denominational outlets, as well as to other religious and secular publishing operations. Thus, almost all of the out-of-state news which Southern Baptists read in their state convention newspapers comes through or from Baptist Press.

Baptist Press is not a religious counterpart of Associated Press or United Press. It is responsible to the SBC Executive Committee through the Executive Committee's public relations "work group". BP's director also handles public relations for the convention and its agencies through the Executive Committee. It is hardly a free press, for it tends to protect agencies against outside challengers, including conservatives who do not enjoy the access to BP which agencies do.

BP Director, Wilmer C. Fields is respected and appreciated by religion writers of the secular press who say almost uniformly that BP, under Field's direction, operates the most efficient and cooperative newsroom of any denomination. Fields draws a comfortable salary from Cooperative Program funds. He could likely make much more as public relations director for a Fortune 500 corporation.

He is an agency man who strongly supports "unity amidst diversity." He is carefully guarded in speech. Only twice is he known to have indicated his feelings about the conservative challengers. In 1982, in inviting secular religion reporters to cover the New Orleans convention, he mentioned that news interests would include "a takeover attempt by a dissident group of fundamentalists." In 1984, he told an audience at River Road Baptist Church in Richmond, Virginia.

Keep in mind there is no binding force at work here. They

[the resolutions passed] represent only the opinion of those present at the convention. [The conservatives] may tell us they represent the majority of Southern Baptists, but they are only a tiny group among the 14.1 million Southern Baptists in the nation.[18]

The personal integrity of W.C. Fields is not questioned by conservatives. It is the policy, they say, which allows agencies to report on themselves to the constituency. This policy, conservatives allege, permits coverups of bureaucratic problems in agencies and liberal teaching in seminaries, resulting in Baptist Press sending out slanted and biased stories on what is happening in the agencies. The challengers further claim that every misstep of conservatives has been magnified while transgressions of moderates have often been overlooked or treated as unimportant. Conservatives have also made these criticisms of most of the state papers.

Let us look briefly at how the Baptist Press system works. BP accredits as writers one or more persons in every agency, usually public relations specialists who send out a steady flow of PR stories through regular agency channels. BP also picks up numerous "local" stories with national interest that are written by editors of state papers. BP occasionally assigns a free lance story, usually to a religion reporter of a newspaper in the area where the event occurred. But most BP articles are written by agency employees who work on agency time.

Sometimes the byline of the writer of a story appears in a state paper; sometimes not. Seldom is the writer's employment mentioned, even when the substance of the story is highly controversial. Perhaps more than 99 percent of the time readers do not know that a "news" report about a sensitive happening in an agency was written by an employee of the agency involved.

The journalistic profession has always been fair game for critics. Baptist Press is no exception, and is probably criticized more than any other element of the SBC informational system. BP undoubtedly deserves some of the criticism, while more often it lives up to a recent commendation by the Executive Committee for "timely, acurate, and well-balanced news reporting of, about, and for Southern Baptists." [19]

While much could be said about the positive contributions of BP, we will consider as case studies two controversial stories which may help in understanding the difficulties, both internal and external, in Baptist Press newsgathering. The first story, which I reported on for *Christianity Today*, speaks to the weakness of a reporting system in which an agency head apparently can control the reporting of in-house problems, at least to some extent. It also shows the power of a denominational agency in dealing with a troublesome employee. The second story, which I have only researched for this larger study, concerns alleged unfairness in reporting on a questionable action by Judge Paul Pressler.

In the summer of 1981, Baptist Press reported that the Sunday School Board had lost a civil suit in which a Circuit Court jury had awarded plaintiff Donald Burnett, a former Board employee, $400,000 in damages. The BP story which I read covered only the bare bones of the incident.[20] At the time, I was busy studying for my doctoral comprehensive exams at the University of Tennessee and gave the article only a cursory reading. The next morning, I happened to read a much different and more enlarged report of the trial in Nashville's *The Tennessean*.[21] This story listed several high Board executives as having been terminated from Board employment for problems allegedly related to litigation brought by Burnett. My interest now aroused, I read again the BP article and saw that the resignations were not mentioned there. I also noted that the bylined writer was a public relations employee of the Sunday School Board. Why had the Board writer not mentioned the executive departures and other damaging information contained in the newspaper article? Why had BP allowed a Board employee to write a story which posed a possible conflict of interest? At this time, I was not aware of how BP reported denominational news.

I sent the clippings to *Christianity Today*, urging the news editor to assign someone else to do the story. But none of the three writers I suggested were available. Partly because some of my secular colleagues had made cynical remarks about the "unethical" journalism of religious organizations, and partly because of my strong belief in human rights, I agreed to do the report. The BP article had not even quoted the former Sunday School Board employee, an ordained SBC minister, who had won the case. I felt that he deserved his day in the "court" of journalism.

In Nashville, I read volumes of court documents and did a round of interviews, including talking with the plaintiff Donald Burnett; defendant Grady Cothen, then president of the Sunday School Board; Baptist Press Director W.C. Fields and News Editor Dan Martin; and the foreman of the jury who said the panel had needed only 45 minutes to decide that Cothen and the Board were at fault.

I learned that the problems related to the trial had begun in August, 1976, when Burnett, then an assistant personnel manager, who had just been named "Employee of the Month" in the Board's internal house organ, had gone to President Cothen with allegations from Board employees about sexual harassment and other misdeeds of superiors. Cothen, who had a long and distinguished career as a denominational executive, including the presidency of New Orleans Seminary, had been at the Board only a year and found Burnett's stories difficult to believe. At Cothen's request, Burnett agreed to be examined by a psychiatrist. Cothen then asked his executive vice-president, who had been at the Board longer, to recommend one. The vice-president suggested a next door neighbor. The examination proceeded and the psychiatrist pronounced Burnett to be a paranoid schizophrenic, potentially homicidal, and in need of treatment.

Cothen then did what later came to be viewed by many as a serious mistake. After consulting with legal counsel, he devised a plan to have Nashville police grab Burnett in a secluded spot in back of the Board's main office building. The police were instructed to take Burnett to a private mental health facility, where a second psychiatrist would examine him to meet a requirement by Tennessee law requiring certification by two psychiatrists before a mentally ill person could be involuntarily committed. Cothen did this without consulting with Burnett's family. The employee's family physician was asked to aid in the commitment, but he refused to have part in it.

The plot went awry. The police became confused and drove into the wrong parking lot in full view of dozens of employee offices. Cothen had to hustle Burnett across the lot where he urged him to get into the police car. Burnett kept protesting. Cothen kept insisting.

Burnett later testified, "I was afraid, if I ran, that people coming out of the Board would say, 'Here's Don and police officers and they're arresting him and he's crazy.' I didn't want to leave that impression."

Burnett got into the car with the officers—under duress, he said later—and was driven to the institution where the second psychiatrist, presumably having been prepped by the next door neighbor of the Board's executive vice-president, was waiting. When they arrived, Burnett told the police, "I think my civil rights have been violated." The officers then permitted him to call his family doctor. The physician asked for the psychiatrist who was to finalize the commitment and warned him not to get involved. When this psychiatrist withdrew, the police released Burnett from custody.

That same day, August 4, Cothen tried to explain to Board employees in chapel what he had attempted to do in the parking lot. "It was," he said, "an attempt on our part, acting upon competent advice, legally and medically . . . to get some help for one of our brothers . . . He has not done anything bad . . . He deserves our prayers." But, added Cothen, "he will not return to the Board until he obtains help, if he needs it."

Burnett asked for his job back. Cothen refused, but put him on paid leave with the promise that he could return after receiving certification of mental health from a psychiatrist. Burnett later testified at the trial that he consulted a therapist in Georgia who found nothing wrong with him. Burnett said he also continued his own investigation of wrongdoing by Board executives and kept passing reports of alleged misdeeds to Cothen who declined to let him come back to work.

Burnett had cited the executive vice president as one he had heard stories about. Cothen learned—not through Burnett—that the man was having a "relationship" with a former counselee. Cothen told the executive he could not accept the relationship as "wholesome and healthy." But he would keep him on at his $50,000 yearly salary if he would break off with the woman. The executive refused and resigned. Two other Board officials, about whom Burnett had made allegations, were subsequently asked to resign.

Burnett ultimately filed suit for $1.5 million. Because of a choked court docket, the case did not come to trial until 1981. He charged the Board with assault and battery, wrongful discharge, gross negligence, outrageous conduct, false arrest, imprisonment and defamation. Burnett further alleged that his reputation had been ruined among Southern Baptists and that he had lost his home and suffered other financial reverses while his suit was awaiting trial.

Third Circuit Court Judge Joe Loser dismissed all charges except the one on defamation. The jury recommended Burnett be awarded $300,000 in compensatory damages and $100,000 in punitive damages. Judge Loser felt this was too much and subsequently reduced the compensation to $80,000.

In trying to get to the bottom of the bizarre happenings, I tried to call the Board's chairman of trustees. He did not return my calls. I finally found a newly elected trustee who said he had called Cothen the week before the trial saying he was concerned about bad publicity on the case. Cothen, the trustee said, had advised that he was watching the reporting process carefully and hoped Baptist Press would let the Board's information officer write the news story for the denominational press. The trustee said that, to his knowledge, no trustee had attended the trial. They had left Board affairs up to President Cothen, who was a defendant in the proceedings.

The story was written for Baptist Press by a Board public relations employee, reviewed and approved by Cothen, then sent across town to the BP office, where BP News Editor Dan Martin concurred with the public relations employee that the names of the "resigned" executives need not appear in print.

Neither the Board writer nor BP had talked to Burnett to this point. After my story appeared in *Christianity Today* [22] and the judge reduced the damages, BP did ask Burnett for his reaction. Burnett responded, "In light of the fact that you've never once called me, during the past five years, for my side, and have printed everything the Board and Dr. Cothen said, I will never give a statement to Baptist Press."

Jury foreman Dr. Rowland Ahrens (a Ph.D. in chemistry) told me that the jurors had not seen Cothen as an "evil man; his desire was to do the best he could for the Board," but they felt he acted unwisely and harmfully against Burnett. I later wrote Cothen, after he had announced his resignation from the Board's presidency on account of ill health, to assure him that nothing personal against him had been involved in my decision to write the story. Cothen replied that he still believed the jury's decision was wrong, that the *Christianity Today* article had caused him "problems," but that the news story for denominational media should "probably not have been handled" as it had.

W.C. Fields, however, defended the news handling. He had been "out of town" during the trial, but said it was BP policy for approved agency personnel to write stories involving controversy about their employers. I suggested that this policy be changed to avoid possible conflicts of interest. Fields said budgetary restraints prevented extensive use of outside writers.

I also talked with C.R. Daley, then editor of Kentucky's *Western Recorder* who served as chairman of the Southern Baptist Press Association Committee on Baptist Press. Daley understood that "several years ago the Sunday School board leadership decided that all the reporting [through Baptist Press] would be done by their staff members." Daley thought the Sunday School Board was the only SBC agency "with this policy." Daley then assured that the BP reporting of the trial would "be on the agenda for the next meeting of his committee." [23]

A year passed, and I continued to note bylines of agency public relations employees on BP stories about problems in their agencies. I then introduced a resolution at the 1983 Pittsburgh convention, commending BP for "efforts at fairness, efficiency, and comprehensiveness in gathering and disseminating news relating to Southern Baptist agencies and activities," while expressing disapproval of "having agency employees report for Baptist Press on their employers in incidents of court suits and controversies of substance" and of the BP practice of "disseminating news of agencies which does not carry the names of writers and their employment." The resolution was referred to the Executive Committee which ordered it printed in the official *Book of Reports* and reported back to the next convention that it had been received as "helpful advice." [24]

I was also invited to present my concerns before the Executive Committee's public relations sub-group which was responsible for Baptist Press. The meeting was attended by several agency heads and most of the state editors. One agency head admitted, "We do have a lot of control over the news in our agencies, perhaps too much." A state editor said, "Hefley has a point. There could be a conflict of interest in the way some news has been handled."

The public relations sub-group reported the discussion back to the Executive Committee. W.C. Fields wrote me that the Committee's response was "positive and constructive all the way through." He added:

> Reporters from our office are doing more reporting on sensitive matters. In some cases, we are sending our people to the scene of the action. In other cases, we are getting the information by telephone.
>
> In some instances that are not particularly controversial but where the agency wanted to be seen as being strictly objective on a matter, they have taken the initiative to ask that we come and do the reporting.
>
> We intend to continue using the bureau system because of its obvious advantages—a cost effective way to utilize personnel and program resources with use of people who are best informed about the news they are reporting and the chance for administrators to prove their accountability to Baptist people by being straightforward and open, even in the most controversial matters.
>
> Furthermore, I have had a round of discussions with SBC agency heads regarding the basic problem of not only allowing but encouraging their newspeople to be open and forthright in their reporting even in the most controversial matters. The latest in that series was a luncheon with Lloyd Elder, the new president of the Sunday School Board, this past week. He said all of the right things. I reminded him that the real test comes in the first serious controversy that comes up.
>
> This is a problem that is never won once and for all.

Each day is a new test, but I am encouraged by the responsiveness of this new crop of leaders.[25]

While no objective study has been done of BP news handling, it appears that more reporting of agency controversies is being done by BP editors and others who do not work for the agency in question. However, it is disconcerting to note that the Sunday School Board's "information officer" wrote the BP story about the brouhaha on the Sunday School lesson commentary about the Devil in the Book of Job.

The second case study, which relates more directly to the Convention-wide controversy, centers on news handling within the BP office of a story involving Judge Paul Pressler.

The basic facts surrounding the judge's alleged "secret tape recording" of a conversation with a student at Southern Seminary are here presented for the first time in print. Judge Pressler had long been interested in Christian education, having taught high school and college students in Sunday School and raised scholarship funds for others at New Orleans Seminary. His involvement in the convention developed from discussions with students whom he "led to the Lord" about Baptist schools they were attending, and what was being taught. He developed a friendship with one student in particular, Stafford Durham, who happened to be the airport driver for Southern Seminary president, Roy Honeycutt had attended a retreat with Pressler's Sunday School class while he and his wife were visiting friends in Houston.

In February of 1984, Pressler was invited to Louisville to participate in fellow conservative LaVerne Butler's fifteenth anniversary celebration at Ninth and "O" Baptist Church. When invited, he contacted Alan Sears, a member of the Executive Committee to see whether a meeting with President Roy Honeycutt could be arranged. The word came back that it could be worked out and Pressler made his airplane reservations to allow him to be free in Louisville for a day for this meeting. When no confirmation of this proposed meeting came from Honeycutt, Pressler called Durham the Sunday morning he was leaving for Louisville to see if he was available for lunch on Monday. Durham said he lived several miles from Louisville and couldn't be in town that day. The brief conversation ended with Pressler's expression of hope that they would see each other at the Kansas City convention.

In the fall of 1984 at a convocation in the Seminary Chapel, Honeycutt declared "holy war." Among many other charges, he alleged that "one of the Texas leaders of the inerrantist political party recently invaded the privacy of my presidential office, to say nothing of my personal life."

None of the "Texas" conservatives say they knew what he was referring to. Later it was revealed by his office that he was making the charge against Pressler. Pressler says he had forgotten the conversation but after the accusation was made against him, he went to his files, discovered Durham's name, and realized that Durham was the only Southern Seminary student he had talked to over the phone for several years. Pressler called Durham on September 1, 1984 to see whether Durham actually drove for Honeycutt. Feeling his previous conversation with Durham had been misrepresented, Pressler took the precaution of taping the conversation which was legal under Federal, Texas and Kentucky law.[26] The tape was not to be used unless necessary. In this conversation, Durham said that, in the previous conversation, he did not tell Pressler that he drove for Honeycutt, that Pressler did not say that he knew that he drove for Honeycutt, that Durham just assumed that Pressler knew and that the whole thing had been blown out of proportion. Three days later, Durham gave a statement to the *Houston Chronicle* that seemed to contradict what he had said in the telephone conversation. When the *Chronicle* called Pressler to tell him of Durham's comments, Pressler told them that they should know the full story and allowed them to listen to the tape so that their article would reflect all the statements of Durham. Then either acting individually or upon the advice of people from the Seminary, Durham evidently decided to make a frontal attack on Pressler for having made the tape.[27]

Pressler says he did not know of Durham's attack until he drove into Nashville on Friday afternoon for his first executive committee meeting. He learned that Dan Martin was trying to reach him and called Martin on arrival. Martin came by the hotel and he and Pressler visited briefly that afternoon. Martin told him he wanted to interview him about the Durham accusations and Pressler said that he was willing to do it then. Martin had family obligations and they agreed that Pressler would come to his office at 9:30 o'clock Monday morning. When Pressler went to Martin's office, he gave him a written statement. He was on a ten-minute break in a sub-committee meeting and could not discuss the matter at greater length. Martin released Durham's story about noon Monday without using any material from Pressler.[28] This story contained allegations that the actions of Pressler were illegal and contained no rebuttal information. The focus in Baptist Press became the taping by Pressler rather than the seeming inconsistencies of Durham.

On Tuesday morning, the Tennessee state paper, the *Baptist and Reflector*, was made available to all members of the Executive Committee. In it was the story of Durham's attack on Pressler with no rebuttal from Pressler. Pressler immediately went to W.C. Field's office. Fields advised him that it was his decision to release the story without any rebuttal. Most of the other state papers, hearing the objections raised on Tuesday, combined the Monday story with a BP Tuesday release on the incident which included a rebuttal from Pressler.

Pressler, who had been alleging unfairness in previous stories about conservatives by Baptist Press and denominational papers, asked for an investigation by the Executive Committee on BP's news handling. After spirited debate, the Executive Committee voted in Pressler's favor and assigned the investigation to the public relations work group.[29]

In December of 1984, Pressler received a call from Bob Terry, editor of Missouri's *The Word and Way*, asking him that he write down the objections he had to the story. Terry did not contact him again. Pressler received a letter on January 23, 1985 from Dr. John Mott of the journalism department at Memphis State University stating that he was researching the controversy over the stories and asked Pressler questions concerning them. Pressler immediately responded to Dr. Mott by asking him who he was and why he was making the study. Mott, according to Pressler, never responded to Pressler. The fact developed at the hearing before the Executive Committee that the committee of three were hired by the representatives of the state Baptist papers in early December, that they met with all the participants in the controversy from Baptist Press's side and did not contact Pressler until the letter dated January 23 was received by him on January 26 or 27. The final draft of their report was ready on February 6. This "study" did not help the conservatives' feeling of distruct toward Baptist Press or the state papers.

Pressler brought a large file of BP releases and asked that the panel consider if there had been a pattern of unfairness by BP toward conservatives over a period of time. The professors said their instructions were to deal only with the two stories about the taping incident. Within this perimeter, they said the two articles were newsworthy and accurate and showed no "direct or circumstantial evidence of deliberate bias against Judge Pressler." As for releasing one story ahead of the other, the committee "found it difficult to fault" BP for the decision [which] is one made every day by many news organizations practicing the highest standards in our profession." [30] The Executive Committee, however added, in its official report,

Because the September 17 article appeared separately

and without an appropriate rebuttal from Mr. Pressler, said article must be deemed as an unfortunate and untimely procedure for reporting of the incident.[31]

However one judges Baptist Press on handling of the Sunday School Board trial and the Pressler taping story, it is obvious that BP is at best only partly free and subject to pressures from within and without the agencies. Would BP be more free if it had separate agency status? A motion to that effect was made at the Los Angeles convention in 1981 by messenger Jimmy Stroud, and referred to the Executive Committee. They concluded there would be no guarantee of greater freedom if BP answered to a board of trustees, instead of a sub-committee of members of the Executive Committee. The Executive Committee study also found that more money would be required for BP as a separate agency to maintain the current level of news operation.

Some of the 34 Baptist state editors operate directly under their state executive board, with the editor reporting to the state convention's top executive, and some are edited by the top executives. A young editor, who had previously worked for a city newspaper, confided to me at the Dallas convention the dilemma he was in with this arrangement. "We have some serious personnel and financial problems in our state office," he said. "I think the people have a right to know. My state executive thinks otherwise. Since neither of us will yield, it looks as if I may have to resign." Within a month he was gone.

Other editors answer to a separate board of directors, elected by church messengers at the state convention. Their offices are generally in the same "Baptist Building" with the state executive. A long-time editor friend whom I greatly respect for his courage says frankly, "I cannot write everything I want. The shadow of the executive is always there."

Whatever their place in the state convention structure, the Baptist state papers are the major communication channel between national agencies and the churches. Organizationally independent in structure and mutually dependent in operations, Baptist Press and the state papers are, in Walter Shurden's words, "the informational glue of denominationalism." [32]

The smaller papers are almost completely dependent upon Baptist Press. Larger publications can afford staff writers to write state features and rewrite Baptist Press dispatches to meet local needs.

The current coterie of Baptist state editors are better educated in journalism than their predecessors. Some are skilled in investigative journalism and can handle tough subjects as well as seasoned religion reporters on big city secular newspapers. Most, however, tend to tread softly when problems in state and national agencies arise.

When I became aware that the Baptist Press story on the Sunday School Board trial had been written by a Board employee, I called several state editors and urged that they investigate the situation and write their own stories. Only one editor saw the need of going beyond Baptist Press. "Well, I'll look into it," he said. "I'll call Grady Cothen and get a statement from him."

"Shouldn't you also talk to the man who won the trial, or a member of the jury?" I pressed.

"No, that won't be necessary. Grady will tell me the straight of it. He and I once served on a board together."

It is not that the state editors see themselves as public relations specialists, but they are Southern Baptist denominationalists all. Many worked for other agencies before coming to their present positions. Bob Terry of Missouri, for example, once wrote news for Southern Seminary and edited the school's alumni bulletin, *The Tie*. He also served as an assistant editor for C.R. Daley at Kentucky's *Western Recorder*, as did six other present state editors.

The dedicated state editor reports significant activities in the churches and associations of his state. This includes what the agencies are doing in the kingdom, for they are an extension of the ministry of the churches. Tennessee's Alvin Shackleford says ". . . Our task is to promote the total program of the Tennessee Baptist Convention and the Southern Baptist Convention." [33]

The purpose of Shackleford's paper is

> To unite Tennessee Baptists in advancing the cause of Christ by providing news, inspirational material, features, and information concerning the ministries of the Tennessee and Southern Baptist conventions and to inform, inspire, promote, and enlist the interests of Tennessee Baptists in these ministries.[34]

Negative stories about SBC agencies in other media tend to draw mixed reaction from state editors. Consider the response to my report in *Christianity Today* on the Sunday School Board v. Donald Burnett. One editor accused *Christianity Today* of "yellow journalism," although he did not dispute the facts in the story. Two editors mildly criticized the Sunday School Board and its president for the bungled attempt to commit Burnett to a mental institution without his or his family's permission. One editor came down hard on the executive vice president for his alleged role in the proceedings which led up to the trial. No editor praised the *Christianity Today* aticle.

Almost two years after the article was published, an assistant state editor drew me aside in the newsroom at the Pittsburgh Convention. "Is it true that you're the uncle of Donald Burnett? Is that why you wrote the story about the Sunday School Board trial?" I assured him I was not. I could only presume he had read a column by the president of the Sunday School Board in the agency's newsletter stating that he had heard that relatives of Burnett influenced the publication of "negative" articles on the court suit. Also at Pittsburgh, the assistant editor of another state expressed his thanks for "telling what really happened at the Sunday School Board. I once worked for one of those executives who was involved in the mess," he said, "and believe me, it was pure h _ _ _ _." Then he added, "Please don't ever quote me on this. I just wanted you to know."

In the "court" of state editors, Pressler vs. Baptist press was no contest. Baptist Press was the good guy and Pressler the villain, with the Executive Committee receiving brickbats for alleged knuckling under to Pressler's call for an investigation.

Missouri's Bob Terry eloquently lambasted the Executive Committee public relations work group's handling of the investigation.

> What is . . . unbelievable is that not a single member of the public relations workgroup asked if FCC charges had been filed or if the comments from the student [Durham] were accurate quotes. Not a single member asked if Pressler had, indeed, taped the conversations and played them for a *Houston Chronicle* reporter as alleged. No one asked if the story was factual.
>
> One workgroup member asked if Christian journalism does not preclude reporting things that are hurtful. In response, one must ask if there are Southern Baptists whose deeds are protected by immunity from public knowledge? Of course, Christian journalism is concerned about the impact of stories on individuals. That is why the motto of Southern Baptist journalists has long been, "Tell the truth and trust the people." [35]

Terry was relieved and pleased when the panel of professors gave their verdict.

> It is difficult to fault BP for the decision [in writing and releasing the stories a day apart] that it made . . . The decision . . . is one made every day by many news organizations practicing the highest standards in our profession . . .

> It is reassuring to hear that, according to three of the best journalism educators in America, the work of Baptist Press reflects the highest standards of conduct and performance.[36]

Terry's reaction to the investigation of BP's handling of the "secret taping" story is somewhat typical of the position taken by other editors who commented on the incident. Jack Sanford of Kentucky's *Western Recorder*, for example, takes BP's side [37] and says the panel of professors made a "good decision in exonerating BP. [38]

The secret taping incident was big news in SBC media because of Paul Pressler's prominence in the big controversy. The continuing conflict, the partisan rivalry at conventions, the activities of major personalities, and statements made by leaders on both sides has consumed more SBC media space than any other story. Yet several of the smaller papers in "pioneer" areas have reported little of the controversy, while coverage in other state papers has ranged from light to heavy.

Baptist Press stories about the controversy have been the mainstay, with the "hottest" reports written by BP News Editor Dan Martin, who, despite his handling of the taping story, is regarded by many conservatives as among the best and the fairest of the denominational journalists. Also, in making assignments to cover events of the controversy in distant areas, Martin has sought to obtain writers who are not employed by an agency under fire. State editors with staff writers have augmented BP's coverage with stories of controversy-related happenings in their own localities. Presnall H. Wood's *Baptist Standard* probably leads in such independent coverage, simply because so many personalities in the conflict live in Texas.

Most state editors probably agree with Kentucky's Jack Sanford as he expressed himself in an editorial, of which a portion of the following was cited earlier in this chapter:

> Agony and pain over the continuing strife in our beloved Southern Baptist Convention is shared by all of us at *Western Recorder*, but most especially the editor who has final responsibility for the paper. We are right in the middle, constantly besieged by both sides in the controversy to tell their story in a way that is acceptable to them, when what we most want to do is find a way to keep the peace.[39]

In this respect, the great majority of state editors appear not to believe that the SBC has a serious theological problem, as leaders in the conservative movement allege. They do not see it as essential for denominational employees to believe in an inerrant text, and certainly not as an issue so important as to risk splitting the church body. How different it is from 1962 when 16 of 28 editors joined in criticizing the commentary on Genesis by Ralph Elliott. Ross Edwards and Joe Odle, the most vocal then, would likely disagree with the majority of their colleagues today.

C.R. Daley, retired from the *Western Recorder*, is a hero among SBC moderates, although some cringe at his candor. While editor of the Kentucky paper, Daley ran a virtual training school for many present SBC state editors. Said Daley, when he lectured at Southern Seminary,

> With the exception of two or three smaller, less influential papers, like Indiana . . . all of the old line, established state papers are remaining loyal to the denomination in opposition to attacks by fundamentalists.[40]

As for Indiana, Daley apparently speaks in reference to editorials of David Simpson, editor of the *Indiana Baptist*, relating to the controversy. Some examples:

> At the heart of controversy in the Southern Baptist Convention remains the nature of the Bible. What is the Bible? Is it totally reliable or partially reliable? Is belief in scripture without error a viable option or must it yield to critical research?

Simpson presents an enlightened history of higher criticism, then defines and critiques neo-orthodoxy in a way that pleases SBC conservatives:

> "Neo" is a term meaning new as contrasted to the "old" orthodoxy. While much of the same language of "old" orthodoxy is retained, the words have different meanings. In effect, both sides use the same vocabulary but use a different dictionary. This system emphasizes experience. Its obvious weakness is subjectivity—the same as classical liberalism. The priesthood of the believer, soul competency and Christian liberty are easily abused. Establishing doctrine is difficult. Neo-orthodoxy is much like a house built on shifting sand. Doctrinal positions change according to the ever-vacillating tide of culture. Doctrinal shifts permit ethical fluctuation and new "norms" are developed. Instead of being a thermostat helping to regulate the standards of a culture, churches become a thermometer reflecting them. Neo-orthodox theology is intentionally vague while stressing interpretation. It allows man to be the final rule while calling for an ever-expanding parameter of pluralism.[41]

Simpson sharply rebukes seminary presidents Dilday and Honeycutt for entering the controversy.

> The use of their platform for speech making must be questioned. Is it the business of seminary presidents to set theological agenda? Do they have a right to be sectarian in interpretive matters when all the people provide for the ongoing of the institution they serve? Does their protection in a seminary setting permit them to make questionable accusations? How is the student sitting in the chapel for convocation to feel while hearing a conviction he holds ridiculed by the label heresy? [42]

Simpson further diverges from other editors in criticizing the appointment of an ordained woman by the Home Mission Board. He notes that "the church [which decides to ordain a woman] is autonomous but the boards and agencies of the SBC are not." By giving financial support to an ordained woman, Simpson argued, the Home Mission Board is "placing fellow Baptists in the awkward position of supporting something or someone that violates their conscience." [43]

Simpson printed a hard-hitting interview with Roy Honeycutt, unlike that of any other state editor, asking the Southern Seminary president, among other things, about his theology, call for a "holy war" against "independent fundamentalists," and his refusal to debate Paige Patterson. The interview consumed over two large-sized pages in the *Indiana Baptist*.[44]

Indiana's Simpson is the exception among denominational editors in raising many of the questions which conservatives want agency executives to answer. In his questions and criticisms, Simpson challenges what has virtually become a corporate dogma for moderates and many agency people, that of "unity amidst diversity." Simpson is bold enough to wonder out loud if the diversity in theology has not gone too far.

Simpson's paper has only 8,500 circulation. Certianly not a power to be reckoned with when compared to the circulation of Daley's "old-line established state papers," which Daley says have remained "loyal" to denominational structures and the accomodation of diversity on the nature of Biblical truth. Does this "loyalty" entail a middle-ground or partisan position in the controversies?

A content analysis study of editorials in all state papers should be made. Here we will only examine and compare editorials relating to the controversy from October, 1984, through September, 1985, in four papers: Kentucky's *Western Recorder*, Missouri's *Word and Way*, Tennessee's *Baptist and Reflector*, and the *Arkansas Baptist Newsmagazine*.

The four papers rank in number of editorials relating to the subject as follows: *Western Recorder*, 21; *Word and Way*, 16; *Baptist and Reflector*, 14; *Arkansas Baptist Newsmagazine*. 2.

In one editorial relating to the controversy, Arkansas Editor Everett Sneed suggests characteristics which church messengers might consider in voting for new officers in Dallas: doctrinally sound, proven denominational commitment, encourager of major denominational interests, and high integrity.[45] Hardly political. Sneed's second editorial merely declares Biblical doctrine to be "the bedrock of evangelism." [46] Sneed obviously endeavors to steer a neutral course between both warring camps.

In 1983, *Baptist and Reflector* Editor Alvin Shackleford endeared himself to conservatives by stating that he was "disturbed" by what he had "found" in the Hollyfield thesis which indicated a decline of orthodoxy as students progressed through their studies at Southern. Shackleford said "the thesis must prompt a serious examination of the current state of Southern Baptist theological education" by trustees, administration, faculty, and the denomination.[47] But, in the period of this study, he is more neutral in the conflict. However, he is less restrained than his Arkansas colleague in commenting directly on problems, as he sees them, and personalities active in the conflict.

In one editorial during the recent 12 months studied, Shackleford suggests that Satan might be behind the controversy.[48] The editor does not say that Satan inspired the theological drift alleged by conservatives, or that the Devil fired up the conservatives to try and destroy fellowship in the SBC, as many moderates claim. He let readers decide.

Shackleford commends Charles Stanley for sermons on love and reconciliation.[49] He does not commend Stanley for allegations of liberalism in some agencies.

Personalities, theology, diversity or conformity, and control or freedom are all issues in the controversy, Shackledford says. But there is one additional issue "which overshadows everything written [in this editorial] Do Southern Baptists love, trust, and respect each other and each other's beliefs?" [50] Does he mean to criticize conservatives who do not "respect" the employment of denominational teachers who do not believe in inerrancy? Again, he let readers decide.

In other editorials, Shackleford calls for prayer, a moratorium on resolutions, a reconciliation committee, and restraint from both sides. There is nothing here to rankle either side.

Shackleford ventures into deeper waters than Arkansas' Sneed, but does not align himself with either camp.

In two editorials during the period, Missouri's Bob Terry speaks of convention "politicians". [51] In three opinions, Terry raises the flag for SBC seminaries: he reports on abstracts of belief which professors at his alma mater, Southern, are required to sign;[52] he prints a guest editorial by Southern professor, Page H. Kelley, "On What the Bible Means to Me;" [53] he writes about "what's right" with the Southern Baptist Convention.[54]

Terry says the Devil must be "laughing" at the controversy.[55] In other editorials, he asks for prayer, a special study committee, a professional parliamentarian for the convention, and the pursuit of peace.

In still another, he notes that Charles Stanley's church sponsored 78 "independent" missionaries, then commends the Atlanta pastor and SBC president for saying that the church needs to give more money to SBC missions.[56]

The Missouri editor adroitly manages to laud and criticize both moderate Kenneth Chafin and conservative Paul Pressler in one editorial about comments made by the two men in public media. First, on their appearance on the Donahue television show, where Pressler "responded to Donahue's questions [about whether Jews will go to Heaven] with a very clear statement about the Baptist position that faith in Christ is the only way to salvation." Chafin, Terry notes with dismay, "unexpectedly dodged the issue [and] said the Bible says one is to 'love God and love our neighbor as ourselves. That pretty well sums it up.' "

Second, Terry refers to a story in the *Richmond Times-Dispatch* which presents Chafin as offering a "cease-fire in the convention's holy war," so "Southern Baptists [can] get back to the tasks of evangelism, missions, and education." Terry notes that in the same article, Pressler reportedly said, "Peace and harmony . . . will return" when agency leaders realize their "responsibility to the rank-and-file Southern Baptists which they have not been fulfilling. The problem is liberal theology, not the talking about," Pressler is quoted as saying. Pressler then, according to Terry, "suggested that a cease-fire at this time would be a disadvantage to the conservative-fundamentalists. 'We are now in a position to deal with [liberal theology] and it can no longer be pushed under the rug."

Declared Terry:

> Pressler was right when, with clarity, he articulated the Baptist commitment to salvation . . . Chafin was wrong when he allowed other concerns to prevent him from a clear declaration of the way of salvation.

Chafin was right when he evidenced a cooperative spirit by offering a cease-fire in the holy war. Pressler was wrong when he seemed more interested in contending for his positions than in cooperating to bring wholeness back to Southern Baptists.[57]

Terry's editorial aptly illustrates the concern of the great majority of state editors. They do not believe the theological diversity in the agencies is so broad as to be of alarm. If the conservatives would lay down their "arms" and get back to the table of cooperation, the trouble would be over.

Jack Sanford, editor of the *Western Recorder*, the fourth state paper in this survey, offers little comfort to SBC conservatives in his 21 editorials during the period. "The basic problem among Southern Baptists," he says, "is lack of respect for each other.[58] All Baptists believe the Bible is inspired.[59] Baptist institutions are under fire for being liberal. They are not." [60]

Sanford uses the phrase "child's play" for Jimmy Draper's warning that his church might escrow its gifts to the Cooperative Program, should Stanley not get elected in Dallas.[61] Sanford commends Charles Stanley for saying he wants to become more involved in Southern Baptist missions.[62]

In the same editorial, Sanford admits he didn't vote for Stanley in Kansas City—which is no surprise to most readers. In both editorials, Sanford calls for support of the Cooperative Program and SBC agencies.

Sanford can be critical of moderates, though not for theological reasons. He slams Duke McCall for participating in an interview with Paige Patterson about SBC problems for Jerry Falwell's *Fundamentalist Journal*. Sanford can "understand" Patterson lending his name to Falwell's magazine, but why should McCall sully himself in such a publication.[63]

Sanford is unhappy with moderates Mr. and Mrs. Robert Crowder for their intention to go to court against the SBC unless their grievances against Stanley's parliamentary rulings in Dallas are redressed by the Executive Committee. He concedes that their "chagrin and sense of injury is no doubt shared by thousands of messengers who were disappointed and angered by the parliamentary procedure at Dallas." [64] Yet he thinks "little good can come from brothers taking brothers into court to settle a dispute which is past history. Such an event will only open the wounds more widely and set back any hope of immediate peace." [65] (See chapter 10 for more details of this looming court case.)

Editorials are traditionally an editor's private opinion. The editor, if allowed independence, also plays the role of gate keeper in selection, placement, headlines, and all the other decisions which go into publishing news. The job description for Tennessee's editor states:

> [The editor] studies and appraises (1) all phases of Baptist work, both state and convention wide, (2) matters concerning other denominations, and (3) general state, national, and world-wide trends. [He] interprets them as they affect Christian life by expressing his position and ideas in editorials and other types of editorial content.[66]

The controversy has been most evident in the letters to the editor section of the state papers. Both sides have been well represented. Since Dallas, moderates appear to have used this opportunity more. Moderate letter writers and some editors in editorials have recently pounded Harold Hunter, a conservative pastor in Jacksonville, Florida who reportedly told a rally of conservatives that messengers from his church should "vote like I vote." Moderates call this "arrogance" and violation of the principle of soul liberty. Hunter counters that the pastor, as overseer of the church, "should do everything within his power to see that his church's wishes are expressed by the messengers. If the church is "overwhelmingly conservative in its theology, its messengers ought to reflect the same. If liberal, then liberal." [67]

Conservatives, in the Tennessee paper's letters to the editor column, have recently criticized editor Al Shackleford for comments on a letter from Jim Stroud, a pastor in Knoxville. Stroud, in objecting to Southern Seminary professor E. Glenn Hinson's leadership of a seminary extension study at Tennessee's Carson-Newman College, cited five quotations from Hinson's book, *Jesus Christ* (Consortium Books, 1975), indicating that Hinson believed the Gospel writers had embellished statements by Jesus. Shackleford printed Stroud's letter, adding the comment, "I have not read Hinson's book, but I am told by those who have read it that your five quotations are taken out of context and are not representative of the book's premise." [68]

Stung by the editor's accusatory comments, Stroud demanded that he name the persons who had said his allegations were "taken out of context." Stroud further challenged Hinson to "a public discussion of his book! If he will name the time, date, and place, I'll be there."

Three other writers came to Stroud's defense in the column. Alan Smith, of Knoxville, notes,

> . . . Hinson writes: "Some embellishment undoubtedly occurred"; . . . concerning the temptations of Jesus he

says, "In the interest of presenting Jesus as the Messiah-Servant, they or their sources could have created the account" . . .

Smith concluded, "I am in favor of removing Hinson or any other professor from our institutions who question the inspiration, inerrancy, infallibility, and historicity of the Bible."

The second Stroud defender, Edward (Tommy) Futrel said he had read Hinson's book with Stroud's letter in hand and had "found the book to be even worse than reported." Futrel quoted from Hinson's book (p. 57), " 'In the case of the gospels, one can safely conclude that a kernel of fact underlies the early church's handling of the material.' " Futrel suggested that Editor Shackleford read Hinson's book for himself" and then point out where Stroud quoted out of context or else offer a public apology" to Stroud.

The third defender, Thomas E. Gatton, said he had also read the book "and it is in the hands of 20 other pastors here in Knoxville, and I'm positive [Stroud's] quotes are in context." Gatton added that Shackleford's "kind of editorializing is one of the causes of discord in the Southern Baptist Convention."

Moderates, in defending Hinson, noted that the book was 10 years old, claimed that quotes were taken out of context and that attackers had acted unethically in distributing xerox copies of the book.

The shape and tone of the state paper is determined by the editor. He decides which articles to use from those submitted by agency executives and writers, outside of Baptist Press channels, and from other Southern Baptists. Occasionally, he may request an agency head to write something on a topic that relates directly to questions in the state about his institution. Take a recent situation in one state.

The editor was invited to "cover" a meeting of the state conservative fellowship. Around 100 pastors were present at this meeting, including some serving churches of over 2,000 members. Two of the pastors gave testimonies of how their faith had been damaged in a SBC seminary in the state. One said higher criticism had almost caused him to leave the ministry. Another recalled a professor asking in class, "Do any of you believe the Bible is without error?' When a few of us raised our hands, the professor laughed and said, 'Well, everybody deserves to be wrong at least once.' "

The two pastors named the seminary they had attended, but their testimonies were not reported in the state paper. Several weeks later the paper published an article on Biblical authority by the president of the seminary in question. No reference was made to the meeting of conservative pastors or the testimonies of the two pastors. But the president declared that every professor in his school stood behind the "authority of Scripture." [69]

Many such articles by heads of agencies under fire have appeared in state papers in recent years. Conservatives, when complaining of theological and other problems in agencies, can usually only gain access in letters to the editor.

Some articles are defensive, obviously intended to defuse criticisms by pastors and churches. Some are irenic, some combative. Sometimes emotions may cloud logic, as in a piece written by a former seminary dean, and published in several state papers. He wrote:

> The issue [between conservatives and moderates] is not "parity" of points of view [requested by Paige Patterson and Jimmy Draper] within our six seminaries. Paige Patterson does not have nor does he want theological parity at Criswell Bible Institute.

The writer did not note that the Criswell Center for Biblical Studies is owned and financially supported by the First Baptist Church of Dallas, in contrast to SBC seminaries which are owned and supported by all Southern Baptists, through the Cooperative Program, including members of First Baptist Church, Dallas.

The writer then continued his illogical course by lambasting a Southwestern Seminary trustee from FBC, Dallas.

> Ralph Pulley, a Dallas layman and member of the Southwestern Seminary board of trustees, made a motion at the recent meeting of that board for president Russell Dilday to stay out of denomiantional politics. Pulley is a member of First Baptist Church, Dallas, where W.A. Criswell is pastor and Paige Patterson is on the staff. Will Pulley balance his act by going to his local church and introducing a motion to instruct Criswell and Patterson to stay out of denominational politics? No, he won't. Here's why. Pulley wants to control Dilday. And Criswell wants to control Honeycutt.[70]

Again, the writer is, in effect, comparing "apples" and "oranges" in institutional ownership. Trustee Pulley has the "right" to oppose Dilday, since all Southern Baptists support Southwestern Seminary. What Criswell does is only the business of FBC, Dallas.

The Texas *Baptist Standard* provides a clear example of how opinion can be injected into reporting. A Baptist Press release of November 16, 1982, was written by Dan Martin. When the Standard reprinted it, they changed the designation of the moderate group from the phrase "moderate-conservative" faction, as used by Dan Martin, to "biblical conservative supporters of the convention."

A new paragraph was then inserted in the article under Dan Martin's byline, although he did not write the material. Seeming to discredit the conservatives, the new paragraph read:

> The Southern Baptist Convention has been torn the last four years by a group of biblical inerrantists seeking control of denominational institutions in the hope they can move the convention to a more fundamentalist-conservative stance. They have been opposed by a biblical conservative group who believes the Bible is 'truth without any mixture of error' as stated in the *Baptist Faith and Message* statement and who have defended the convention's agencies, institutions, and Cooperative Program plan of mission support.

Some conservatives have hinted at a conspiracy among state editors. Conscious or unconscious, some collusion probably does occur. It happens among partisans in all organizational struggles. The temptation is always there to take advantage of reported problems among one's critics.[71]

A state convention executive director of my acquaintance happened to be in Nashville shortly after the story broke on Judge Pressler's "secret" taping of his phone conversation with the Southern Seminary student. "I had to visit the bathroom," he recalls, "and had just entered a stall, when a couple of our state editors happened to come in. Not knowing I could hear every word being said, they discussed how to get the most possible mileage out of the story. I'm no fan of Judge Pressler's. I don't even know the man. But I was sickened by their plotting of how and when they would schedule their stories on the incidents. After they left, I went back to my hotel, packed my bags, and flew home without telling anyone why."[72]

The incident is, hopefully, not typical. Some state editors keep on "safe" ground by printing only material on which both sides can agree, and avoiding articles and editorials on differences, especially on the nature of Biblical inspiration. Some show their moderate "colors" in editorials. Baptist Press has improved in reporting adversarial incidents, although some agencies are still allowed to report on themselves in disturbing instances.

Overall, with the noticeable exception of the editor of the *Indiana Baptist*, state news journals tend to reflect the tilt in most agencies to the status quo of "unity amidst diversity" which moderates are desperate to maintain. This could hardly be expected otherwise since state papers, which are linked to national agencies through Baptist Press and other denominational media, are enmeshed in agency structures, from which they receive their subsistence. Right or wrong,

SBC agencies are under attack by conservatives, who claim the institutions they help support have violated sacred trust by permitting doctrinal deviation. Right or wrong, the denominational media tends to defend these agencies against those who are disturbing the corporate peace.

The struggle, as Nancy Ammerman succinctly indicates, is between elective and agency power. She is correct in observing that most staff [agency] power is still in the hands of moderates. This includes the SBC media, who can probably be expected to stand with the agencies, whether controlled by moderates or conservatives. To control the denominational media, the conservatives must elect sufficient numbers of trustees who will make policy and personnel changes in agencies. They can take charge of the national agencies by consistently winning elections at the national convention. State conventions may pose a more difficult challenge, especially in the Old South where moderates are strongest. The challengers could win on the national level and lose in most of the states. In such a case, the state editors will remain loyal to the structures in their respective states, whether conservative or moderate.

So the struggle continues between two powerful forces in what is presently the nation's largest non-Catholic denomination. What are the options? Where will it end? Which side will come out on top? We will consider these questions in the closing chapter.

REFERENCES

1   Mark Kelley: " 'Concerned' Arkansas Pastors Condemn 'Liberal Drift,' Call for 'Proper' Ballot in Dallas," *Arkansas Baptist Newsmagazine*, March 14, 1985, p. 11.

2   Jack Sanford: "Sanford's Perspectives," *Western Recorder*, April 9, 1985, p. 2.

3   See *The Quaterly Review*, July-August-September, 1985, p. 96 for a complete list of circulation figures of state papers.

4   See reference in chapter four to Odle's address.

5   Linda Lawson: "Sunday School Board Acknowledges Errors," *Baptist and Reflector*, July 17, 1985, pp. 1, 2.

6   "Trustees Adopt Response to Job Lesson Errors," *Arkansas Baptist Newsmagazine*, August 15, 1985, p. 13.

7   "Consultation of BSSB Staff Explores Biblical Authority," *Baptist and Reflector*, January 15, 1986, p. 2.

8   Jack Sanford, op. cit., August 25, 1985, p. 2.

9   Nancy Ammerman: "Organizational Conflict in a Divided Denomination: Southern Baptists and Abortion," Candler School of Theology, Presented to the Meetings of the Society for the Scientific Study of Religion, Savannah, Georgia, and the Conference on Religion and the Political Order, Hilton Head Island, South Carolina, October, 1985, p. 19.

10   Claude W. Howe, Jr.: "From Houston to Dallas: Recent Controversy in the Southern Baptist Convention," "The Controversy in the Southern Baptist Convention," A Special Issue of *The Theological Educator*, Published by Faculty of New Orleans Baptist Theological Seminary, 1985, p. 44.

11   *The Tie*, September-October, 1984, pp. 4, 5.

12   Ibid.

13   Ibid., July-August, 1985, p. 5.

14   Ibid., November-December, 1985, p. 5.

15   Norman Jameson: "Anti-abortion Efforts Grab Top Attention," *Baptist Messenger*, December 19, 1985, p. 8.

16   James M. Dunn: "Reflections," *Report from the Capital*, October, 1985, p. 15.

17   Richard V. Pierard, "The Christian Right Threat to Evangelical Christianity," *Report from the Capital*, November/December, 1985, p. 4 (adaptation of a paper delivered as a Theological Fellowship Lecture at Southwestern Theological Seminary).

18   *Southern Baptist Advocate*, September/October, 1984, pp. 1, 14.

19   *Book of Reports*, Southern Baptist Convention, 1985.

20   The BP story appeared in most, if not all of the state Baptist papers. See, for example, *Rocky Mountain Baptist*, August 6, 1981, p. 4. To my knowledge none of the state papers reprinted stories from *The Tennessean*.

21   Kirk Loggins: "Baptist Board Must Pay Ex-Worker $400,000," *The Tennessean*, July 24, 1981, p. 1.

22   James C. Hefley: "Former Southern Baptist Sunday School Board Officer Wins Settlement," *Christianty Today*, October 2, 1981, pp. 46-50. Several volumes of depositional testimony are available for review in the archives of the Third Circuit Court in Nashville. Board trustees declined to pay for a printed record of the trial.

23   Correspondence from C.R. Daley, September 16, 1981.

24   *Book of Reports*, op. cit., p. 12.

25   Correspondence from W.C. Fields, May 8, 1984.

26   Baptist Press Release, 9-20-84.

27   Telephone Interview with Pressler.

28   Correspondence from Judge Paul Pressler, March 12, 1986.

29   Follow-up of September 17th article, Baptist Press, September 18, 1984.

30   *Word and Way*, February 28, 1985, p. 2.

31   *Book of Reports*, op. cit., p. 8.

32   Walter B. Shurden: "The Erosion of Denominationalism: The Current State of the Southern Baptist Convention," Address Delivered at Annual Meeting of the South Carolina Baptist Historical Society, November 12, 1984.

33   Alvin Shackleford: "Editorial," *Baptist and Reflector*, February 21, 1985, p. 4.

34 *Baptist and Reflector*, p. 5, August 21, 1985.

35 Bob Terry: "Thoughts," *Word and Way*, September 27, 1984, p. 2.

36 Ibid., February 28, 1985, p. 2.

37 Jack Sanford, op. cit., February 12, 1985.

38 Ibid., February 26, 1985.

39 Ibid., April 9, 1985.

40 From taped lecture to Southern Seminary class, as cited in previous chapters.

41 David Simpson: "Simpson Says...," *Indiana Baptist*, May 21, 1985, p. 2.

42 Ibid., September 18, 1984, p. 2.

43 Ibid., January 8, 1985, p. 2.

44 David Simpson: "Personal Interview with Dr. Roy L. Honeycutt, President, Southern Seminary, *Indiana Baptist*, November 20, 1984, pp. 2, 3, 8.

45 J. Everett Sneed: "The Editor's Page," *Arkansas Baptist Newsmagazine*, May 23, 1985, p. 3.

46 Ibid., August 29, 1985.

47 Alvin Shackleford, "Editorial," p. 4, March 17, 1982. The *Southern Baptist Journal* reprinted the editorial and gave it wide distribution. The title of the 1976 thesis, cited earlier in this book, is: *A Sociological Analysis of the Degrees of "Christian Orthodoxy" Among Selected Students in the Southern Baptist Theological Seminary*. It was approved by G. Willis Bennett (Chairman), E. Glenn Hinson, and Henlee Barnette of the faculty.

48. Alvin Shackleford: "Editorial," p. 4, March 27, 1985.

49 Ibid., February 27, 1985.

50 Ibid., May 8, 1985.

51 Bob Terry: "Thoughts," as cited above, April 11 and June 6, 1985.

52 Ibid., November 15, 1985.

53 Ibid., April 25, 1985.

54 Ibid., May 30, 1985.

55 Ibid., April 11, 1985.

56 Ibid., October 18, 1985.

57 Ibid., August 15, 1985.

58 Jack Sanford, op. cit..

59 Ibid., November 6, 1985.

60 Ibid., June 11, 1985.

61 Ibid. April 16, 1985.

62 Ibid., November 13, 1985.

63   Ibid., May 14, 1985.

64   Ibid., September 10, 1985.

65   Ibid., September 24, 1985.

66   *Baptist and Reflector*, August 21, 1985, p. 5.

67   Bill Moore: "Insults to Lay People" and Harold F. Hunter: "Hunter Responds," "Letters to Editor," *Baptist and Reflector*, January 15, 1986, p. 5.

68   The "letters to the editor" were printed in the February 12 and 19, 1986 issues of the *Baptist and Reflector*. By quoting statements which the letter writers to be in Hinson's book, my purpose is to illustrate reader and editorial reaction in "letters to the editor." Readers should not make any judgments on Hinson's book from these comments, but should read the book themselves before forming an opinion.

69   I was present at the meeting.

70   Walter B. Shurden: "What Happened to the 'Baptist' Part in 'Southern Baptist?'" *Western Recorder*, August 5, 1981. The article was carried in a number of other papers.

71   Article, *The Baptist Standard*, Nov. 24, 1982, p. 3.

72   The executive related this to me at the Dallas, 1985 convention.

10 SCENARIOS AND SOLUTIONS

Country comedian Jerry Clower, a deacon in the First Baptist Church of Yazoo City, Mississippi is an optimist of sorts. "When this fight's over," he says, "there'll be more cats and there'll be more Baptists." [1]

But will they be in the Southern Baptist Convention?

Walter Shurden, staunch moderate and strict denominationalist, is not laughing. Shurden, a respected church historian, sees our Southern Baptist tomorrow as "bleak, very bleak. It is heavily overcast. Let no one distort or pretty-up the picture. It is heavily overcast. This is the worst that we have ever had. It threatens to undo us as a denomination." [2]

Henry Huff, whom moderates elected as Convention second vice president at Dallas while many conservative voters were away, says only three conditions can change the direction of control by conservatives: God's will must be "preeminent"; The Peace Committee must "accomplish a great deal"; Moderates must have more votes than conservatives in Atlanta.[3]

H. Franklin Paschall, a former SBC president and retired as pastor from First Baptist Church, Nashville, a "conservative in theology" with the Bible as "the Book of my life," warns that "a split or splintering is not only possible but inevitable unless we mend our ways." [4]

Shurden and Paschall are talking about division, Huff a conservative takeover. W. A. Criswell does not forsee a split so much as a gloomy future for conservatives. "I think we will . . . gradually acquiesce [to liberalism]." [5] Criswell is pessimistic in predicting the future of Baptist educational institutions in light of the history of other mainline denominations. "All the great old universities of the world were established by the church for religious purposes—to train the ministry and godly lay people. All of us know the great old schools are now completely secular. All are lost to the faith. They are infidel institutions." 6

Criswell has in mind such institutions as the University of Chicago (established by Baptists) and Vanderbilt University (founded by Methodists). Both have religion departments, of high academic reputation, but which hardly represent the conservative Biblical faith of their founders.

Criswell believes "infidels" are slowly taking over Southern Baptist colleges and seminaries. He sees irreversible trends indicating that the denomination is following the downward path of the United Methodists, Presbyterians, and other mainline denominations which have drifted from Biblical moorings, downgraded traditional evangelism, and concentrated on structures and social salvation. "The death that I see in these old-line denominations is coming to our Southern Baptist Convention . . . little by little," he laments.7 Moderates, of course, deny this passionately, but in truth many similarities between beliefs and practices of SBC moderates and their counterparts in the more liberal mainline denominations can be seen.

Jimmy Draper, who preceded Charles Stanley as SBC president, is not quite as gloomy as the man on whose staff he once served. But Draper does believe "we have problems" which we must face. "They are not insurmountable . . . they are not unscalable. But we do have some things which need to be addressed." 8

The one thing on which leaders on both sides agree is that the crisis is real and very grave.

These facts are clear:

The division is between two factions of "true believers," each contending for a different orthodoxy around which they say Southern Baptists must unite.

Conservatives rally around Biblical inerrancy, which, they say, is the belief of the founders and the foundation of the denomination. The historic belief that the Bible is without error, conservatives say, is now being replaced in institutions with a leaky neo-orthodoxy that allows man to decide what is truth and what is error in the Bible. They want agencies to reverse this "doctrinal drift" and shore up the Biblical authority and doctrine held by the founders. There is a limit to the theological diversity which conservatives will allow.

Moderates, who acclaim Biblical authority in their own way, hold to "unity amidst diversity" upon which, they say, the denomination was founded and by which it holds together, enabling Baptists who differ on doctine to do evangelism, missions, education, and benevolence together. Moderates say there is more that presently unites than divides Southern Baptists.

Both sides appeal to the denominational heritage, conservatives to the theology and moderates to the ecclesiology, of the founders. Both are right. The founders, and almost all the influentials until around 1940-50, with the possible notable exception of E.Y. Mullins, held to inerrancy. They also were committed to "unity amidst diversity" expressed in cooperative stewardship and ministry. But, conservatives say, this is now negated because the denomination has moved to the left, with some elements having trampled down the doctrinal hedge which the founders erected.

The struggle between the orthodoxies of theology and ecclesiology and uniformity versus diversity is mirrored in the history of many denominations. Southern Baptists, having been insulated in the South for over a century, are latecomers to the battlefield. In asserting that a doctrine of Biblical errancy leads into classical liberalism, institutional decline, and decay, the conservatives have history on their side. In claiming that the theology of neo-orthodoxy dampens evangelism and chills church growth, conservatives have denominational demographics in their "corner". Moderates can hardly argue otherwise and so they seldom deal in comparisons of church growth.

Each side, in respect to its orthodoxy, accepts the "slippery slope" theory, holding that, once departure from the norm is sanctioned, the rush downhill will begin. Conservatives fear that, if they are turned back, the agencies will "slide" more rapidly into "liberalism". Moderates fear that, if conservative churches are allowed to support only the agencies they like, the Cooperative Program method of financing will soon be lost.

The differences also run deep on the role of the church in society. This can be seen in the trans-denominational alliances in which each faction participates. Many conservatives are allied with the so-called Religious Right in the crusade to return the nation to traditional values. So, they support amendments to overturn the Supreme Court ruling on abortion, restore school prayer as allowed before 1962, and return "traditional values" to textbooks.

Moderates are concerned about moral values, too, but they are more schizophrenic on moral legislation than conservatives. Moderates, for example, support laws against racial discrimination (as do conservatives), but generally are generally passive about legislation regulating personal sexual morality.

Moderates, who see the religious right as a threat to society, network with ecumenists and others who have a different agenda. Some see not humanism or secularism as the enemy, but the conservative drum-beaters for a religious and moral reformation.

SBC conservatives and moderates tend further to hold different perspectives on politics, foreign policy, and the economy.

But the bottom-line is always theology and specifically whether the Bible "has . . . truth" or is "truth, without any mixture of error."

Where does the struggle now stand?

First, a brief recap of developments. Moderates first campaigned for the presidency, electing Jimmy Allen, a personal conservative who would stave off the threat of a perceived conservative militant and uphold the status quo in agencies.

Conservatives triumphed in 1979, and have won every presidential election through 1985. Moderate vote percentages have ranged from 39.0 percent to 48.64 percent of the vote. Their best showing came in 1979.

With seven presidential victories and five slates of conservative trustees, the conservatives have demonstrated elective power. After seven painful losses, moderates see their influence slipping in agencies.

The heat is on in every agency, some more than others. No seminary administrators or professors under fire from conservatives have resigned. Some seminary teachers have transferred to Baptist colleges where more diversity in theology is acceptable and there is less pressure from conservative pastors. Students holding to inerrancy are becoming bolder. The conservative "Spurgeon Club," for example, recently gained administrative approval at Midwestern Seminary and conservative students were elected to student offices.

Two of the agency heads who have attracted much conservative ire, Foy Valentine and James Dunn, are standing their ground on principles they have espoused. Valentine's Christian Life Commission, however, has been forced by adoption of "Sanctity of Life Day" to provide churches more help in fighting abortion.

Except for the one statement from Keith Parks, the Foreign Mission Board has been neutral. The head of the Home Mission Board has not positioned himself on either side.

The Sunday School Board, under a new administrator, is turning back to the conservativism which reigned before the Elliott commentary on Genesis was published. Some editors may privately hope for a moderate comeback in convention elections. If so, they are keeping quiet. There will be no daring publishing departures from traditional doctrine in the foreseeable future.

Baptist Press is being watched closely, as are some state papers. But the denominational press system continues to be linked closely with agencies. While making extra efforts to show balance in news stories of controversies, BP and most of the state papers will not be cheering the conservatives on.

Conservatives hold elective power at the moment. Moderates still have the majority of staff power, but their grip is weakening.

The controversy has, of course, spilled over into many state conventions. Here—especially in the Old South states—conservatives are much weaker than on the national level, perhaps because moderates in states with the largest Baptist population have more friends in state convention bureaucracies, or perhaps because moderates are becoming more skilled in ecclesiastical politics. Moderates in North Carolina won all state convention offices in 1985. Their campaign was reportedly led by a "pro" from the Democratic Party.

Because the conflict is most heated on the national level, Baptist colleges excepting Baylor, have been little troubled. Conservatives, however, see a continuing secular drift in some colleges, particularly in eastern Old South states, evidenced by fewer ministerial students, less preaching in chapel, and hiring of more non-Baptist faculty. Colleges with larger endowments are finding it less necessary to depend on Cooperative Program support.

Currently a furor is raging over the decision by Wake Forest trustees to establish themselves as a self-perpetuating board.[9] Wake Forest's president is a Presbyterian. Chapel attendance is low. Endowment is high. A big chunk of the endowment comes from the R.J. Reynolds tobacco fortune. Moderates and agency executives in North Carolina bemoan the step taken, which will probably lead to greater secularization, something which goes unmentioned.

So the situation stands at this writing. Conservatives have the momentum. Moderates are desperately trying to make a comeback at the national convention level and shore up lost influence in agencies. They can only do this by electing a president who will do their wishes, or get appointment power, leading to trustee nominations, moved to the states.

Because conservatives have not been winning by large majorities, the moderates could, by herculean efforts, stage their comeback at the next convention, which is held in Georgia where moderates are strong. Atlanta could be the moderates last "hurrah" in their fight to prevent a conservative takeover.

Whatever the predictions for Atlanta, an uneasy calm prevails, while the Peace Committee is striving to find compromises with which both sides can live.

All the while, a troublesome court suit, brought by lay moderates Robert S. and Julia Crowder [10] and Henry C. Cooper against the SBC and its Executive Committee, simmers. The petition, filed in federal district court in Atlanta, charges that the plaintiffs were "irreparably harmed" by "erroneous rulings" of Charles Stanley representing the SBC as its presiding officer at the Dallas convention. They allege that Stanley violated their "rights" by "depriving" them "of the opportunity . . . to vote" on matters relating to the Committee on Boards." The plaintiffs are asking the court, on the basis of Bylaws 16, 32, and 35, to declare the election of the Committee on Boards in Dallas invalid, and to allow "any individual or a slate of individuals" to be nominated by messengers in opposition to persons offered by the Committee on Committees. Should the court decide in plaintiffs' favor, two Committees on Boards could conceivably be voted on at Atlanta. The Executive Committee is a defendant in the case, because it voted after Dallas to "affirm" Stanley and the conservative majority vote at Dallas. [11] Former Attorney General Griffin Bell has been hired to defend the SBC.

The Executive Committee has voted to recommend to the Atlanta convention that two sentences be added to Bylaw 16, allowing nominations to the Committee on Boards and Standing Committees from the floor. The additions would require that no messenger be allowed to nominate more than one person at a time. This would prevent a messenger from presenting a slate of nominees. It could also result in long business sessions, as each challenge is debated.

The Executive Committee action has not succeeded in persuading the plaintiffs to drop their suit. The Executive Committee reports that it has already incurred over $100,000 in legal expense in preparation of the defense. Total defense expenses are predicted to run as high as $250,000, and perhaps even more if, as expected, a decision in plantiffs' favor is taken up the appeal ladder to the Supreme Court. All expenses will have to be paid from Cooperative Program contributions from churches.

With the concern over the suit, much attention has centered on the Crowders and Cooper, who originated the suit. They apparently have substantial financial backing from unknown sources.

The Crowders, who tried in previous conventions to change SBC bylaws to require minimum Cooperative Program giving by candidates for Convention office, are members of Southside Baptist Church, Birmingham. Cooper is a deacon of First Baptist Church,

Windsor, Mo. Their pastors have been vigorous in opposing the conservative movement in their respective states.

The suit has gained widespread national attention, even though, if successful, it would merely allow Convention messengers to make substitutions on the Committee on Boards as they are already able to do with trustees offered by the Committee on Boards.

Many denominational executives have joined conservatives in expressing dismay over the legal action. Paige Patterson says the lawsuit is in "direct contradiction to the clear and lucid instructions" of Scripture forbidding Christians to go to court against one another.

Moderates tend to agree with the Biblical injunction. But, says David Sapp, a Georgia pastor, "we should not allow our objections to the lawsuit to obscure the wrong that was done in Dallas. Every Baptist should ask what has driven a fine Christian like Bob Crowder to such an action."

Former SBC Second Vice-President Gene Garrison, pastor of First Church of Oklahoma City, whose church defied the local association in ordaining women deacons, "understands Bob Crowder's frustation . . . The abuse of parliamentary procedure and the totalitarian tyranny of the presidential chair [at Dallas] is probably the most frustrating thing I have ever experienced at any meeting of any kind." Garrison, however, does not think a lawsuit "is the way to handle this. I am afraid the reaction to the suit [will] be even more negative than was the reaction to the way the president ignored parliamentary procedure."

SBC attorney James P. Guenther of Nashville, believes the "real controversy" is deeper than an argument over Robert's Rules of Order and that "every event . . . is placed, or shoved into the context of the current theological debate. Mr. Crowder's complaints about parliamentary procedure are merely symptoms of fundamental differences within the Southern Baptist Convention." [12]

The Peace Committee, with its diversity of members, brings together leaders from both factions and respected persons who have not identified themselves with either group. There have been summits before, but always off the record, with participants from both sides only saying afterwards, "We came out as divided as we went in."

The Peace Committee, in a sense, is an extended summit. It has a tough-talking chairman, Charles Fuller, who maintains that neither the "moderate" nor the "fundamental" position is "the center" of SBC life. "The true center is where we keep faith with what we have been historically." [13] Finding such a center may not be easy.

The Peace Committee has heartened conservatives with two important findings: One, the dispute is basically theological and concerns the nature of Bible truth. Two, the concern for sound doctrine is directed at institutions. The issue is not a creed for the churches, as moderates once maintained. In Chairman Fuller's view, it focuses on the balance between the accountability an employee owes to his employer (what agency people owe to SBC churches) and the accountability a believer owes to God.

Fuller further notes that the first meeting of the Peace Committee focused not just on whether there is a diversity of ideas, but on what impact such diversity would have "in seminary classrooms, lesson preparations, and roles of denominational leadership. We are all aware that, as Baptists, we firmly believe that everybody has a right to their own interpretation." The critical question is "how much diversity of interpretation can we have and still work together in denominational undertakings." [14]

Jimmy Draper, in 1983, urged the appointment of a "blue ribbon committee" which would "draw up . . . a set of [theological] parameters, and then present [them] for convention debate and possible adoption." [15] Draper's "irreducible minimum theology"— that "a person must subscribe to in order to be acceptable as a professor at one of our schools, or as a worker, writer, or policymaker in one of our agencies"—includes Christ's Deity, substitutionary atonement, "literal, bodily" resurrection, and justification by grace through faith. Draper does not omit Scripture, which he says must be taken as "the final authority" and basis for these "deep beliefs and convictions." [16]

Draper's parameters have been rejected by moderates as another attempt to creedalize Southern Baptists. After two presidential losses following Draper's presidency, moderates are reportedly now taking a closer look at "basic" doctrines. Jack Harwell, editor of Georgia's *Christian Index*, predicts that the Peace Committee will "come up with something approximating" Draper's bottom-line doctrines. Some now say that moderates dropped their marbles when they didn't accept those minimums when Draper proposed them." [17]

Draper did not use the term "inerrancy" in his presidential sermon at Pittsburgh where he presented his "irreducible" minimums. Should moderates agree to his parameters, the knotty argument over whether the Bible is without error in text or only in message will remain.

This is not the first time church bodies have, in seeking to preserve unity, wrestled over words and phrases. The great dispute in the fourth century was over the relationship of the Son to the Father in the Trinity. One faction, led by Arius, held that Christ was of a different (*heteros*) essence or substance from the Father. Christ was divine because of his virtuous life and obedience to God's will, they said. The group led by Athanasius declared that Christ had existed from all eternity with the Father and was of the same essence (*homoousios*) as the Father, although he was a distinct personality. Passionate and sometimes violent disagreement raged among church leaders for years, until Athanasius' view prevailed over most of the Church.

Arianism became the heresy which, in time, led to the Socinianism of the 16th century, which helped create the climate for humanistic and naturalistic interpretation of Scripture.[18]

Many theologians today believe that the nature of the Bible is the critical battleground of the 20th century. The fourth century dispute over the nature of Christ ultimately ended in division. They could not find a middle ground between *heteros* and *homoousios*. It may be so among Southern Baptists on the question, What is "truth, without any mixture of error for its matter?"

The Peace Committee was chosen to be representative of right, left, and middle in Southern Baptist life. Assuming the committee can agree on a bottom-line theology for denominational employees, how will this be enforced in agencies?

When Charles Stanley asked faculty at Southeastern Seminay about Biblical truth, he was answered with stony silence. Stanley had no authority to demand answers. In 1986, the convention-elected Peace Committee will have sent sub-committees of four members each, going to 11 of the 20 national SBC agencies before the Atlanta convention. The purpose of the subcommittees, said Committee Chairman Charles Fuller, is "neither a whitewash nor an inquisition. I think the [Peace] Committee is genuinely trying to avoid those extremes." They "go in the spirit of love and candor and with the major purpose being to sensitize agencies to convention concerns and to solicit their active participation with us in the peace-making process." This is all well and good, but Fuller lists no specifics of inquiry.

Each sub-committee will have included both moderates and conservatives. They have met with the chief administrative officer, the chairman of the trustees, and, at seminaries, with the chief academic officer. Guidelines specified that "any faculty member or agency employee whose name enters into the discussion," may appear before the sub-committee or present a written statement if he or she wishes.[19]

Larry Lewis, the most active college president in the conservative camp, thinks the visits are a "good idea. Representatives of academic accrediting associations visit our campus and ask questions of faculty. We don't particularly enjoy this, but we cooperate in order to have the association's stamp of approval. I can't see why any seminary which needs the approval and gifts of Southern Baptists would object to such 'certification' from a duly appointed committee. We already require our faculty to affirm a strong statement of faith, which includes Biblical inerrancy. But if there was any question of our commitment, we would not object to a team elected by the Missouri Baptist Convention coming to our campus for interviews."

Lewis questions whether the sub-committees will dig deeply enough. "The concern of conservatives is with those who are teaching in the seminary. What do they believe about the Bible? As I understand the guidelines, teachers can volunteer to appear before the inquirers. Otherwise they will not be interviewed. If administrators give the standard answers they've been telling the press and if teachers in question are not interviewed, then, from the perspective of some of us, it could be another whitewash. Nothing will be solved. Everything will go on as before. The accrediting people who come to our school nose around. They talk to students and to any teacher they wish. They go into files. I'm not proposing that these investigators from the Peace Committee go to these extremes but I do think they need to find out what the teachers believe about the Bible and Christian doctrine."

Lewis sent a letter, to conservatives and "middle-roaders who believe the Bible with us" on the Peace Committee, "spelling out the importance of thorough inquiries." He expresses "hope that [interviewers] will do a thorough and complete investigation so there will be a full disclosure. If there are doctrinal problems in our institutions, we need to know that and set about to correct it. If not, we need to know that too." [20]

Shortly before this book went to press, the Peace Committee reported the findings of the inquirers. The "significant theological diversity" uncovered was no surprise to SBC insiders. The Peace Committee statement marks the first time a high-level denominational committee, composed of both conservatives and moderates, has gone on record in admitting that such diversity exists. The statement indicates that many of the allegations made by conservatives for many years, and given little credibility by most of the denominational press, are true. So that readers can judge for themselves, the complete statement is presented here.

The Peace Committee has completed a preliminary investigation of the theological situation in our SBC seminaries. We have found significant theological diversity within our seminaries reflective of the theological diversity within our wider constituency. These divergencies are found among those who claim to hold a high view of Scripture and who teach in accordance with, and not contrary to, the *Baptist Faith and Message* statement of 1963. Examples of the diversity include the following, which are intended to be illustrative but not exhaustive: (1) **Some accept and affirm the direct creation and historicity of Adam and Eve while others view them instead as representative of the human race its creation and fall.** (2) **Some understand the historicity of every event in Scripture as reported by the original source while others hold that the historicity can be clarified and revised by the findings of modern historical scholarship.** (3) **Some hold to the stated authorship of every book in the Bible while others hold that in some cases such attribution may not refer to the final author or may be pseudonymous.** (4) **Some hold that every miracle in the Bible is intended to be taken as an historical event, while others hold that some miracles are intended to be taken as parabolic.** (Author's emphasis)

The Peace Committee is working earnestly to find ways to build bridges between those holding divergent views so that we may all legitimately coexist and work together in harmony to accomplish our common mission. Please pray that we may find ways to use our diversity to win the greatest number to faith in Christ as Savior and Lord.[21]

The "cat" which so many denominational public relations people, along with most of the denominational press, has kept in the "bag" for so long is now out for all to see. The diversity now must be admitted by all. Some (how many, the report does not say) professors do not think early Genesis is real history. Some do not accept certain other Biblical events as stated by the "original source" as historical. Some do not think certain Biblical miracles actually happened as the Biblical writers say they did, but are to be interpreted as "parabolic."

Those who hold these views, the Peace Committee report says, "claim to hold a high view of Scripture and teach in accordance with and not contrary to the *Baptist Faith and Message* . . ." "Claim" likely indicates that some members of the Peace Committee do not believe that the *Baptist Faith and Message* is necessarily being honored.

Next on the Peace Committee agenda is a study of politics,

messenger registration and irregularities, presidential powers, "ongoing political activities in the convention", and "the effects and advisability of negative designation" in Cooperative Program giving to national and state Baptist Convention agencies and institutions.

The last item is of most concern to denominational agencies and workers. If churches are told they can exclude certain agencies from their Cooperative Program giving, many agencies may be forced to rearrange their budgets. Some agencies may benefit. Others may be hurt. The Cooperative Program method as practiced for over 50 years will be in disarray.

How will churches decide which agencies are "worthy" of financial support? Will denominational papers provide information on theological diversities at various institutions so churches can make good conscience decisions? Such information, pro and con, will, in the immediate future, more likely flow through independent papers and grapevines among both factions.

Many seminary professors and other denominational employees are understandably nervous about their job future. One SBC teacher, when preparing to give blood, was asked by the nurse if he was engaged in a hazardous occupation. "Yes," he answered, "I am a theologian."

Charles Stanley's reelection at Dallas was "deeply distressing" to one state editor who has survived attempts by conservatives to remove him from office because of his personal beliefs about Scripture. Another SBC moderate, active in the women's ordination movement, saw "[denominational] people frightened over their jobs; people hurting because of public accusations against their theological positions; . . . a male organization [of] committees seeking out heretics for censure or dismissal; the denial of the basic right of personal interpretation of scripture and, with that, the loss of the heart of Baptist life—the priesthood of believers." [22]

Whether such fears are realistic or not, there is real concern—"a circling and drawing in of the wagons," as one visitor to Southern and Southeastern seminaries recently put it—among denominational employees who have expressed controversial theological views in recent years. The fear is there because of the recognition that conservatives are dealing from strength and getting stronger, and because of statements from conservatives which give moderates in institutions little cause for comfort. As Tennessean Clay Frazier declares, " . . . The Dallas convention said to our institutional leadership, 'You can't ignore us any longer; you don't own the institutions, we do, and we demand they be run according to our convictions.' " [23]

Conservatives are not generally sympathetic to uneasiness among denominational employees who feel threatened. They say fear over the loss of once secure jobs, with good pay, is understandable, but ask where these employees were when some conservatives suffered career loss from speaking their convictions.

Millions of Southern Baptists pray that the Peace Committee will find solutions, acceptable to a majority, that will restore harmony to the denomination. The Committee was charged by the Dallas convention to

> determine the sources of the controversies in our Convention, and make findings and recommendations regarding these controversies, so that Southern Baptists might effect reconciliation and effectively discharge their responsibilities to God by cooperating together to accomplish evangelism, missions, Christian education, and other causes authorized by our constitution, all to the glory of God.[24]

Whether and to what extent the Committee will succeed in reaching these goals remains to be seen. Beleaguered moderates see the committee, in Roy Honeycutt's words, as "our best hope." [25] Conservatives appear to have adopted a wait-and-see attitude.

Beyond the Peace Committee, whatever its success, where are Southern Baptists going? At this point we will speculate on three possible scenarios and consider the results of each.

1. **What if the conservatives keep winning until they have an unquestioned majority of trustees on every agency board?**

There will certainly be no wholesale massacre in the agencies. Some executives and policies may be changed, just as happens when a new administration comes to power in Washington, but the new guys on the block will find themselves dependent upon the bureaucracies. In any case, many denominational employees will have already become "cooperative" with the conservative trustee majority. Long-time observer Louis Moore, religion editor for the *Houston Chronicle*, noted, as far back as 1983, that the rank-and-file of the Southern Baptist bureaucracy, "the curia," will go with the perceived winners, although in private they have sided with moderates.[26] Large scale firings do not occur when political parties change power in national and state governments. This will not happen in the case of a "takeover" by conservatives in the Southern Baptist Convention. Should such even be attempted, and even if the denominational press becomes captive to conservatives, the adverse publicity in independent journals and secular newspapers would be so great that trustees and administrators would retreat.

The future could be more clouded for agency heads who mounted public campaigns to defeat the conservative presidential candidate at Dallas, as did Roy Honeycutt and Russell Dilday, and Randall Lolley to a lesser extent. Still, conservatives stress that their first priority is not to fire any present employees, but to tighten doctrinal requirements for new adminstrators, teachers, and editors. To repeat Judge Paul Pressler: "When your house is flooding, you first try to stop the water coming in before you start cleaning up the mess." [27]

This is the "house cleaning" which some denominational employees fear. Shudders ran through seminaries when one state paper quoted Paige Patterson as saying that if he were president of a denominational seminary, "existing" faculty members would be replaced with teachers who believed in Biblical inerrancy. It was a typographical error. Patterson had actually said replace "exiting" teachers.[28] This would undoubtedly happen in cases where targeted individuals are nearing retirement age. They would be allowed to depart with grace and dignity.

James Bryant, pastor of Grand Avenue Church of Fort Smith, Arkansas, reflected the feelings of many conservatives when he told "concerned" pastors in Little Rock that doctrinal, not political motives are "behind" the conservative movement, adding,

> They [SBC moderates] are our brethren. They know and love the Lord . . . I can't be very hard on anybody else when I look at my own human sinfulness in the light of the Lord Jesus. As He has forgiven us, we ought to forgive one another.[29]

Forgiveness, however, is not likely to mean that a denominational administrator or professor, who blatantly steps over policy and doctrinal bounds, will be kept on. Warnings would first be given, then the individual given time to look for another position. In all situations, expect "old school" ties and traditional southern courtesy to allow denominational workers extensive "hearings," if they so desire, and special severance benefits in case resignation is recommended. In most instances, employees whose teaching and beliefs are perceived to be "out of bounds," would be given months to look for another job.

Moderates and institutionalists are also fearful that conservatives in command would kill the Cooperative Program. They cite low Cooperative Program percentages in churches pastored by some conservatives and conservative threats to escrow CP funds. Yet, these same conservatives say their churches will give more and the CP be strengthened when problems are solved, meaning a tightening of doctrinal standards and changes of some personnel and programs.

Adrian Rogers declares, "Every time we try to promote an increase for the Cooperative Program in our church, it seems that a professor or administrator in one of the agencies says or does something that is contrary to the conservative conscience and cools enthusiasm for giving more. Our church wants to give more, but we feel it is illogical and immoral to be asked to support what is inimical to our convictions." [30]

Exactly the opposite of what moderates have been predicting could happen. The Cooperative Program could take on new vigor as bellwether conservative churches up their percentages. However, some agency programs could suffer or even be killed by being cut out of the Cooperative Program or by permitting churches to exclude them from CP designations.

The Christian Life Commission and the Baptist Joint Committee on Public Affairs, two of the smaller agencies, would probably change leadership, assuming that the present executives do not make adjustments in programs desired by conservatives. Christian Life Commission pronouncements on "liberal" social causes and "leftist" revolutions in Latin America would probably be curtailed, if not entirely eliminated. Under new staff, the Christian Life Commission might then become a leader in the pro-life movement's crusade for a constitutional amendment to outlaw abortion.

The press system, which permits employees of agencies to write news stories about in-house problems and controversies, might not change. Human nature is the same when it comes to the temptation to hold back or cover up bad news in one's institution. The conservatives who now assail Baptist Press for protecting agencies could very well praise them for doing the same when they are in power.

As for state Baptist papers, conservatives will undoubtedly enjoy the editorials and the story selections more than they do now.

Conservatives have been complaining that much of what now passes for evangelism in agencies is something less. If conservatives take full control, more attention will be given to revivalistic and soul winning techniques from the "old-time religion." Baptisms will probably go up overall in the SBC under the leadership of persons who have a proven track record in local churches.

What will happen to the three "alternate" conservative seminaries—Criswell, Mid-America, and Luther Rice—with conservatives enthusiastically promoting denominational seminaries? Efforts will probably be made to bring the independents under the denominational umbrella, but trustees and administrations will probably say, "thanks, but no thanks" and remain independent. There is already at least one precedent for an "independent" school receiving Cooperative Program money from a state convention. William Jewell College, in Missouri, has its own self-perpetuating board of trustees. New trustees are presented to the Missouri Baptist Convention for "approval," and the convention counts Jewell as an institutional ministry. The same could happen with the three independent seminaries noted above.

SBC moderates have not yet given up the fight to turn back the conservative challenge. How will they respond to clear-cut conservative victory?

Moderates will likely continue giving through the Cooperative Program so long as conservatives do not move too fast, especially in the seminaries. If major changes, such as the firing of some presidents and several professors, should occur, then look for moderates to caucus and perhaps take drastic counteraction. Cecil Sherman has already said, "I will advise my church not to support a 'Jerry Falwell' [fundamentalist controlled] seminary. They may not listen, but I will tell them" [31] Many moderates would do what they castigated conservatives for threatening to do before Dallas: escrow funds designated for the Cooperative Program.

It is no secret that many, if not most, SBC seminary professors are unhappy about the conservative challenge and agenda. How would they respond to the firing of administrators and teachers who do not subscribe to inerrancy, or to pressure from administration and trustees to conform?

The upheaval in the Lutheran Church—Missouri Synod's Concordia Seminary immediately comes to mind. In 1974, Lutheran moderates, who held views on the Bible roughly similar to SBC moderates of today, were faced with a doctrinal crackdown by an administration, backed by a majority of trustees, holding to inerrancy. Forty-three faculty members and 400 students went on a sit-down strike. The administration waited a month, then issued an ultimatium of "no work, no pay." Most faculty members resigned, leaving only five teachers pledging loyalty to the seminary, and formed the breakaway Concordia Seminary in Exile. The new seminary later moved to Chicago where it is incorporated today as Christ Seminary— Seminex, an institution of the small Evangelical Lutheran Church, led by moderate pastors who left the Missouri Synod after the inerrancy crackdown. Christ Seminary reported 227 students in 1984. Concordia Seminary has 735 students, about the same number as when the walkout occurred.

Roy Honeycutt doesn't see Seminex as a possible "outcome" of seminary defections by Southern Baptist moderates. "We aren't going anywhere. There's no place to go." [32] But the Missouri Synod moderates did set up their own seminary and small denomination, and dissident SBC moderates could do the same.

Southern Baptist seminaries now enroll over 12,000 full-time students, plus over 14,000 engaged in part-time continuing education. How many would "defect" in a worst possible situation where administrators and numbers of faculty resign? One would be naive to assume that all would stick with the seminaries in such an eventuality. Presidents Honeycutt, Lolley, and Dilday all received resounding student and faculty applause in making chapel speeches opposing Charles Stanley and a conservative "takeover." Many of these students could follow them out.

A new denomination could result from seminary professor walkouts, student dropouts, and church pastor pullouts, just as happened among the Missouri Synod Lutherans. They might take the Cooperative Baptist Convention as a name for their denomination. This is hardly scare talk. It could happen. Already moderates and conservatives have held separate pastors' conferences before the annual convention. The two groups have also held separate meetings before or during many state conventions.

A denomination of Southern Baptist moderates would probably become more centralized to reflect the enthusiasm of moderates for strong agencies. They could be expected to develop strong fraternal ties with the American Baptist Churches in the U.S.A., which, with 1.6 million members, survives from the old Northern Baptist Convention. The two denominations might eventually merge to form one national American Baptist denomination. The combined groups would not likely be as large as a conservative controlled Southern Baptist Convention.

A denomination of SBC moderates would be strongest where moderates are now strongest, in such Old South states as Virginia, North Carolina, Maryland, Georgia, and Kentucky. State Baptist conventions in these states might align with the new moderate denomination, with a minority of churches electing to remain in the SBC. The so-called "pioneer" and "frontier" state conventions are believed to be more conservative and might be expected to remain virtually intact within a conservative-dominated SBC. An unassessable factor which might favor conservatives holding state conventions is the loyalty to SBC institutions built up through years of religious education. Even if they felt "mother" had become too narrow, many with less-than-conservative beliefs might stay in the fold and hope for the beloved parent to loosen the theological reins on her "children" in agencies.

However, many members of SBC "Women in Ministry" (WIM)

would likely affiliate with a denomination of moderates where they already have support for women's ordination. WIM is hardly appreciated by conservatives at the moment. None seem interested in seeking to remedy the tax disadvantage suffered by non-ordained women church staffers. A male "minister" of Christian education can receive a house allowance tax free, provided he is ordained, and many male staffers have been ordained for that reason. An unordained woman "director" of Christian education cannot. It may be that in pressing for women's ordination, which most conservatives conscientiously oppose, the WIM group has alienated sensitive conservatives who might have helped them in other areas. Or it may be that many conservatives are too chauvinistic and insenstive to tackle financial inequities dealt to women church professionals.

Should conservatives take full control, and should moderates split away to form their own denomination, would the new church body of moderates grow? The greatest increase might come during the first few years as sympathetic pastors and churches dribble out of the old SBC. The the new church body could then reach a plateau and start dropping in membership. Moderates together would likely have a much lower ratio of baptisms to members than is now true of the SBC. Churches which already have low baptisms would not likely improve in a new denomination.

A new denomination of moderates could be expected to follow the trend in mainline American denominations whose growth has been stymied by more liberal theology, more investment in social programs, and less attention given to evangelism. According to Harvard University scholar William Hutchinson, Presbyterian, Methodist, Episcopal, and similar mainline church bodies dropped from 76 percent of America's Protestant population in 1920 to 53 percent in 1984. Not only did they fail to gain substantial numbers of new members through evangelism, they were also unable to plug the leak of members to secular society. These mainline churches, Hutchinson found, lost members to secular society at twice the rate of conservative churches.[33] United Methodists, champions of religious pluralism, have seen Sunday school attendance drop from 4.2 million to 2.1 million in just the past 20 years! [34]

What of the denomination left behind with conservatives at the helm? It will obviously have an immediate drop in membership, stewardship, education, and missions, if a substantial number depart to join a new church body led by moderates. Then, if the leadership can rouse the grassroots for aggressive evangelism and missions, the old SBC could rebound and, within a few years, surpass the membership of the present SBC. This assumes that the conservative leadership will join in promoting the kind of cooperative missions and evangelism which flourished in the SBC in the 1950s.

SBC moderates now charge that conservatives are bent on taking the denomination away from its historic moorings to become a loose network of independent churches, much like the Baptist Bible Fellowship of ministers who get together once a year for only a super-charged pastors conference. This is not likely to happen.

Almost all of the conservative pastor leaders in the SBC attended denominational seminaries. Most are pastors of large churches with deep roots in denominational life. Tradition, loyalties, and a web of continuing relationships in denominational entities should keep these men loyal to the denomination.

A conservative dominated SBC could attract many rapidly growing independent Baptist churches. Some moderates think Jerry Falwell would even lead his flock of associated churches and fast-growing Liberty Baptist University into the SBC fold. Falwell might be more welcome on SBC platforms, but it is doubtful that he would submerge his power base to the interests of a wider fellowship.

2. **What if moderates and their allies should decisively turn back the conservative challenge and restore the much hallowed "unity amidst diversity" which characterized the SBC before 1979 and allowed neo-orthodoxy to develop in some institutions?**

Heretofore, moderates have tried to slow the conservative drive with five parliamentary actions: One, elect presidents who will appoint persons to the Committee on Committees who favor pluralism. Two, establish a minimum percentage for Cooperative Program giving from a presidential nominee's church, or at least require that the nominee's church stewardship record be made known to messengers before they vote. (With the almost ubiquitous denominational media, the latter now seems irrelevant.) Three, trim presidential appointment powers by requiring assent of the first and second vice presidents for naming members of the Committee on Committees. Four, require that members of the Committee on Committees be elected officers from state conventions. (They have been unsuccessful at this.) Five, provide that substitutions for nominees to the Committee on Boards be made from the floor of the Convention. They could win the fifth in the federal district court of Atlanta.

The election of officers comes early at the annual convention. If moderates could elect a candidate of their choosing (one who valued diversity over doctrinal purity) at the next convention, they might then move on at this and future conventions to pass bylaws limiting presidential appointment power and perhaps prevent conservatives, who are strong in popular voting, from ever making a comeback. The SBC would then be back to the pre-1979 "unity amidst diversity" which allowed denominational employees to affirm the *Baptist Faith and Message* while personally believing that the Biblical text contains errors.

Board nominations would again be made primarily on the basis of individuals' commitment to cooperation with agencies. Serious questioning of an agency's program or teaching at a seminary would disqualify anyone from consideration. Personal belief, no matter how conservative, would be respected, as was true before 1979. But, conservatives perceived as change-minded would be passed over, as happened before 1979.

With friendlier trustees, agency administrators would then feel more secure in developing programs other than those that might be attempted with conservative trustees. Resolutions by conservatives at conventions on such "divisive" issues as inerrancy would be heard, then ignored in policy decisions, even when passed by a majority, as happened before 1979.

The seminaries would be at peace, with professors who were formerly targets of conservative protests rejoicing that the invasion of the "barbaric" fundamentalists had been quelled. Some teachers and agency executives could become more bold in talking openly about so-called errors and contradictions in Scripture, "inspired" folk myths in the Old Testament, and "church" accretions in the Gospels and Epistles.

If the pattern established by other mainline denominations in rejecting Biblical truth is followed, disavowals of such fundamental doctrines as the virgin birth of Christ might eventually occur. Kenneth Kantzer, long-time theological educator and former editor of *Christianity Today*, knows "of no instance in which an institution has preserved complete doctrinal orthodoxy on all points except that of inerrancy for as long as a full generation." Kantzer, who does not believe inerrancy should be made a test of church fellowship, adds, "Let those who argue for a limited inerrancy prove just once that they and their institutions can remain on that thin knife-edge." [35]

Promotion of women's ordination would likely be stepped up, with inspirational stories on women pastors appearing frequently in the denominational press. Agencies would lead the way in educating the grassroots for the cause of women's ordination. This might not happen within one to five years, but it could be expected, if previous patterns in other mainline denominations are to be taken seriously.

Agency public relations departments and most state papers would trumpet peace, unity, and progress. Evangelism would be much talked about but not aggressively practiced in many churches.

Agency budgets and employees could be expected to increase. In time, the structure might be changed to allow more control from "headquarters." Nashville might really become "The Baptist Center." Ecumenical links with other mainline denominations would likely be made. Eventually, the SBC might seek membership in the National Council of Churches, although the constitution would have to be changed for that.

As more and more diversity in doctrine is allowed, the SBC would probably in time become much like other mainline denominations. Growth would slow to a standstill and, for the first time in SBC history, the membership might begin to fall. It has happened with other mainliners.

Some state Baptist colleges would be held to the Bible and Baptist theology by conservative trustees in state conventions. Others would likely follow the drift of such schools as the University of Richmond and Wake Forest and gradually lose the identity established by their founders, thus fulfilling Criswell's prophecy.

One need only look at the ratio of ministerial students to total enrollment to perceive that certain schools are becoming less Baptist and more secular. In 1984, the University of Richmond, founded and now only partially controlled by Virginia Baptists, reported only seven ministerial students out of an enrollment of 11,022, a ratio of around one to 1500. Wake Forest University, which has broken ties with the North Carolina Baptist Convention, has only one ministerial student for every 280 students enrolled. The Virginia and North Carolina state conventions are largely controlled by moderates.

Compare Wake Forest and Richmond to two strongly conservative Missouri Baptist schools, Southwest Baptist University and Hannibal-LaGrange College, which have ministerial students in ratios to total enrollment of one to eight and one to thirteen respectively.[36] Conservatives are probably stronger than moderates in the Missouri Baptist Convention, with a large contingent of middle-roaders endeavoring to keep the two groups in the same structure.

With the reduction of ministerial students in SBC colleges drifting towards secularism, other changes would be noticed. Compulsory chapel would be eliminated. Voluntary chapel attendance would drop steadily. Less and less identification with the founding denomination would appear in yearly catalogs and bulletins. Statements such as now appear under "purpose" in the University of Richmond's catalog would be common: "The University, related to the Baptist General Association of Virginia affirms its commitment to Judeo-Christian values in an atmosphere free of sectarian bias, inviting and serving individuals of all faiths and persuasions." [37]

A decisive turnback of SBC conservatives would probably hurt SBC seminary enrollment, certainly in those seminaries perceived most accomodating of neo-orthodoxy. Within ten to fifteen years, enrollments would likely drop noticeably, following the pattern seen in other mainline denominational schools. The independent Criswell Center for Biblical Studies and Mid-America and Luther Rice seminaries would probably be helped as more students and money were diverted to those schools by conservative churches. Other independent seminaries might spring up. Mid-America has already opened a branch in up state New York. One need only compare enrollments in United Methodist seminaries with Asbury Seminary, an independent Wesleyan school, to see what could well happen in Southern Baptist theological education. In 1984 Iliff School of Theology enrolled 276; Garrett-Evangelical Theological Seminary, 363; and Methodist Theological School of Ohio, 241. These are three of the healthier United Methodist schools. Asbury, which receives no denominational support, enrolled 722 theologues in 1984, with most being United Methodist. Similar comparisons can be made between other mainline denominational schools and independents. Fuller Seminary, an independent evangelical institution, enrolled 2,728 in 1984, which included an estimated half of all mainline Presbyterian students in seminary.[38]

What would the future hold for SBC missions? A leveling off of increases experienced in recent years, followed by decreases might be seen, paralleling missionary decline in other mainline groups in the U.S. Religious News Service cites these losses in certain mainline church bodies during a 20-year-period from 1960-80: Episcopal Church—79%, Lutheran Church in America—70%, United Presbyterian Church—70%, United Church of Christ—68%, Christian Church (Disciples)—66%, and the United Methodist Church—46%. [39]

This invites the critical question: What actions would conservative pastors and churches in the SBC conservative movement take if they perceived their cause of "turning the denomination around" to be hopeless?

In stewardship they would probably issue warnings, as Jimmy Draper did before Dallas, that Cooperative Program gifts would be cut unless agencies became more "representative." He previously charged faculties at "some of our educational institutions" with granting "only token acknowledgement to conservative views at best. In some classrooms, when students reflect the beliefs of the churches that nutured them, they are ridiculed for those beliefs. This is not to be tolerated." In this context, Draper declared, "No longer can we expect thousands of churches to contribute to institutions that contradict what the churches believe and stand for in their communities." [40]

Agency heads would probably try to "reason" with the recalcitrants having a history of giving large amounts to the Cooperative Program. Promises would be made. But, if conservatives judged agency deeds to be inadequate, their Cooperative Program funds would go elsewhere. It is because of insufficient agency response, some conservatives say, that their churches presently give small budget percentages to agencies through the Cooperative Program.

First Baptist Church of Atlanta already supports a sizable number of missionaries (church members) who are serving in non-Southern Baptist missions. In the case of a conservative defeat in the SBC, other conservative churches might begin supporting their own "independent" missionaries. Eventually, these churches could endorse or establish one or more mission "boards" of their own, or endorse certain independent boards, as has the conservative Presbyterian Church of America, composed mostly of congregations which defected from the mainline body of Presbyterians.

Would a sizable bloc of conservaties "pull out" of the SBC? The denomination has lost local churches before in conservative protests, but not in substantial numbers. J. Frank Norris, after years of fighting with SBC denominationalists, finally established his own World Baptist Fellowship in 1931. He also set up a "seminary" of disputed academic quality in his First Baptist Church of Fort Worth. Yet, Norris and his sympathizers never came close to getting inside the SBC denominational structure as the conservatives of the 1970s and '80s have done.

A fair number of other churches have left the SBC more quietly and are counted within the loosely structured Baptist Bible Fellowship. In the more distant past, the SBC lost churches to the Landmark party which objected to denominational boards.

Beyond these departures, and excluding the Landmark defection, which was not over the nature of Scripture, there is no precedent in the SBC for what could happen if leading churches in the present conservative movement should begin breaking ties. A landslide could develop or the defection might be held to a few hundred congregations.

A number of historic analogies can be found in other Baptist bodies. In 1887, the gifted pulpiteer Charles Spurgeon led a small minority to leave the British Baptist Union after failing to persuade his denomination to adopt a binding doctrinal statement which included inerrancy. The defectors never became a powerful force. The theologically diverse majority which retained the institutions and denominational name never again became a dynamic church body. From 1980 to 1985, the Baptist Union of Great Britain and Ireland, dropped in membership from 155,501 to 148,000. During this same period, Muslims increased in England from 600,000 to 900,000.[41]

Forty years after Spurgeon left the Baptist Union of his country, the Ontario-Quebec Baptist Convention of Canada excluded T.T. Shields, pastor of Jarvis Street Church in Toronto for his noisy protests of modernism at McMaster University. Shields then helped organize the Union of Regular Baptists which never made a significant impact in central Canada. The Baptist Federation, which now includes Ontario and Quebec, still champions theological diversity and numbers today only 130,943. In recent years, Southern Baptists from the notably conservative Northwest Baptist (Washington and Oregon) Convention have made healthy inroads into Canada, much to the chagrin of the static Baptist Federation. Canadian Southern Baptists are now in the process of establishing their own seminary.

Closer to home, the Northern Baptist Convention, now the American Baptist Churches, U.S.A., was racked by theological controversy during the first half of this century. Unlike Southern Baptists, isolated in their cultural womb of the old south, Northern Baptists were directly exposed to and infiltrated by liberalism. Prominent conservative preachers first protested against liberalism in schools, then pulled out when action was not taken to their liking. T.T. Shields and William Bell Riley, with assistance from J. Frank Norris, who pastored a mega-church in Detroit along with his Fort Worth congregation, formed the Baptist Bible Union in 1923, which, in 1932, was absorbed into the General Association of Regular Baptists (GARB).

The next sizable departure from the Northern Baptist Convention came in 1947 with the organization of the Conservative Baptist Association of America (CBA), composed of churches objecting to the parent denomination's refusal to require creedal tests of denominational workers. Conservatives in the Northern Baptist Convention had attempted to get a motion passed in 1946 requiring that the Convention and its agencies "not employ" as denominational executives or appoint as missionaries any persons who refused to affirm the Biblical record of the incarnation, the miracles of Jesus, and inerrancy of the New Testament. A substitute motion was voted, replacing the original motion, calling only for the denomination to "reaffirm our faith in the New Testament as a divinely inspired record and therefore a trustworthy, authoritative, and all-sufficient rule of our faith and practice." [42] Northern Baptists lost other churches during the tumultous fundamentalist-modernist controversies, but the GARB and the CBA comprised the major defections.

The Northern Baptists did not so much split as hemorrhage. Only two state conventions, Wyoming and Oregon, voted to go with the CBA, and none opted to support the Baptist Bible Union and the later GARB. In 1984, the GARB reported approximately 300,300 members, up from 243,000 in 1982, and the CBA 225,000, showing no gain during the past two years. Taken together, the two denominations are still less than one third the size of the parent American Baptist Churches, U.S.A. which has experienced a decrease in membership since the modernist-fundamentalist dispute in the first half of the century.

If a groundswell should develop among SBC conservatives to organize a new denomination more to their preference than a structure dominated by the "unity amidst diversity" party, could they attract a large following? How many state conventions and associations would cut ties with the national SBC and support a new and untested denomination? The conservatives would probably be rejected by most or all of the state conventions in the East, though a number of individual churches might join. Moderates in control of the SBC would be greatly helped by the traditional loyalty of churches to their "mother" denomination.

Conservative chances would probably be better with state conventions in the west and northwest, which, even moderates admit, are conservative strongholds. But would these "frontier" SBC state conventions, which presently receive large supplements from the Home Mission Board and aid from other agencies, readily cut their institutional umbilical cords? A conservative split from the SBC might gather less than 1,000 churches. Conservatives or moderates, in attempting to start a new denomination, would likely find ties and traditions that go back for generations hard to break.

Would a denomination of conservatives, even though small at the beginning, grow? The record of the GARB and CBA withdrawals from the Northern Baptist Convention offer little encouragement, and we should remember that Northern Baptists were then more accomodating of liberal theology than Southern Baptist institutions are now. Still, defecting conservatives might steadily increase as more churches became disenchanted with an SBC moving steadily to the theological left.

Conservatives departing from the SBC would have to deal with the pension problem. They would also be short on experienced institutional leadership, since the present movement is directed by dynamic, "rugged individualist" type super-church pastors. Could these pastors, accustomed to yielding strong power at home, cooperate in institutional endeavors? Fundamentalist pastors leaving the old Northern Baptist Convention had difficulty working together.

It appears more likely that defeated SBC conservatives would take no immediate action to organize their own denomination. Their churches would remain, nominally at least, Southern Baptist. They would simply ignore the agencies and send their ministerial students and missionary money elsewhere. They would convene for pastors' conferences and fellowships, with some pastors emerging as an unofficial "council of bishops." Many might stop coming to the annual convention altogether, as a good number did before Adrian Rogers' election to the presidency in 1979. Smaller churches and new congregations would look to the mega-churches for specialized resources. These mega-churches would, in effect, assume the role once played by denominational agencies.

3. **What if the SBC should lapse into a see-saw power struggle, with moderates and agency loyalists winning the presidency for two or three years, then conservatives making a comeback?** (This assumes that the moderates would be unable to cripple the appointive powers of the president.)

Democratic institutions tend to experience pendulum swings from right to left. The SBC is no exception. However, each party in the present conflict perceives the other as trying to move the denomination to an unacceptable extreme. Given present inclinations, the infighting seen during the past few years might actually increase. Evangelism and missions would be hurt. The denomination could become the laughing-stock of the nation, as some think it already has.

None of the three scenarios projected in this chapter are inviting. None are likely to bring the peace and progress so fervently desired by so many Southern Baptists. Is there not another way? Cannot the elected Peace Committee, or some other representative group, bring reconciliation?

The Peace Committee brings leaders of both sides together. To this point, the Peace Committee agrees only that the nature of Biblical truth, as held by teachers and administrative employees of agencies supported by CP funds, is the core of the controversy. Shades and hues of other doctrines affecting evangelism and women's ordination, to mention only two, are at issue, as well as roles and policies of agencies.

The Committee could propose doctrinal perameters, similar to what Draper suggested. It might recommend that some seminaries be designated as more diverse in theology than others. It might advocate that the two most controversial agencies, the Christian Life Commission and the Baptist Joint Committee on Public Affairs, be removed from the Cooperative Program with contributions for their operations coming from special offerings given by churches that agree with their programs. Chairman Fuller says "selective support" (the term he prefers to "negative designation") is one possible compromise that might be reached, allowing contributors to the Cooperative Program to exclude some agencies from receiving any of their gifts while still having the contributions considered as CP giving.[43]

The Peace Committee might further recommend that Baptist Press be made an independent agency and given sufficient budget to provide independent news coverage of agency operations, with an elected board strong enough to resist coverups of problems in agencies.

The Committee might devise a questionnaire on which all key denominational employees can state what they believe about the Bible. One section could list Biblical narratives, personages, and miracles which conservatives allege are not accepted as historical by some in agencies. The responses could be tabulated by computer and the denomination made aware of where large numbers of its employees stand, without specific dissenters from the *Baptist Faith and Message* being identified. An inquisition? It is no more than what many Christian institutions have done, albeit in a variety of ways, in making certain that their teachers and other influentials share the beliefs of the majority of supporters.

A new or revised confession of faith might help pacify many conservatives, but it would have to spell out what is meant by "truth, without mixture of error . . . " Conservatives have passed resolutions stating, in effect, that this should mean that the Bible is historically, scientifically, philsophically, and doctrinally without error. This would be acceptable to the conservative side in a new confession, but moderates would undoubtedly balk and refuse to affirm the new statement.

Can language on Biblical truth be found which will satisfy both sides? That was the intent with the 1963 *Baptist Faith and Message*? The tumult of the past 23 years indicates that it has not worked. The hard truth is that moderates and conservatives live in two different assumptive worlds as regards the Bible. They think and reason differently on Bible authority. This affects their interpretation of

many Biblical passages and doctrines, particularly on the question
of women's ordination. Conservatives take the passages dealing with
qualifications for church officers as literally applying in the first century
and today. Moderates take them as bound to culture and interpret
the verses in terms of principles in the "whole" of the New
Testament.

The Peace Committee has not, to this point, considered the dis-
mantling of the convention. Still it may not be able to bring the contending factions together. Denominations have split before.

The committee might then simply decide that the differences in
the denomination are too great for bridging and propose, (as some
moderates and conservatives may have already decided) that the
instituional resources be amicably divided. Former conservative
SBC President Bailey Smith knows "of nobody who can bring us
together because the issues are so deep and strong. We have two
denominations now; we should just admit it and move on."

On the moderate side, C.R. Daley stated, at Southern Seminary,
before Dallas:

> . . . Some [moderates] are arriving at the conclusion that
> maybe we have walked together as long as' we need
> to . . . Somebody suggested to me this week that
> if . . . the tide is not stemmed; if Mr. Stanley is reelected,
> somebody ought to rise—and this is a very responsible
> person who said this—and say, "Friends, it is obvious that
> the time has come when we cannot live together. I move
> that a committee be appointed, including the presidents
> of the state conventions plus ten or twelve or fifteen at
> large, to study the advisability, the desirability of dividing
> the convention's assets and bring back a report next year
> letting us have a plan whereby we could depart from each
> other in peace." [44]

If the Peace Committee cannot effect reconciliation, the proposal
noted by Daley might be next on the agenda. Yet the great, great
majority of Southern Baptists surely must hope that we never reach
this point of no return.

At this time, we can only be certain that the controversy has not
run its course. We do not know what history and the sovereign will of
God will bring. Some will may play more active roles than others.
All of us can be mindful of Charles Stanley's call in his first address
as SBC president to board members of an agency:

> We've got to stop arguing with each other and start pray-
> ing for one another. You can't fight a man you pray with,
> you can't even argue with a man you pray with. If you

pray long enough, you'll love [him] . . . If you're going to have an impact on this nation, the one thing this unbelieving world has got to see from us is love and fellowship and forgiveness and acceptance among one another.[45]

J. Terry Young, professor of theology at New Orleans Seminary, urged in a 1985 New Year's plea: "We must start talking to the Lord instead of talking about each other. We'd better heed 2 Chronicles 7:14 while we still have time. God may grow weary of our petty bickering and raise up some other group in our place." [46]

Finally, whatever our differences, we should hear and heed Roy Honeycutt's statement after the tumultous Dallas convention:

> Of this I am sure: the ultimate resolution of our controversy rests beyond us in the presence of God and His intervening grace. Never before in our 140-year history has there been a time when we Southern Baptists have needed the presence of God's Spirit any more desperately than we do today. Doing our best to resolve our crisis and committing outselves to be used of God as He chooses in the process, let us pray that the Lord Himself will lead us and that His will may prevail through all our actions.[47]

May it be so. Amen.

REFERENCES

1   Baptist Press Convention Reports, June, 1985.

2   Walter B. Shurden: "In Defense of the SBC: The Moderate Response to Fundamentalism," "The Controversy in the Southern Baptist Convention," A Special Issue of *The Faculty of the Theological Educator*, Published by the Faculty of New Orleans Baptist Theological Seminary, 1985, pp. 11-14.

3   James B. Cox: "Three Conditions Can Effect Change in SBC Life, Veep Henry Huff Says," *Western Recorder*, July 2, 1985, p. 1.

4   "Paschall Offers Proposal to Resolve Crisis in SBC," *Baptist and Reflector*, November 21, 1984, p. 1.

5   Jim Jones: "Criswell Claims Erosion Will Cause SBC Decline," *Baptist and Reflector*, February 2, 1983, p. 3.

6   Helen Parmley: " 'Schools Going to Liberals,' Criswell Warns Baptists," *Baptist and Reflector*, October 6, 1983, p. 1.

7   Jim Jones, op. cit.

8   "Face SBC Problems, Draper Tells BSSB," *Baptist and Reflector*, August 11, 1983, p. 3.

9   R.G. Puckett: "Wake Forest Trustees Set Self-Perpetuation Board," *Baptist and Reflector*, December 25, 1985, p. 3.

10 Mr. and Mrs. Crowder came to see me in Chattanooga months befor Mr. Crowder became active for the moderate cause. Mr. Crowder said a state Baptist editor had recommended me as someone who might help them put their concerns in writing. They obviously were committed to doing their part to "save" their beloved denomination. After I declined to assist them, I next saw them at the Pittsburgh convention where they had their crusade well under way.

11 "Missourian Joins Suit Against SBC," *Word and Way*, December 12, 1985, p. 3.

12 Dan Martin: "Baptist Leaders React to Pending Bylaws Suit," *Word and Way*, December 12, 1985, p. 3.

13 "Fuller Expresses 'Optimism' for SBC Solutions," *Baptist and Reflector*, August 7, 1985, p. 4.

14 "How Diverse Should Baptists Be?" *Word and Way*, October 17, 1985, p. 1.

15 James T. Draper, Jr.: *Authority: The Critical Issue for Southern Baptists*, Fleming H. Revell, Old Tappan, N.J., 1984, p. 108.

16 Ibid., pp. 105, 106.

17 Personal Interview, Dallas, June, 1985.

18 Earle E. Cairns: *Christianity Through the Centuries*, Revised and Enlarged Edition, Zondervan Publishing House, Grand Rapids, Michigan, pp. 133-134.

19 Dan Martin: "Peace Committee Subcommittees to Visit SBC Agencies," *Arkansas Baptist Newsmagazine*, January 2, 1986, p. 12.

20 Personal Interview, Hannibal, Mo. January, 1986.

21 Dan Martin: "Peace Panel Adopts Statement on Diversity," *Baptist Standard*, March 5, 1986, p. 3.

22 Libby S. Bellinger, "A Reflection on the 1985 SBC," *Folio*, Autumn, 1985.

23 "Letters to the Editor," *Baptist and Reflector*, July 24, 1985, p. 5.

24 "Best Hope for Southern Baptists," *The Tie*, July/August, 1985, p. 5.

25 Ibid.

26 *Southern Baptist Journal*, January, 1983, p. 4 (reprint from *Houston Chronicle*).

27 Personal Interview, Kansas City, June, 1984.

28 "Patterson Misquoted . . . ," Editor's note in "Lettters to the Editor," *Baptist and Reflector*, April 4, 1984, p. 7.

29 Mark Kelly: "Concerned" Arkansas Pastors Condemn 'Liberal Drift; Call for 'Proper' Ballot in Dallas," *Arkansas Baptist Newsmagazine*, March 14, 1985, p. 11.

30 Personal Interview, Kansas City, June, 1984.

31 Personal Interview, Pittsburgh, June, 1983.

32 Telephone Interview, October, 1984.

33 "America's 'Mainline' Denominations Are Losing Ground," *Word and Way*, August 15, 1985, p. 1.

34 Bishop Richard Wilke: "Rise up and Walk," *Good News*, September/October, 1985, pp. 34-38.

35   Kenneth S. Kantzer: "Evangelicals and the Inerrancy Question," *Christianity Today*, April 21, 1978, pp. 17-21.

36   *The Quarterly Review*, July-August-September, 1984, p. 58.

37   *University of Richmond Bulletin*, 1982-84, p. 7.

38   Enrollment figures from *85 Higher Education Directory*, Higher Education Publications, Washington, D.C., 1985.

39. James T. Draper, Jr., op. cit., p. 95 (*from an editorial in the Baptist Standard, December 2, 1981*).

40   Ibid.

41   *U.K. Christian Handbook 1985/86*, Edited by Peter Brierley, MARC Europe, 1985, p. 112, 117.

42   *Baptist Life and Thought: 1600-1980*, William A. Brackney, Editor, Judson Press, Valley Forge, Pa., 1948, pp. 382-3.

43   26. Toby Druin: "Peace Panel Won't Bar Member Nominations," *Baptist Standard* January 29, 1986, p. 5.

44   C.R. Daley: Lecture to Class at Southern Seminary, as previously cited.

45   Michael Tutterow, Baptist Press, July, 1984.

46   "Guest Comment: New Year's Yearning to Solve SBC Division," *Illinois Baptist*, January 2, 1985, p. 2.

47   Roy L. Honeycutt: "President's Journal: Best Hope for Southern Baptists," *The Tie*, July/August, 1985, p. 5.

ACKNOWLEDGMENTS

Because this is a "reporting" book and not an opinion, it could not have been done without aid from many sources. Mine go back at least to seminary days in the 1950s. But I did not begin writing in any depth about the Southern Baptist Convention until 1976 when my wife Marti and I were commissioned by a national trade publishing house to write a book on Jimmy Carter and his denomination (*The Church That Produced a President*, Wyden/Simon & Schuster, New York, 1977) Publisher Peter Wyden said his eyes were opened when he read the manuscript. "I always thought of Southern Baptists as a monolithic group of southerners set in the same mold," he said. "You have shown them to be a great diversity."

Jack Harwell, editor of the *Christian Index*, was an extraordinary help in providing research assistance for the earlier book. Persons in many other denominational agencies helped, including W. C. Fields, Director of Baptist Press; Walker Knight, then editor of *Home Missions* magazine; and Lloyd Householder, director of the office of communications for the Sunday School Board. Scores of prominent Southern Baptists gave us time for interviews, including Dr. Jimmy Allen, then president of the SBC, five former SBC presidents, and Foy Valentine, Executive Director of the Christian Life Commission. I mention the assistance of these because resource material from the earlier book (available now only in libraries) provided valuable background material for this writing, particularly for chapters three and four.

The Church That Produced a President is heavy in history. *The Truth In Crisis* focuses more on recent events, and particularly on the conflict between "conservatives" and "moderates." Many who helped before also provided resource material for this writing.

In retrospect, I can now see that *The Truth In Crisis* (both the book and the conflict) has been in process for over a decade. When I "covered" the annual Southern Baptist convention for *Christianity Today* in 1975, I hardly thought that the controversy would mushroom as it has and demand a book. Now that it has, I must cite my indebtedness to the scores and scores of Southern Baptists who shared information and insights with me during and between conventions of the past decade for articles written for *Christianity Today* and other national publications. These include every SBC president during the period covered, along with other newsmakers, both conservative and moderate, and many persons in denominational agencies, including five of the present six seminary presidents. Particularly helpful were conservatives W. A. Criswell, Paige Patterson, and Paul Pressler and moderates Cecil Sherman and the late Don Harbuck, a friend for over three decades until his untimely death from a brain tumor in Chattanooga where he was pastor of the First Baptist Church.

As to printed material my most fruitful source was Baptist Press. W. C. Fields, Baptist Press Director, and Dan Martin, Baptist Press News Director were always willing to help. I'm sure they didn't always agree with my approach, but they were always cooperative. Baptist Press appears frequently in my source references, as does state Baptist papers, particularly Bob Terry's *Word and Way* and Al Shackleford's *Baptist and Reflector*. Except for editorials, most articles referenced to these and other state papers originated with Baptist Press. I also read regularly a number of other denominational periodicals, including the *Review and Expositor*, published by the faculty of Southern Seminary, one of the most thought-provoking theological journals on the scene.

W. C. Fields, Dan Martin, and state editor colleagues have themselves willingly or unwillingly entered into the great conflict. In seeking to understand their roles, I wish them to know that nothing personal is involved in whatever light they have appeared and that their research assistance for my articles and this book is not unappreciated.

I mention four other journalistic friends who have been particularly helpful. Bill Powell, now retired as editor of the independent *Southern Baptist Journal* was always available. Bill, in my judgment, has been a powerful influence in the controversy. He and I have not always agreed and on one occasion I scolded him severly for hitting moderates below the belt. Whatever else is said of Bill, he is dedicated and has strong convictions. At great personal sacrifice, he has given the prime of his life to the conservative cause.

Russ Kaemmerling, former editor of the conservative *Southern Baptist Advocate*, came along later in the controversy. I have watched the *Advocate* mature into a respectable journal. Russ and the *Advocate* have been of immense help, particularly with background on certain personalities and events in the conservative movement.

Walker Knight, founder and editor of *SBC Today*, is close to moderates, of whom many serve on his board. A man of great integrity, Walker never gave me less than straight answers to tough questions about issues in the controversy.

Louis Moore, a fellow Southern Baptist who happens to be religion editor of the *Houston Chronicle*, is, in my opinion, next to Ed Plowman, the best investigative religion reporter in America. I have probably discussed the SBC controversy with Louis more than with any other journalist. Louis has been aggressive and hard-hitting in covering the controversy, but always eminently fair to both sides.

I have dealt only cursorily with the SBC "women's movement." No group is more committed in my judgment—whatever one believes about ordination of women—to their goals than SBC Women in Ministry. Reba Sloan Cobb, editor of WIM's *Folio*, helped me understand WIM on many sensitive points.

I also thank the editors of *Christianity Today* for their confidence in commissioning me to cover the annual convention for past years. The prestige of being *Christianity Today's* man opened many doors through which I could not have gone on my own. I particularly thank Ed Plowman, Tom Minnery, and Ron Lee, the *Christianity Today* news editors under whom I have worked.

Larry Lewis, president of the college where I am writer in residence, must be given the blame or credit for instigating this book. Larry urged only that I report the story as "you've seen it happen." As a leader among the conservatives, he provided insights and understanding of what went on behind the scenes of some important convention decisions.

I am deeply grateful to all of the above and many others who provided help. Most of all I thank my dear wife who has never been much for "preacher politics," but has always been understanding of my commitment to write about the struggles within our denomination. I've found that when all other views have been considered that her insights are usually the most sensible.

None of the persons cited should be faulted for my sins of omission or commission in this book. The responsibility is wholly my own. Much more will be written. Much more deserves to be, especially work based on sound survey research. The most insightful study to date has probably been done by Nancy T. Ammerman, Director of the Center for Religious Research at Candler School of Theology. Dr. Ammerman's initial paper is based on her research of the "organizational conflict" as it relates to Southern Baptists and abortion. I thank her for sharing this paper with me.

Many of us who write about the SBC have much more than an academic or journalistic interest in the outcome of the controversy. Because we do not take strong "stands" does not mean that we are not concerned. We stand near and yet apart from the conflict, sometimes breaking our silence in personal conversations and meetings with friends, while striving to understand and interpret for a wider audience what is happening and the meaning for the future. That has been my intention and that is why I have written.

Hannibal, Mo., January, 1985.

James C. Hefley
Hannibal, MO
January, 1985

PUBLISHED BY:

Criterion Publications
P.O. Box 214749
Dallas, Texas 75221-4749

Please send me **The Truth in Crisis** by James Hefley.

ORDER INFORMATION • PLEASE PRINT

MAIL TO: _____ Books x $7.95 _____

Criterion Publications   Total _____
P.O. Box 214749
Dallas, Texas 75221-4749   Texas residents:
                              Add 5% sales tax _____

Postage and Handling   _____   Books x $.75 _____

                                  Grand Total _____

Name_____

Address_____

City_____ State_____ Zip_____

Send no cash!

Check Enclosed ☐   MasterCard ☐   VISA ☐

Signature_____

Account No._____

Expiration Date_____